D0859716

THE ASJA Guide to Freelance Writing

808.
02
ASJ

THE ASJA Guide to Freelance Writing

* * *

A Professional Guide to the Business, for Nonfiction Writers of All Experience Levels

EDITED BY Timothy Harper

Foreword by Samuel G. Freedman

ST. MARTIN'S GRIFFIN ✶ NEW YORK

FINKELSTEIN
MEMORIAL LIBRARY
SPRING VALLEY, N.Y.

3 2191 00673 8834

The American Society of Journalists and Authors (ASJA) is the national organization of independent nonfiction writers. Founded in 1948, the Society includes more than one thousand freelance writers of magazine articles, books, and other forms of nonfiction writing who have met ASJA's exacting standards of professional achievement. For information, write to ASJA, 1501 Broadway, Suite 302, New York, N.Y. 10036, or visit the Web site at www.ASJA.org.

THE ASJA GUIDE TO FREELANCE WRITING. Copyright © 2003 by American Society of Journalists and Authors. Foreword copyright © 2003 by Samuel G. Freedman. All rights reserved. Printed in the United States of America. No part of this book may be used or reproduced in any manner whatsoever without written permission except in the case of brief quotations embodied in critical articles or reviews. For information, address St. Martin's Press, 175 Fifth Avenue, New York, N.Y. 10010.

www.stmartins.com

Book design by Richard Oriolo

LIBRARY OF CONGRESS CATALOGING-IN-PUBLICATION DATA

The ASJA guide to freelance writing : a professional guide to the business, for nonfiction writers of all experience levels / edited by Timothy Harper ; foreword by Samuel G. Freeman.—1st St. Martin's Griffin ed.
　　p. cm.
　ISBN 0-312-31852-9
　1. Authorship Vocational guidance.　I. American Society of Journalists and Authors.　II. Harper, Timothy, 1950–.
　PN145.A79　2003
　808'.02'023—dc21

2003009125

FIRST EDITION: September 2003

10　9　8　7　6　5　4　3　2　1

COPYRIGHT ACKNOWLEDGMENTS

"Freelance Writing Today—and Tomorrow" copyright © 2003 by Jim Morrison

"Planning a Writing Business" copyright © 2003 by Erik Sherman

"The Writer's Office and Tools" copyright © 2003 by Samuel Greengard

"The Mystery of Ideas" copyright © 2003 by Jack El-Hai

"Seven Secrets of a Successful Magazine Query" copyright © 2003 by Lisa Collier Cool

"How to Sell a Book" copyright © 2003 by Sherry Suib Cohen

"Writing for the Web" copyright © 2003 by Lisa Iannucci

"Why Literary Agents Need You More Than Ever—And How to Get the Agent You Need" copyright © 2003 by Michael Larson, AAR

"Research: Finding the Right Stuff" copyright © 2003 by Minda Zetlin and Steve Weinberg

"How to Find Experts" copyright © 2003 by Estelle Sobel

"Writer-Editor Relations" copyright © 2003 by Megan McMorris

"Collaborations: The Pleasure and Perils of Shared Bylines" copyright © 2003 by Sarah Wernick

"The Serendipity of Specialization" copyright © 2003 by Claire Walter

"Self-Publishing: Alternatives for Getting Books into Print" copyright © 2003 by Marilyn and Tom Ross

"Networking" copyright © 2003 by Sandra E. Lamb

"This Pen for Hire: Leveraging Your Skills" copyright © 2003 by Anita Bartholomew

"Op-Eds and Essays: Leveraging Your Knowledge" copyright © 2003 by Larry Atkins

"Reprints, Re-Slants, and Other Ways to Resell Your Work" copyright © 2003 by Kelly James-Enger

"Making Pictures" copyright © 2003 by Barbara DeMarco-Barrett

"Employing a Writing Assistant" copyright © 2003 by Lester A. Picker

"Contracts: Protecting Writers' Rights" copyright © 2003 by Richard A. Marini

"Creating Brand You: Promoting Yourself and Your Work" copyright © 2003 by Jennifer Pirtle

"Writers and the Law" copyright © 2003 by Sallie Randolph and Timothy Perrin

"Taxes and Deductions" copyright © 2003 by Julian Block

"Forays into Fiction" copyright © 2003 by Kathryn Lance

"Moving to Full-Time Freelancing: It's Not a Leap" copyright © 2003 by Robert Bittner

CONTENTS

FOREWORD

by Samuel G. Freedman

Few words conjure more romantic visions for any aspiring writer than "freelance." Those two syllables summon images of the stringer in wartime, the magazine stylist, the book author, all of them beholden to no one but the muse. I know, because I came of age in the 1970s enthralled by such figures—Michael Herr painting the chaos of the Vietnam War in *Esquire,* Cameron Crowe interviewing Neil Young in *Rolling Stone,* Robert Sam Anson investigating the death of Karen Silkwood in *New Times.* And I know the allure shines as brightly now, as I watch my students at the Columbia University Graduate School of Journalism aspire to become the next Susan Orlean or James B. Stewart.

Yet I often find myself warning them, not against the aspiration, but against the fantasy of a freelancer's life. It is a life of multiple rewrites, myriad rejections, editors who over-assign, checks that come too late and for too little, and in which there is no such thing as a paid vacation. I give them my personal advice, to move to a city where the rent is cheap and the competition less strenuous than in New York or Los Angeles. I tell them to plan for the long term, because the most successful freelancer I know, now a National Magazine Award finalist for *Esquire,* made just $12,000 the year after he left a staff reporting job at the *Washington Post.* I recall the actress I once profiled for the *New York Times,* who told me that her job had two parts—working, and looking for work.

The ASJA Guide to Freelance Writing, then, offers a degree course in the real world. This book doesn't destroy the myth of the footloose freelancer, typing all morning in pajamas, then jetting off to the next assignment in the afternoon. It tells you, in its precise and candid and canny way, how to transmute myth into reality. This is a book by writers who get paid for writing. Some write only what they love. Some write only what they're good at. Some write only what sells best. Most, I would suspect, combine all three. The important thing, the baseline fact, is that they make their living at it.

Chapter by chapter, the working writers who wrote this book share the concrete details of the writing life, from office furniture to databases, from pitch letters to research assistants, from contract language to literary agents. What you read in these pages is what you would hear working writers talk about over coffee or cocktails. You need not agree with it all; I don't. But you ought to seriously consider it all.

In reading *The ASJA Guide to Freelance Writing*, you are being admitted to a kind of private club, albeit one that always has room for another talented member. And that helps give you a sense of community, because freelancing can be lonely, isolating work.

At another level, *The ASJA Guide to Freelance Writing* is a manual for running a business. And, as such, it is a backbone-stiffener, a reminder that doing the work you love is no reason not to be paid, paid well, and paid promptly for it. In some way or another, almost all writers want to express a literary impulse, change the world, or both; negotiating a deal and tabulating tax deductions don't come naturally to many of us. But when I teach a seminar at Columbia about writing non-fiction books, I urge my students not to fear the marketplace element of publishing. "You're not selling Agent Orange or the Dalkon shield," goes my standard advice. "You're selling your talent."

In my own case, I haven't held a staff position on any publication since I resigned from the *New York Times* in 1987 to begin researching my first book. Though I am tenured as a professor at Columbia, my writing life is entirely a freelancer's life, ranging from books for Harper-Collins and Simon & Schuster to cultural features for the *New York Times* to Op-Ed columns for *USA Today* to essays for *Smithsonian*. The thrill has never gone out of seeing my byline, and the satisfaction has never gone out of depositing the check. So read deeply, think hard, and get to work.

SAMUEL G. FREEDMAN is the author of four books—*Small Victories* (HarperCollins), *Upon This Rock* (HarperCollins), *The Inheritance* (Simon & Schuster), and *Jew vs. Jew* (Simon & Schuster). He has been a finalist for the Pulitzer Prize and the National Book Award and has won the National Jewish Book Award and the Helen M. Bernstein Award for Excellence in Journalism. His seminar on nonfiction books at Columbia University has resulted in contracts for twenty-five students. He can be visited on the Web at *www.samuelfreedman.com*.

ACKNOWLEDGMENTS

This book, from start to finish, probably should have been a difficult, prolonged, contentious project. After all, freelance writers are typically independent, strong-minded people, more than willing to forcefully express their views. All too often, getting two of them to work together is enough to send at least a few sparks flying. Getting a couple dozen of them to work together on this project at first seemed like a job better suited to a ringmaster than to an editor. But it wasn't like that at all. From conception to publication, this book had remarkably few bumps in the road. It wasn't a difficult, prolonged, contentious project. More than anything, that is no doubt testament to the spirit of generosity and cooperation that so many of the contributing writers have created together under the umbrella of the American Society of Journalists and Authors.

The idea of the book was born in an ASJA committee chaired by Florence Isaacs, a longtime member and one of the most respected freelance writers in America. Her committee members, all of them known for their willingness to share the secrets of their successful freelance careers, included Claire Berman, Lisa Collier Cool, Suzanne Loebl, Melba Newsome, and Terry Whalin. The committee was instrumental in outlining the scope of the book, constructing a preliminary outline, and choosing an agent. Longtime ASJA member Norman Schreiber helped Florence prepare her presentation to the board of directors of the ASJA, which quickly endorsed the project.

Jim Morrison, who was president of ASJA until May 2003, was instrumental in keeping the project on track. Invaluable support came in many different ways from the staff at ASJA headquarters in New York—Executive Director Brett Harvey and her assistant, Zeleika Raboy. Lisa Collier Cool, who succeeded Jim as president of ASJA, helped shepherd the book through the last stages to publication. Sallie Randolph, the freelance writer-turned-lawyer who routinely provides so much legal aid and moral support to fellow ASJA members, helped work out the intricacies of various legal documents and contracts, including the ever-important rights issues.

ASJA member Nancy Love, the literary agent who represented the book, offered to take a significant reduction in her fee, and then worked as hard to sell this guide as she has on any of the bestsellers her agency has sold to major publishers. Nancy is known for finding the best home for her clients' books and she did it again with this one, negotiating the sale of the book to St. Martin's Press.

One of the biggest reasons that St. Martin's was the best home for this book was Senior Editor Marian Lizzi, who bought the project and did so much to shape it from proposal to manuscript to finished book. Marian and her colleagues proved again and again that St. Martin's is a writers' house. Among those colleagues at St. Martin's were Julie Mente, the assistant editor who took care of the nuts and bolts; Wah-Ming Chang, the production editor responsible for the book's smooth appearance; Lisa Force, who designed the cover; Kathryn Parise, who directed the design of the interior of the book; Richard Oriolo, the designer; Amy Wolosoff, the lawyer who sorted out the complicated rights and other legal issues; Penny Makras, who supervised publicity; and Diana Drew, the Randolph, New Jersey, freelance copy editor who deserves unreserved thanks from every ASJA contributing writer, and especially from the editor. Together, the St. Martin's editors made us professional writers look even more professional.

Special thanks go to Samuel G. Freedman, professor and associate dean at the Columbia University Graduate School of Journalism, who wrote the foreword that says so much that is so true about freelancing in general and this book in particular. Besides being one of the nation's leading journalism educators, Sam's parallel career as a freelance journalist and award-winning author allows him to offer insights and reflections on the challenges and the benefits, financial and otherwise, of the life of the independent writer.

Most of all, thanks to the ASJA writers who contributed to the book and made the job of editing the manuscript not only enjoyable but educational. The writers who wrote or collaborated on chapters went to extraordinary lengths to selflessly share their time and expertise; I cannot imagine those at the top of any other profession, craft, or trade going to similar lengths to help others in their field, and to raise the level of competence and success for their business in general. Similarly, thanks to the dozens more ASJA members who contributed tips—little nuggets of wisdom heretofore most likely to be shared among writers who are friends. There's a lot to be said for working with and learning from the best, and these writers are the best.

ABOUT THIS BOOK

Freelance writing is often a solitary business. Perhaps that's why so many nonwriters or would-be writers don't consider it a business at all. They prefer to think of the artist in the garret, carefully crafting words and sentences. Well, there are some aspects of art and craft to what we do as freelance writers. But make no mistake. Freelance writing *is* a business. If you say you are a freelance writer but you don't operate in a businesslike fashion—paying attention to everything that a big corporation does, from maintenance and inventory to marketing and sales—then what you have is not a business. It's a hobby.

This book is written by and for freelance journalists who are in business to make a living. The more than two dozen writers who have contributed the twenty-six chapters in this book, and the dozens more who have offered brief but detailed nuggets of advice in the "Tips from the Pros" appendix, are all freelancers who make a living from their writing. They are not interested in suffering for their art. They are interested in profiting from their craft—to raise families, pay mortgages, take vacations, and fund their pension plans. Most of them have been in the writing business long enough and have been successful enough to make more than a million dollars apiece from their nonfiction.

These contributors are all members of the American

Society of Journalists and Authors, the foremost organization of nonfiction freelancers in the United States. For many members, ASJA helps counter the isolation that comes with our solitary work. The organization is a means for sharing information through programs, workshops, seminars, a monthly newsletter, an annual conference, and electronic forums and bulletin boards. Through those programs and the ASJA Web site, *www.asja.org,* more than a thousand of America's best nonfiction magazine writers offer each other encouragement and advice on how to do their jobs better and how to be more successful—both as writers and as businesspeople.

This book is an example of the best of ASJA, offering specific pointers for both experienced, successful freelance writers and for those who think they might want to become full-time freelancers some day. Each chapter is a mix of the contributor's reflections and expertise in a certain area, along with pertinent anecdotes and advice from other ASJA members. For example, Lisa Collier Cool discusses breaking into bigger and better magazines, author Sherry Suib Cohen and agent Michael Larsen talk about how to write strong book proposals, Anita Bartholomew looks at how to branch out into corporate writing and consulting, Jennifer Pirtle explores how writers can "brand" themselves, and Robert Bittner discusses the so-called "leap"—he doesn't think it should be a leap at all—from a staff writing job to full-time freelancing.

The focus of the book is on nonfiction, since ASJA is primarily an organization of independent journalists. But many of the business principles apply to both fiction and nonfiction writers, and there is a chapter specifically on fiction by Kathryn Lance (fifty books, fiction and nonfiction), including advice from bestselling novelist and ASJA colleague Mary Higgins Clark.

Most of the contributors have included contact information in the brief bios at the end of their respective chapters. If you have questions or comments, feel free to get in touch with any of us, or with the American Society of Journalists and Authors at *www.asja.org*. There's nothing we'd rather talk about than writing—and the business of writing.

—Timothy Harper
New York
www.timharper.com
September 2003

Freelance Writing Today—and Tomorrow

Jim Morrison

People inevitably ask what it's like to be a freelance writer. My guess is that's a polite way of broaching the question they really want answered: Is that a *real* job? My answer is always that I get paid to learn. What could be better?

I've climbed and slept in a 243-foot-tall redwood. I've hiked high into the Sierra Madre Mountains of Mexico to visit the endangered winter sanctuary of 150 million monarch butterflies. I've walked onto the lush green of Yankee Stadium to interview baseball stars. I've interviewed CEOs and rock stars to discover how they built their companies and careers. I've spent weeks talking with teens, administrators, and judges in the juvenile justice system, looking for solutions to their problems. I've watched doctors and nurses work their postbirth miracles in a neonatal intensive care unit. I've had publications pick up the tab for trips to Venice, Aspen, New York, London, Paris, Toronto, and dozens of other places. It makes for a surplus of cocktail-party conversation starters and an unbeaten record in Trivial Pursuit.

It's easy to romanticize the freelance life. After all, you get paid to travel across the country—or the world—and talk to fascinating people. But that's only half the story. There are two pillars for building a freelance career: writing ability and marketing ability. One makes for great conversation. The other makes for a fat bank account. You need to be good at both. I've seen a remarkable number of writers who are creative thinkers and beautiful stylists, but they don't understand that it's necessary to work just as hard on the marketing end. You've got to keep banging on doors until they open or your head wears out from the pounding.

I've also seen writers who think getting assignments is all about marketing. Just find the right markets, get a few good contacts, and you'll have work. Well, at a certain level that may be true. There is a demand, even in tough times, for competent work. But never forget that the better a writer you become, the more editors will be calling.

In the quest for that next big story or big book, it's easy to lose sight of the simple fact that freelancing is a business, a business that in many ways has changed dramatically over the past decade. No matter how good a reporter and writer you are, no matter how passionate a journalist, you will not get published and earn a living unless you know the business by doing the same kind of research you would if you were working on a magazine story or a book. This book is designed as a one-stop guide to improving your business.

Those same cocktail partygoers who enjoy my stories often mistakenly assume that a freelance writer is a dilettante, not truly a professional. They're right in one way: It has never been easier to become a freelance writer; the bar has never been lower. All you need is a computer and some time. Plenty of writers contribute the occasional story to a local newspaper or small magazine, never coming close to earning a living wage. But anyone who thinks you cannot have a fascinating, rich work life *and* earn a good living as a freelancer is not aiming high enough. Every year at ASJA's conference we run a panel of writers who share their secrets to earning a six-figure income. They can do it and so can you. In truth, saying there are "secrets" is hype. Mostly, it's a matter of smarts, of thinking about writing as a business. You have to plan well. You have to be disciplined. You have to be creative. And you have to be persistent.

Web Working

I entered the freelance life after nearly a decade as a staff writer for a metropolitan newspaper. Talk about good timing. I became a freelancer just as the World Wide Web was becoming a remarkable resource. Through the Web, I not only could research my stories; I could also research my career by reaching out to writers I'd never met. How, I've often wondered, did freelance writers survive before the world was at their fingertips?

Today, it's easier than ever to find ideas, whether by tagging a program that sends you every story with the word "endangered" from the *New York Times* or simply by playing around with a search on Google (*www.google.com*) or Electric Library (*www.elibrary.com*) or cruising the dozens of online news-tip sources. Finding sources is a snap, whether you search online or you put a request in at a site like Profnet (*www.profnet.com*). Increasingly, useful research can be found online, whether you're looking for a General Accounting Office report about school lunch nutrition or the latest from the California task force investigating a pathogen killing oak trees. Of course, you still need to get out from behind your desk and rummage through library stacks and interview live people. For more, see Chapter 9 about doing research online and offline.

The overall effect has been to make freelance writers more efficient. Of course, it's made my competitors more efficient, too. Once, freelancers had to frequent East Village bars in Manhattan to talk shop. There's still something to be said for going out for a drink with other writers once in a while, no matter where you live. Perhaps the biggest transformation facilitated by the Web has been to remove the isolation of freelancing, whether you work from a ranch in Wyoming, a brownstone in Chelsea, or a suburban home outside Los Angeles. No matter where you are, you can connect with other freelancers and get their advice about the business. Over the past decade, I've participated in bulletin boards for freelance writers on Compuserve, Freelance Success (*www.freelancesuccess.com*), and now on ASJA's Web site (*www.asja.org*).

In addition to chatting online, I've come to rely on databases and resources, especially on the ASJA site. There, I often use Paycheck, a database of how much publications pay for stories, and the Query Project, examples of letters or e-mails that netted writers assignments. Before I take a shot at querying a new market, I often post a note on a writers' bulletin board or check ASJA's membership directory, which is searchable online by publication credit. It's that attention to detail and access to inside information that provides an edge. It's something I could not have conceived of doing a decade ago. Because I take the time to understand the market for my work, I know, for instance, the magazines most likely to give me a raise if I ask for more money. I know the magazines that initially offer odious work-made-for-hire contracts but then come up with a more writer-friendly First North American Serial Rights contract if I ask for one. And I know which editors are notorious for never responding to queries from new writers. I know what a book proposal that netted a six-figure advance looks like because I've seen one, thanks to a connection made online. I know how to find and evaluate an agent to sell that book proposal. And I know how to work publicity when that book hits stores. Much of that advice comes from other ASJA members, including those who have contributed to this book.

Freelancing Today

So what about the freelance market today? Like every other industry in recent times, it's been shaken and stirred enough to warrant a martini or two.

The late 1990s were a modern-day Gold Rush for freelancers. First, there was the boom of publications, online and in print, voraciously gobbling up story after story. Magazines, especially technology magazines, doubled as castle doorstops they were so large. Editors could not find enough good writers to fill their pages. Payments rose. Magazines such as *Fast Company, Real Simple, Martha Stewart Living*, and *O*, the Oprah magazine, launched and quickly established themselves. Online sites like *Salon, Feed*, and *Slate* pioneered journalism on the Web. Then came the bust. Magazines folded. Web sites disappeared or drastically dropped their rates. The already-small number of slots for freelance stories, even at the big papers, dried up. But even on the down side of that bust, as I write this introduction, there's a silver lining. Never have there been more outlets for good, solid reporting and writing. Magazines. Web sites. Custom publishing. Ghostwriting. Books.

For help with the long view of the industry, I called Samir Husni, a professor at the University of Mississippi. Husni isn't just any academic. He's "Mr. Magazine," an industry observer for twenty years. He was encouraging. "We definitely now have more freelance opportunities than ever before," Husni says. "Yes, the times have been tough. But it's not like we're seeing any letdown in terms of the new magazines that are being published." He guesses there were about 1,500 magazines in the 1960s. When he began studying the market in 1978, there were barely 2,000 magazines. A quarter-century later, that number had mushroomed to more than 6,000.

Why? Specialization. The magazine world—and publishing in general—is more niche-oriented today. To survive, freelancers also need to have a specialty or three. Husni uses the bridal story market as an example. No longer are there just one or two magazines devoted to getting married. There are the various bride magazines, city magazines devoted to brides, wedding magazines, spin-offs from magazines like *Martha Stewart Living* and *Elle* devoted to weddings, family magazines, divorce magazines, and even "mother of the bride" magazines. How specialized have magazines become? During a recent newsstand visit, Husni counted twenty-two magazines devoted to tattoos.

He also sees custom publishing—magazines published for companies, but containing journalism—as a growth market. They are as diverse as *Departures*, the upscale travel-and-luxury magazine published for American Express gold card members, and *Tomorrow,* published by Daimler/Chrysler and the UAW for union workers. Advertisers, Husni says, are learning that custom publishing is a way to target a specific group of people and appeal to them through their lifestyle.

The other thing that has changed over the past few decades is the emphasis of magazines. Once, only a few magazines like *House and Garden* offered service journalism—news you can use—to readers. Now, service journalism is ubiquitous. "If you don't have service journalism, you don't exist," Husni says. That doesn't mean that writing a penetrating analysis of an issue or telling a good, dramatic story has gone out of fashion. It hasn't. Great narrative ideas or a creative way of looking at an issue remain valuable currency.

"There is still room for people who want to tell stories," Husni says. "What's changing is you have to tell your story in a package as opposed to starting on page one and ending on page fifty. You need more entry points, more exit points. You have to help the reader.... Now we write for the eye as well as the brain. You have to grab the eye first with the visual. Our readers are television viewers first, skimmers second, and readers third. If we can turn them into skimmers and then readers, they will sit down and read that lengthy article. But I have to get them excited to get them into that lengthy article to start."

Freelancing Tomorrow

The market has changed and will continue to change. Technology has made freelancing easier. But that doesn't mean it's easy. If there is one failing I've seen in freelancers over the years, it's giving up too easily. A couple of years ago, I was having a drink at a party with a good friend of mine, a writer with a decade-long track record at places like *GQ*, *Rolling Stone*, and other major magazines. Someone sidled up, introduced herself, and—as people always do in New York—asked us what we do. We told her we were writers. Well, she wondered, what was the most important talent for someone in our business? Almost in unison, we answered: "Accepting rejection and moving on."

The most important skill a freelancer can hone is the ability to take being rejected—or being ignored—by an editor and to move on, whether you offer that same editor a new idea or you offer that idea to another editor. There are those wonderful exceptions. Take my first *New York Times* assignment. When I query a new market, I always call to find the right editor to pitch. Sending a query to a name on the masthead to me seems akin to tossing it in the trashcan under my desk. The editor may have left. She may not be responsible for assigning features. And the *Times* doesn't even have a masthead for its Sunday sections. So one afternoon, I dialed the *Times* and asked for the Styles section, which uses a lot of freelance material. When a man answered, I sputtered that I was a writer with a story idea and I wondered which editor to query.

"Me," he said. "You can send the query to me." He gave me his name, then paused. "Since you're on the phone," he added, "why don't you tell me the idea? We're looking for stories." I ran through it nervously.

Sounds good, he said. Who have you written for? I listed my credits.

Sounds good, he said. Can you have a written query and some clips over here tomorrow?

Um, yes. I dropped a package at the *Times* office on 43rd Street the next morning. By that afternoon, I had an assignment to do a 1,300-word feature for the Styles section. That was a combination of luck, timing, and a great idea—all necessary in this business.

Too many freelancers—and would-be freelancers—underestimate the work necessary to break into good markets and to make a good living from their writing. They give up too easily. Publishers rejected the first offerings of Walt Whitman, Herman Melville, H. G. Wells, John LeCarré, and Jane Austen. Mark Twain had to resort to self-publishing *Huckleberry Finn*. John McPhee, a Pulitzer Prize winner, suffered years of rejections before his byline appeared in the *New Yorker*.

Yes, freelancing has changed since then, and it continues to change. But the same persistence is required. When you read the advice in the pages that follow, remember that you need to use and apply that knowledge with passionate persistence. Do so and your business will grow.

JIM MORRISON, a full-time freelance writer since 1990, has written for *Smithsonian*, the *New York Times*, the *Wall Street Journal*, *George*, *This Old House*, *Family PC*, *Good Housekeeping*, *Playboy*, *Biography*, the *Washington Post*, *Reader's Digest*, *Utne Reader*, and various in-flight magazines, among others. President of the American Society of Journalists and Authors 2001–2003, he speaks often about writing and can be reached at *jimmor@aol.com*.

Planning a Writing Business

ERIK SHERMAN

Writing can be many things: a craft, an art, a passion, an obsession. Yet for those who lack a trust fund, a wealthy spouse, or a bursting portfolio, spending significant time writing requires something else. It must be a business. And every business needs a business plan. Some amateur writers mistakenly believe that their writing will suffer, or their attention to their craft will be diverted, if they take a businesslike approach to their writing. True professional writers, however, realize that they are running a business, and managing their writing careers like a business allows them to devote more time, energy, and creativity—not less—to their writing.

The dichotomy between craft and commerce is thousands of years old. In *The Republic,* Plato noted that the art of making money is inherently separate from the art of a vocation, and the proper practice of one does not guarantee the success of the other. One can hone writing skills; getting paid, as every writer finds, takes a completely different set of skills. The difficulty is striking the balance, honoring the craft's demands while finding a way to make a reasonable profit. To continue to write, a writer must learn business. Many of us, at least initially, find business a collection of such daily chores as record keeping, mailing, and even filing. But it is far more than that. Even marketing and sales are only like the parts of an auto, components that must work together to make the car move in a given direction. To put the parts together for optimum performance and choose a direction in which to move, the writer needs to plan the business.

The first step to intelligent business planning is an understanding of what it is *not.* Many people think that business plans are thick stacks of paper, detailing everything from organizational structure to market strategies, which then reside forgotten in drawers. But a business plan is more than words on paper; it is a process requiring constant adjustment and reconsideration. Inadequate design—or a lack of monitoring ongoing business performance—can lead to both short- and long-term difficulties. Planning a writing business is important, and also complex. The process must address a range of topics, including:

* Monetary requirements

* Client management

* Cash flow

- Marketing
- Sales
- Time management

Financial investment in the business, long-term client development, and even planning for subcontracting work to others are also fair game for the business plan.

Defining the Business

Formal business planning usually starts with a definition of the business: goals, strengths, weaknesses, and operating philosophy. But having talked with many writers over the years, I've come to believe that a slightly different approach is most helpful. When most businesspeople plan their activities, there is an underlying assumption that money is important, and that a goal central to the operation of the business is the accumulation of profit. Many writers, however, fail to keep monetary motives in mind and must first thoroughly understand their economic needs and circumstances.

Small-business consulting books offer a variety of techniques that can be useful. In one common model, the writer—and we can shift to second person, for that is you—must sit down with paper and pen to list expenses. Calculate everything from housing, food, and clothes to gas for the car, summer camp for your children, and how much you spend on books. Determine the money you need each month to live, and not merely at a subsistence level. Don't tell yourself, "Oh, I can get by on eating packaged macaroni and cheese every day." If you don't fully accept both what you need and what you want, your business will not have the impetus to grow. Once you have the list, add money for retirement, health insurance, life insurance, taxes, and investment. Add 10 percent for your profit, because the business should generate money above what you pay yourself. This is no time to be forgetful. The final total is the amount you want—no, *need*—to make each month.

Now figure the amount of time you have available to work each month. In the average 4.3-week month, there are roughly twenty-one working days. Subtract at least four days for marketing (more on that later) and another two days for vacation, sickness, holidays, and other time you will be doing something else. That leaves you fifteen days of actual labor. With eight hours in each day—or ten, if you are like many of us—you have 120 to 150 hours of time. Take the amount of money you want to make each month and divide it by the number of hours available to you in the same period of time. That result is the amount of money you should be making every hour, on average.

Take a deep breath, because the amount will seem daunting. Yes, it really is that large. Let it be for now. You do not have to reach this figure immediately. This is a goal and, as you will eventually see, a realistic one. There are many writers who regularly make $75, $100, $150, or more per hour of their time, although the people paying for the services may not see them charged in such a fashion. For example, a magazine editor might pay by the word, a marketing director by the brochure, and a radio producer by the minute of airtime. This is immaterial as long as you know how much you are receiving and how long it takes to do a particular project. Remember three things about this financial goal. First, it is an average. There are days you will make more and days you will make less. Sometimes you may happily take lower-paying assignments because of other benefits they offer, such as interesting work, a valuable networking opportunity, or quick payment. Second, if your writing does not currently offer this level of remuneration, it's a goal to aim for. Do not give yourself the out of giving up because you are not yet making the money you wish. Third, a financial goal is an attempt to set a floor, not a ceiling. If you do better than your plan, then increase the difficulty of the goal.

Once you have determined your financial needs, it's time to plan.

This is complicated, because you must juggle three things: client management, cash flow, and sales. But with practice it becomes second nature. To meet your goals, you must ensure that you book enough work. This is more difficult than it sounds. Each piece of your income results from doing a project for a client, whether the client is a magazine, an advertising agency, a multinational corporation, or the local newspaper. When considering revenue, you must look at both the nature of the project (sales) and working with the client (client management). Sales affect cash flow (how quickly you are actually paid), cash flow affects the amount and types of sales you need to make, and the nature of clients affects everything. Every pairing of project and client incorporates the following six factors:

* Income

* Time

* Satisfaction

* Reliability

* Payment speed

* Annoyance

The income is the amount of money you will earn from the project. How much simpler could a concept be? Much. Some clients will try to reduce the size of a project after it is under way—often seen in the magazine world where a title contracts for payment by the published, not submitted, word. Others, whether due to organizational upheavals like a new editor or manager or financial problems, will cancel projects. Some will expand projects and pay more. Over time, you will get a sense of the likelihood that a project will be changed in one of these ways. Do not worry about suddenly finding yourself making more money than you expected, as this is a rare and delightful problem. Instead, look at how much of your income, on average, is lost, through project cancelation or reduction, as a percentage of your total income. Subtract that number from 100, and you have your real income percentage. For example, if, on the average, you sell $4,000 a month in writing, your total income should be $48,000 a year. Say that a $1,500 brochure was canceled and a $2,500 article was shortened; you received only $2,080. You would have lost $1,920, which is 4 percent of your total revenue. Therefore, the real income percentage is 96 percent of the revenue you booked. Perform this calculation over the duration of time you have been in business, and you will have a reasonably good idea of how much of your expected income actually comes in. Take this factor and multiply your expected revenue per month for a realistic view, over the long term, of what you will actually see. This is not a perfect system. There will be months when your income shortfall is greater. Over the long term, though, this planning and tracking will give you a better understanding of what you should expect to be making.

You should also track the revenue losses by each client, which is part of client management. There are good customers and bad customers. At times, you will radically improve your business by replacing bad customers with better ones. One customer who regularly reduces the scope of work might be responsible for an overwhelming portion of your lost income. If you have other reasons to keep the client, such as a high volume of work or rapid payment, then be sure to perform the lost revenue percentage calculation *just on that client.* Finding the real income percentage for that client allows you to appropriately discount the value of any work coming in from that company. Such focused attention can improve your overall accuracy at predicting income.

As you get a better feel for your real income, you can also analyze your expectations for any particular month and figure out how much you must still make in sales to meet your goals. (Don't count on a flush month to make up for a bad one. Better that you keep the same efforts and bank the extra money whenever possible.) Either in a spreadsheet program or on a paper grid, list the months of the year. Under each month, show a detailed accounting of the jobs you have scheduled as well as their expected income, multiplied by the real revenue percentage, and your best guess as to the number of hours the work will require. Add the figures for each month, and you begin to have an understanding of your business's financial health in advance and not just in retrospect. If a month needs sales attention, you can determine how much more you must make to meet your goals and how many hours you have to do so. Next, take the target revenue per hour you calculated when determining your financial needs and compare it to the total revenue of a potential project divided by the time it will likely take to complete. You can now see whether the work helps you meet your goals or fills time with low-paying work that will require you to toil even longer. Look at the total number of hours you have booked in the particular month to decide whether you have time to complete a project, or if you need a more manageable bit of writing. This is part of job satisfaction; sometimes it feels right and makes sense to take a relatively low-paying assignment. One of the joys of this business is being able to choose what we work on, for whatever the reason.

Sales planning is a critical part of the process. You probably do a variety of writing jobs, whether press releases, book or product reviews, feature articles, or brochures. When you know the amount of money you need to make and the time you have available, you can better target your sales efforts. Save longer projects, which typically take more time to sell, for the future whenever possible. Selling one to two months ahead is a fine goal that, when reached, greatly reduces working stress. Shorter, more readily available projects can be used to fill in small holes in a current month when necessary.

There is more to life than money, and the character of the client can affect your work experience greatly. An annoying client is one you'd prefer to avoid if at all possible. Why put up with aggravation in addition to the work necessary for an assignment? It is best to arrange your sales efforts to minimize the frustrations that might make you wish you were pushing a broom for a living. One of the worst client problems—other than numerous revisions, which increase the amount of time a project uses and decreases your revenue per hour—is late payment. Money unreasonably delayed affects cash flow, the rate at which money flows into and out of your business checking account, and that must become a major consideration when working for a publisher or a company. Many businesses find themselves in danger because, while doing well on paper, actual payments come in too slowly. As you plan sales and work schedules, note how long clients take to pay invoices. On a similar grid to the one you have just used for sales, plot when you reasonably can expect checks to arrive. As you determine your target income, add together all the expenses that absolutely must be met in a typical month. This shows the minimum cash flow that you need; any shortfall will need to be met by dipping into savings or credit lines. If you see that an upcoming month is a problem, consider rearranging your work schedule to increase the amount of funds that will show up by appropriately placing work that, even if lower in value, will more quickly result in cash.

To make the sales, you must also market yourself. Marketing involves approaching potential clients about projects. The rule of thumb is to spend 20 percent to 25 percent of your time actively marketing your services. Do not be fooled by stretches of plenty. I know a writer who let her usual torrent of queries slacken one year when work was plentiful and financially rewarding. But clients come and go, and prudence directs the constant cultivation of new ones to replace those that will leave. By taking that break from her marketing, she found herself in trouble a year later and she still hadn't fully recovered two years later. It is imperative that you never let up the process of searching for work. Set aside time every week for prospecting for corporate clients or pitching new story ideas, and remember to plan for volume. As experts in the field note, successful selling is a matter of numbers. The more pitches and queries you send out, the more responses you get and, in the end, the more checks you cash. Increase the volume of marketing, and you will increase the volume of money. By keeping the financial aspects of business at a hum, you make room for the craft and even artistic considerations. Income is important, but deadening if that is the only reason left for writing. Plan for a variety of assignments and types of work that will feed your creativity and tighten your grasp on the craft of writing.

Successful planning takes time, as well as management of that irreplaceable resource. I would heartily suggest an approach that started helping me a dozen years ago: the FranklinCovey planner. Break all of your marketing, sales, and even writing tasks into small items that can be listed and checked when completed. Listen to the tapes on time management and follow them with a quasi-religious fervor. Business planning may seem tedious when compared to being creative at the keyboard—except maybe when you're under a deadline crunch—but it is vital to your success and ability to work and live as a writer.

ERIK SHERMAN is an award-winning and widely published journalist and author. He has written for such publications as *Newsweek, US News & World Report, Continental, Men's Journal, Chief Executive, CIO Insight* and the *New York Times* Syndicate. He is also a photojournalist. He can be contacted through *www.eriksherman.com.*

3

The Writer's Office and Tools

S AMUEL G REENGARD

G reat writing skills simply aren't enough to ensure success as a freelancer. Without a well-equipped and
smartly designed office, it's almost impossible to work in
a professional manner and present a professional image.
If you don't have the right tools, it's tough to meet tight
deadlines and produce high-quality articles, books, and
other work.

The digital office of the twenty-first century is a much

different environment from that which existed a quarter-century ago. Now, writers face a dizzying array of choices about desks, chairs, lighting, office equipment, computer software, telecommunications, and more. Assembling the right gear and creating an optimal work environment isn't only a good idea; it's crucial. After all, time is the freelancer's most precious commodity. Because independent writers typically work on a per-project basis, greater efficiency translates directly into a higher income. If you can research and write an article in two days rather than four, you can use the remaining time to develop queries and write additional articles.

Yet speed isn't the only consideration. It's also essential to create an office environment that fosters creativity and allows you to produce high-quality work. Since we live in the Information Age, it's increasingly important to use tools to manage data, information, and knowledge. The Internet might put the world's largest research library at your fingertips, but it's up to you to uncover the right information and manage it effectively. For example, your hard drive can hold a wealth of data, but it's useless without tools that can help you find what you need quickly and seamlessly.

There are also the general requirements of operating a business to consider, such as choosing phone and Internet services, bookkeeping software, and banking solutions (for example, you should always have a separate checking account and credit card for your business). You should have a budget for putting together and maintaining your office. You might also consider hiring an assistant to handle basic tasks like transcribing, fact-checking, and running errands. And don't overlook attractive stationery and business cards. When putting your office together, don't put desks, tables, files, and equipment into the room in a haphazard, slapdash fashion. Think about what works best, what's most comfortable and efficient. Design books, Web sites, and software can help give you ideas about how to lay out your office so it's best for you. More than anything else, it's important to remember that a freelancer is an entrepreneur. Maintaining a professional image, managing your business wisely, and delivering a great product will help ensure a successful writing career.

Putting Investments to Work

Writers need to remember that when they equip themselves and outfit their offices, they are investing in their business. How much to spend and whether it's worth the cost are issues that even multinational corporations with huge resources must confront. While technology for technology's sake is an absolute waste, when you create a professional environment and you use the tools in a professional way, it stands to reason that you're going to work in a more professional manner and produce a better product faster. If you need an extra incentive, remind yourself that business expenses are tax deductible. Depending on your tax bracket, you're realizing a savings in the neighborhood of 20 to 30 percent on every purchase.

The trap that many writers fall into—and plenty of other entrepreneurs, for that matter—is lagging so far behind the adoption curve that they wind up using horse-and-buggy technology in a world that's moving at light speed. The old axiom "If it ain't broke, don't fix it" is downright dangerous today. Just as the corner drugstore or bookseller has had to adapt to radically different conditions, so do you. That means working within your basic business plan (see Chapter 2 about planning a writing business) to come up with an annual budget that provides for upgrading equipment and software when it can boost your bottom line. It means subscribing to at least one magazine or newsletter that discusses home-office and small-office issues in order to keep up on the latest technology and office trends. And it means constantly adapting—being willing to change the way you work and take occasional risks with new technologies and processes. Ultimately, those who put all the pieces together realize that the act of writing is only one of their jobs.

They're president, chief technology officer, facilities director, and secretary all rolled into one. They know that creating an outstanding office environment requires a healthy dose of vision but also plenty of hard work.

Making Your Space Count

The space you choose for an office and the way you decorate it says everything about your expectations and goals. Your office sets the tone for how you feel—and think. Whenever possible, it's wise to choose a separate room—so a partner or children do not distract you. Not only does this afford you a sense of quiet and privacy when you're on the phone or writing, it provides you with a place to keep your office equipment, supplies, paperwork, and other possessions—away from the busy areas of your house or apartment. An added bonus: A home office is tax deductible for most freelance writers. Consult your tax preparer to determine whether you qualify, and whether there are long-term ramifications (see Chapter 24 about taxes and deductions).

Regardless of where you set up shop, a sturdy, well-designed workstation is essential. If you amortize the cost of a unit over fifteen or twenty years, it isn't worth trying to cut corners over a few hundred dollars. Remember that you will be working at the desk almost every day. Comfort and efficiency are important. Before buying a desk, think about the manner in which you work. A personal computer, fax machine, scanner, printer, and phone can cover lots of real estate—leaving you little space for files and paperwork. Without adequate desk and counter space, you're almost certainly going to feel cramped and frustrated. If you have a room that's large enough, consider a wraparound workstation. It helps you keep equipment and often-used items within arm's reach.

Likewise, the location of drawers, hutches, and filing cabinets can help you stay organized or lead to total chaos. It's important to place high-touch items, such as stationery and office supplies, stamps, calculator, batteries, and checkbooks, as close to your seating area as possible. It's also wise to keep key file folders and business records close at hand. If your editor calls and needs some information about a story you just turned in, it saves time and effort if you have the file folder handy rather than embarking on a time-consuming search-and-retrieval mission.

Finding Your Comfort Zone

Clicking, tapping, typing, and twisting. Plant yourself at a computer for any period of time and you will almost certainly repeat the same movements and motions thousands of times. Even with functional furniture and proper posture, the repetitive nature of many tasks can wreak havoc on fingers, wrists, and necks. Factor in poorly designed equipment and the results can be disastrous. If you want to maximize productivity and minimize fatigue you need to start with excellent lighting. Good general lighting—supplied by indirect sunlight, recessed lights, or standard fixtures on the ceiling—helps illuminate the entire office space. Specialized-task lighting—usually from lamps—is helpful for reading or specific areas.

The chair you select is a key to staying productive. Invest in a chair that's comfortable but also provides adequate lumbar support. And make sure the chair can swivel so that you can reach all areas within your workstation without twisting and turning. The cumulative effect of unnatural body movements can take a toll on your neck and back over time. As a general rule, writers need a chair that's heftier than a secretary's chair but not as bulky as an executive chair. Since you will spend a lot of time typing but also a lot of time on the phone and online, you want to be able to perform a variety of tasks comfortably. Just as a person sitting at a PC for any period of time must adjust the keyboard and mouse to the right height and distance, the proper placement of a monitor can prevent neck strain and headaches. Keep the monitor at least an arm's length away and position the screen at or slightly below eye level. In order to prevent eyestrain and boost productivity, you might also want to consider upgrading to a seventeen-inch, nineteen-inch, or even a twenty-one-inch monitor and then magnify the size of the text onscreen—something that's easily accomplished using the zoom function within a word-processing program.

Finally, invest in a good telephone headset. It lets you keep your hands free for typing or handling other tasks. If that alone doesn't convince you, consider the physical toll from bending your neck when you're trying to cradle the receiver between your head and shoulder. Over a period of time, you're almost certain to wind up with neck and upper back pain. In most cases, an excellent headset costs $150 or more. But it's worth paying the premium. Inexpensive models produce inferior sound quality and may be uncomfortable if worn for more than a few minutes. An ergonomically designed office will help you avoid repetitive stress injury and other chronic muscle and joint ailments. It will help you handle tasks more quickly and efficiently. By paying attention to your body, you can unleash your mind.

Getting Equipped

At the center of today's digital office is the personal computer. Not only is it essential for producing words and editing them, it's your connection to the Internet and your tool for managing information. Buying a personal computer may seem like a visit down the rabbit hole in *Alice in Wonderland*. How many megahertz do you need? How much RAM should you buy? What size hard drive do you require? Should you add a CD-RW drive or a Zip Drive? And what about scanners, printers, and other peripherals? Every month, more powerful computers come along and prices drop. Should you wait? And when do you know it's the right time to buy a new unit?

To a certain extent, buying the right computer depends on your needs and your work style. A good rule of thumb is to purchase a system that's powerful enough for today but equipped to handle new tools and capabilities that could emerge over the next few years. For most freelancers, the "best buy" is a computer that's a couple of notches down in processing power and features from top-of-the-line systems. A more powerful system is likely to cost several hundred dollars more and an inexpensive system will probably become obsolete far too soon. When you're equipping your PC or Macintosh, don't skimp on memory. In many instances, the amount of RAM on a system will affect the actual performance more than processor speed. Having plenty of memory will also allow you to run several applications at the same time and avoid crashes. And because digital files are constantly getting larger and most of us are hanging onto PCs longer before replacing them, it's wise to buy a spacious hard drive. You probably won't want to add storage space later, and you can sometimes double the size of your hard drive for less than $100.

It's impossible to run through every spec for a new computer in a chapter of this length. Suffice it to say, there are a few other important issues to consider, including what type of backup drive, such as a CD-RW, Zip Drive, or other media, to purchase. Today, CD-RWs are a standard feature on many new PCs. They allow you to create your own data CDs as well as audio disks. And because they hold 650 megabytes of data on a single disk, and you can add and delete files, CDs offer unparalleled flexibility. Meanwhile, Zip disks have become the modern counterpart to the floppy disk. They can hold 100 MB, 250 MB, or 750 MB (depending on which version you buy) and are available on new PCs and as an external drive you can connect to your computer.

There's also the warranty and customer service to consider. It's easy to overlook these factors when you're buying a PC, but quality tech support is essential and a solid warranty can go a long way toward maximizing your investment and minimizing costs. You don't want to wind up on hold for forty-five minutes or an hour and then find yourself dealing with a rude or inexperienced tech support person who can't help you. One of the reasons companies like Dell, Gateway, and Compaq have emerged as leaders is that they provide excellent support. Some, like Dell, offer 24-7 support and allow you to purchase three-year, in-home service.

If you spend a good deal of time out of the office, a laptop may be a must. Also consider purchasing a Palm or Pocket PC to complement your computers. These personal digital assistants (PDAs) allow you to carry data with you, so you can find a phone number or an e-mail address the instant you need it. Best of all, these devices synchronize with your desktop or notebook PC to make it easy to keep your data current. If you change or delete an entry on one device, software updates the other device. PDAs also allow you to install handy programs, ranging from reference guides to international dialing codes.

Finding the Right Office Equipment

Even in today's e-everything world, it's essential to have the right office equipment and peripherals. You will need to print documents, and the type of printer you use determines how fast you can do so and what the quality will be. These days, the choice is between laser printers and inkjets. The former are slightly more expensive to buy but less expensive to operate (cartridges are cheaper per printed page) and they offer crisp, clear images in black and white. Inkjets, on the other hand, are less expensive to purchase and more expensive to operate. However, most inkjet models print in color.

Depending on how you use your PC you might also want to buy a scanner, which creates digital copies of paper documents and photos in your PC. Today's scanners create high-quality images and are simple to use. When selecting a scanner, you have two choices: flatbed or sheet-fed. The advantage of a flatbed scanner is that it can make copies from books, magazines, and other bound materials. A sheet-fed unit works with standard 8½-by-11-inch sheets of paper. Either way, it's possible to fax scanned files, attach them to an e-mail, or archive them for future reference. Many scanners also include software for making photocopies, and some include optical character recognition (OCR) software, which lets you scan a letter or article and produce editable text in your word-processing program. Those who prefer a dedicated fax machine over computer-based faxing, or like the idea of consolidating equipment, should consider a multifunction device (MFD). It allows you to fax, scan, and print from a single unit. All major manufacturers produce MFDs, though it's important to compare features to find the unit that best fits your needs. MFDs are the Swiss Army knife of peripherals, though there is a down side to them. If something goes wrong with the device, you lose the ability to fax, photocopy, scan, and print—all at the same time.

A freelancer's office wouldn't be complete without a voice recorder and a transcribing machine. Experienced journalists record most interviews so that they can obtain accurate quotes and protect themselves in the event of a legal dispute. Recording also lets you keep your hands free while you're talking and it allows you to concentrate totally on the interview. You have a choice between using a conventional tape recorder and using a digital recorder. The advantage of tape is that recorders are inexpensive and easy to use. The down sides are that tape is prone to breakage and, if you record a lot of interviews, you have to keep track of where each interview is stored on different tapes and risk losing or erasing something important. A digital recorder, on the other hand, costs a couple of hundred dollars up-front. But you don't have the ongoing expense of tapes and you can e-mail files to an assistant or a professional transcriber and get the text file back within hours. Moreover, it's easy to archive and store files for future reference.

Virtually all digital recorders allow you to transfer the files to your PC. Some vendors, such as Olympus, also include specialized audio software that allows you to transcribe recordings directly onto your computer using a special foot-pedal attachment. The software can speed or slow the recording and also let you backspace. These tiny recorders are perfect, too, for in-person interviews. They typically provide one or two hours of recording capacity. Whether you opt for a digital or tape recording device, you still have to connect the device to your phone. If your telephone has a built-in recording jack, then you simply attach a cable to the recorder and you're set. If the phone doesn't have a jack, the best approach is to purchase a unit that connects between the handset and base of the phone and provides a line-out jack to a recorder (available at electronics stores and through various catalog vendors). While they cost a bit more, these devices provide a better-quality recording than suction cups and other inexpensive gadgets.

The Hard Facts About Software

Most freelancers woefully underutilize their PCs. It's not uncommon for writers to think that a good word-processing program, an e-mail application, and a Web browser are all they need to succeed. But it's important to remember that you're running a small business. That means you need all the powerful tools you can muster to increase your productivity, improve your performance, and grab more assignments.

It's likely that your computer came with Microsoft Word, the de facto standard for word processing today. It's rich in features, simple to use, and virtually all editors and corporations rely on it. If you prefer another program, just make sure it's compatible with Word. If you cannot import and export Word files, you're at a distinct disadvantage. An integrated contact management and e-mail program is also essential. You can store names, addresses, phone numbers, and more in the program, and when it's used right it's like a Rolodex on steroids. You can track calls and e-mail with clients, file press releases and correspondence in folders, keep a calendar, set up alerts and reminders, and much more. For example, several programs—including Outlook and Act!—let you drag an e-mail to the calendar to set up an appointment. At that point, you can also embed a file, such as a list of questions or a project you're working on, for easy access. It's also simple to track your interaction with someone. If you're attempting to break into a new market, for example, you can view a list of queries or review notes of previous contacts with editors.

A Web browser is your link to the Internet. Whichever browser you use—typically Internet Explorer or Netscape Navigator—make sure you're using a recent version of the software and the latest plug-in applications. That way you can take full advantage of the Internet and all it has to offer. Also, familiarize yourself with bookmarks and consider adding specialized toolbars, such as those supplied by Yahoo! and Google. Once you install them into your browser, it's possible to conduct searches and find information more quickly. For example, the Yahoo toolbar includes buttons for Yellow Pages, reference materials such as a dictionary and World Fact Book, and maps with driving instructions.

Indeed, research is a key element of successful freelancing. And with the right tools on your computer, you'll enjoy a competitive advantage. One tool to consider is Copernic (*www.copernic.com*), which uses different search engines to scour the Web simultaneously. It can also narrow a search down to a particular category, including newsgroups, business and finance, family and parenthood, travel, and newspapers. The program, which is available in a free version as well as more-advanced versions for a fee—can also memorize searches for future reference. Another powerful tool is Enfish Personal (*www.enfish.com*). It indexes your hard drive—including Word, Excel, PowerPoint, Acrobat, e-mail, and graphics—and lets you search for specific information by keyword. That makes it possible to find old transcripts, stories, and even press releases sent by e-mail—even when you can't recall the name of the file. It can also help you locate random bits of data. For example, if you type in a phone number that exists anywhere on your hard drive, Enfish Personal can cross-reference it with a name or an organization.

No less important is a program for bookkeeping and managing your finances. Intuit's Quicken and Microsoft's Money are equally adept at generating invoices, maintaining banking records, and generating expense statements for clients. Just as valuable: They can produce end-of-year profit-and-loss statements that you can use to simplify taxes. You simply print a report and hand it to your tax consultant. Two other programs can help you manage and access files more efficiently. The first, Adobe Acrobat Reader (a free download at *www.adobe.com*), makes online papers, reports, and other documents available exactly as they appear in their native application or on paper. Acrobat Writer, meanwhile, allows you to generate PDF documents—if you're inclined to do work electronically. Among other things, that makes it possible to produce an electronic invoice and send it to a client via e-mail as an attachment. It also lets you scan a stack of papers, combine them with documents or graphics from your PC, and send the entire stack to an editor or colleague electronically. You can also sign documents electronically using Acrobat.

Paperless office aficionados, as well as those looking to make it easier to retrieve faxes, e-mail, and voice mail, might also consider using dedicated software such as Winfax Pro (*www.symantec.com*) or J2's fee-based Communicator software, which provides unified messaging. Simply put, you're able to receive faxes and voice mail in your e-mail inbox and send faxes from your computer or PDA through the Internet or via the J2 Web site (*www.j2.com*). Those who travel can find the service invaluable. J2 also lets you listen to e-mail by telephone. Don't overlook various utilities that can make your life simpler—or save it in a crunch. Internet backup services like Connected.com (*www.connected.com*) and @backup (*www.atbackup.com*) can copy key files onto the Internet so you can retrieve them if your system crashes. If you want to store files on the Web and access them from another computer—or share them with an editor or colleague—consider using MyDocsOnline (*www.mydocsonline.com*). And, above all else, make sure that you use a solid antivirus program, such as Norton Antivirus (*www.symantec.com*) or McAfee's VirusScan (*www.mcafee.com*) and that you update the virus definitions on a regular basis.

Making Connections

A personal computer might serve as the brain for the modern office, but telecommunications are the heart and soul. With a solid phone system and the right equipment, it's possible to operate at Internet speed. But the wrong selections can leave you feeling like you're operating a three-wheeled stagecoach. For most freelancers, it's wise to install two phone lines for business: one for voice and another for data and fax. The voice line should be separate from your personal phone line and shouldn't be answered by children. If a single phone line is your only option, then make sure you attach a device to automatically route voice and fax calls. It's thoroughly unprofessional to ask people to call you first so that you can switch on your fax.

Of course, it's not unusual for a journalist to spend several hours a day on the phone, particularly when conducting interviews. As a result, it's wise to pay a bit more for a telephone that can provide all the features you need. The list includes speed dial, volume control, a hold button, a mute button, a speakerphone, and redialing capability. Some phones, particularly those designed for a small office, now provide far more advanced functionality—including jacks for recorders and headsets, Caller ID, distinctive line ringing, and conference-calling capabilities. Whether to use phone company voice mail or an answering machine is another consideration. In today's fast-paced business environment, a busy signal or a line that goes unanswered is unacceptable. The advantage of phone company voice mail is that there's no machine to malfunction or clutter your desk, and it's easy to access, save, and even forward messages. On the other hand, it's typically more expensive than an answering machine.

You might also want to use certain phone company features, such as call waiting, call forwarding, and Caller ID, on your business line. Call waiting notifies you when someone calls while you're already on the line. That can be convenient, especially if you're waiting for an important call. But it can also prove annoying to someone who winds up being interrupted or put on hold. Call forwarding can also pay dividends, especially if you find yourself traveling or out of the office frequently. What's more, there might be times when you want to forward calls to a mobile phone. Caller ID lets you identify a caller before picking up the phone. That way you can know when it's an assigning editor or a pesky phone solicitor.

Long-distance companies offer billing codes, yet another valuable feature for freelancers. If you subscribe to this service, which is available free or for a few dollars per month, you enter a three- or four-digit code when you dial a long-distance number. Later, when your bill arrives, the calls are sorted by code, making it easier to track expenses and saving time when submitting an expense report.

Net Gains

It's no secret that we now live in a wired world. E-mail travels across the globe in seconds and information on almost any topic is available at the tap of a keyboard. By now, almost every writer and journalist understands the value of the Internet. However, not all connections are created equal. Most writers still rely on dial-up service, usually with a 56-kbps modem. For some, this is a perfectly adequate way to surf the Web and swap e-mail. It's easy to connect, and dial-up Internet service is certainly affordable at $20 to $25 per month. However, for a growing number of freelance writers, high-speed Internet—often referred to as broadband—is compelling, despite its $35-to-$70-per-month price tag.

Using a cable modem or digital subscriber line (DSL), you can surf the Internet at ten to twenty times the speed of dial-up service while maintaining an always-on connection. Consider this: If you're downloading a 12-megabyte program from the Internet, 56-kbps dial-up service slogs through the task in 50 minutes while a 1.5-mbps broadband connection takes only about 2½ minutes.

Broadband is a better choice for many writers. Besides loading Web pages faster and saving you time on downloads and uploads, it eliminates several seconds of wait time that it takes for a modem to establish a connection to the Internet. Multiply by dozens of times dialing in and connecting during a typical workday and that can add up to a twenty-minute loss of productive time. What's more, when your computer is connected to the Internet all the time, you can use specialized programs and features (including automated backup and recovery services) and present a more professional image. For example, when e-mail from an editor arrives, you see it immediately and you're able to respond without delay. Choosing between DSL and cable (or a satellite connection in areas that do not have other broadband options) needn't be complicated. If you have a choice, the key factors to consider are price and connection speed. If you opt for a high-speed Internet connection, make sure you install a personal firewall, such as ZoneAlarm (*www.zonealarm.com*) or Symantec Desktop Firewall (*www.symantec.com*). A firewall can protect you from hackers and other threats on the Internet.

SAMUEL GREENGARD is a Burbank, California, writer whose articles have appeared in *Wired, Discover, Modern Maturity, Hemispheres, Chief Executive, Business Finance, Home,* and *Internet World.* He is a past president of the American Society of Journalists and Authors. For more, visit *www.greengard.com.*

4

The Mystery
of Ideas

Jack El-Hai

Early in my writing career a friend kept calling me a *wordsmith*. "How's the wordsmith business going?" he'd ask, or "Was that a tough article to wordsmith?" Aside from the ugliness of the term, something about this label bothered me. A wordsmith sounds like someone who works with words just as a tinsmith works with pieces of metal. Words, my friend implied, were the basic unit of my trade. He seemed to think I mainly concerned myself with selecting words and cobbling them into articles and books. To a non-writer, the process of writing may look like an exercise in words. But our task is really much more challenging and satisfying. Composers manipulate themes and harmonies, not notes; doctors treat patients, not organs; and photographers explore light and color, not pixels. In the same way, nearly every successful writer realizes that ideas—not words, sentences, or paragraphs—are the currency of our work. Ideas are the raw materials for our industry. Anyone can learn to use a word correctly. Only skilled writers can identify promising story ideas and develop them into irresistible articles and books.

Where does a writer find that skill? Where do the ideas come from? Learning the craft of capturing ideas doesn't require formal training or an advanced degree. It demands only a subtle change in the way you think. If you learn to view the world with curiosity, wonder, and an eye for what is incongruous or unexplained, the ideas will come. Once you have learned that craft, generated some good ideas, and built articles or books on them, you'll really know the true value of ideas. You'll feel reluctant to share marketable ideas with other writers. You'll test ways to keep track of them and recall them. You'll devote hours to expressing them clearly. A single idea can keep you busy and prosperous for years, and some writers have grown famous on fewer ideas than you can count on one hand. "Ideas are what get you the job and keep editors coming back to you," says magazine writer Karen J. Bannan.

The Zen of Idea-Making

Generating story ideas is more about a frame of mind than a procedure. Open yourself to your responses to what you've experienced, heard about, or read. "Most often my new story ideas emerge out of events or news items that stir my emotions or my curiosity. I'll see something in the newspaper and tear it out or somebody will say something that makes me want to know more," says Anita Bartholomew, who has written magazine features for *Reader's Digest, McCall's, YM,* and other publications. "Usually, this process doesn't start out as, 'Oh, what a great story idea,' but as simply, 'What's going on here?'" Some writers talk about "a Zen aspect" to story ideas. When they need to come up with ideas, they stop and let their minds wander; maybe they're doing other things, such as mowing the lawn, taking a shower, exercising, driving, or doing the laundry. The ideas make themselves noticeable and bubble into conscious thought. Some writers say that the more they let their minds do this, the more ideas they get.

We all live in a world bounded by our inner experiences, acquaintances, work, interests, family, and what we see and hear from the media. Let your world be your inspiration. Nearly every good idea comes to writers in one of three ways: from what we experience, what we hear in conversation, and what we learn from the work of other reporters and writers. Whatever comes to your attention that raises questions in your mind is a possible idea for a story. "The essence of thinking like a writer is the recognition that what's most interesting is what's unknown, not what is known," notes James B. Stewart in his writing manual *Follow the Story* (Touchstone). "Thinking like a writer prizes the question more than the answer. It celebrates paradox, mystery, and uncertainty, recognizing that all of them contain the seeds of a potential story."

It Happened to You

Things happen to us. Examine every event in your life for its potential as a story idea. Is your life dull? Ask why. Find others who feel that way about their lives. You can turn dull living into a good story.

Florence Isaacs, a veteran freelancer who specializes in articles on family and marriage, relationships, women's issues, and health, finds most of her ideas in her circle of experience. What seemed like an unusual frequency of diabetes in her family led to an article in the *New*

York News Sunday Magazine on the nationwide epidemic of that disease. "I followed that with an article on how to be an effective caretaker while taking care of yourself at the same time," she says. After noticing a large number of mentally ill people on the street in her neighborhood, she wondered why, and why *now*. "I did some digging and sold to *Reader's Digest* an article on the deinstitutionalization of the mentally ill," she says. Isaacs has also harnessed her own experiences in the generation of book ideas. "My difficulty composing a condolence note to an acquaintance whose daughter suddenly died led to the idea for my first book, *Just a Note to Say ... The Perfect Words for Every Occasion*," she notes. "It went on to sell 140,000 copies to date." Her joys and problems with friends resulted in a book on women's friendships, *Toxic Friends/True Friends: How Your Friends Can Make or Break Your Health, Happiness, Family and Career*. "I've found that my own life is teeming with possibilities for both article and book ideas," Isaacs says. "The trick is to be open to noticing them and to do some digging to come up with a larger story."

After Janet Mazur quit her staff writing job to care for her children and freelance, she feared that her new home-based career would kill her inspiration and dull her senses. Instead, she found new sources of ideas and learned to market herself differently, as a writer of articles on parenting issues for such magazines as *Parents* and *American Baby*. For ideas, "I don't have to look much beyond my own two daughters," she says. "I write quirky pieces, developmental stories on topics as thrilling as spit-up, and stories aimed at mothers and the difficult transition they face in our culture, regardless of whether they return to work or remain at home for their kids." When dozens of people stopped her in public to ask about "that thing" she used to carry her infant daughter, she knew it was time to pitch a story on baby slings. And after hiring several teen baby-sitters, she grew curious about their perceptions of the job of minding someone else's kids. She ended up writing an article about baby-sitters' nightmare jobs. "I interviewed girls who told of parents who arrived home drunk; of uncooperative and destructive tots; and of one mother who didn't return home until seven o'clock the next morning, leaving the sitter stranded and scared," Mazur recalls. "Of course, the piece also contained sidebars on classes a would-be sitter can take and helpful hints for both parents and sitters."

A few years ago, Karen Bannan was making her regular visit to her health club. "The girl at the desk handed me a sample of Dove Body Wash. 'Hmm,' I thought, 'this is an interesting way to advertise a new product.' I did a little research and found out that a lot of vendors were using the gym as a place to do sampling," she says. The outcome of her curiosity? "I pitched the story to my editor at the *New York Times* and I got the assignment."

Sometimes a writer wants not to write directly about a personal experience, but instead to chronicle her response to the experience or her means of recovering from it. Andrea Warren has built a successful writing career from the biggest tragedy of her life, the death of her ten-year-old son in 1986. "Since then, I've been on a quest to find out how people survive traumas that made them want to die, or in some instances almost killed them, and go on living fulfilling lives," she says. "I was looking for insight to help me. I suppose I was also looking for people whose hurt was as great or greater than mine. As a result, I've published several drama-in-true-life kinds of stories, including two articles on two different survivors of the Oklahoma City bomb blast, both gravely injured and buried under the rubble for hours." But Warren has also drawn ideas from her son's death in a more unexpected way. She writes nonfiction children's books about kids who lived through traumatic events, such as *Surviving Hitler: A Boy in the Nazi Death Camps* (Harper Trophy). "I am so drawn to children who are tough, who make it through, and who forgive. Such stories, such ideas for stories, are everywhere." Warren's awareness of her own family tragedy is what makes her sensitive to the potential and power of these narratives.

Similarly, Susan J. Gordon conceived her book titled *Wedding Days:*

When and How Great Marriages Began (William Morrow) as a healing distraction. "Usually, I just tell people that my book was inspired by the engagements of my two sons, and that's true," she explains. "But something else was going on. It was a very happy time in my family, but we were also involved in a deeply troubling situation—a rift of unparalleled dimensions between two other people in my family. I was sick at heart, and emotionally unsteady. But out of that sad time, something wonderful happened. Subconsciously or unconsciously, I found a way to protect and heal myself. Out of the blue, the idea for this joyous book materialized, an upbeat and soulfully satisfying project taking me out of myself and out of my sadness. The research was so vast—I investigated the lives of more than one thousand couples—it left me little time to think."

Your personal experience also includes your curiosity about events taking place in your own backyard. Several years ago, writer B. J. Roche seriously examined her backyard when she transformed her problems with her home septic tank into an article for *Country Journal* about how these buried waste disposal systems work. The advice "Look in your own backyard" does not, of course, have to be taken so literally. Your backyard includes your geographic community and the cultural, ethnic, religious, and recreational circles in which you travel. Even writers in the largest metropolitan areas, such as New York City, Chicago, and Los Angeles, can claim territories of their own. When you find story ideas in your own backyard, you often spare yourself the expense and time of travel and the difficulty of tracking down sources in other parts of the country. Your knowledge of the people in your locality gives you a reporting edge over other writers, and you gain the satisfaction of bringing your backyard idea to readers far beyond your community.

Friends and Professional Sources

The novelist Henry James first used the term *donnée*, French for "given," to mean an inspiration that's handed to you as a gift. James gained notoriety for halting friends in full throttle telling an interesting story or anecdote. "Stop!" he would cry out. "I see it now—it's becoming clear to me!" He was experiencing the vision of a short story that he could craft from his friend's anecdote. Interrupting people in conversation, as James did, won't win you any friends, but paying attention to a *donnée* that falls into your lap is a smart practice for any writer. "I recently got a *Woman's Day* assignment from pitching a story about Bunco, which is a game that women on Long Island and across the country are playing," says Karen Bannan. "I knew about it because my friend went to a Bunco party and told me about it."

It often pays to cultivate a group of busybodies, gossips, and terminally curious people who can feed you their stories. Claire Tristram, who writes often about technology, has done just that. She routinely seeks out and keeps in touch with "interesting people who love being informed about everything but don't want to write about it themselves. They're just passionately interested in subjects, take the time to find out everything, and love talking about their interests," she says. "They are often people I've interviewed for past stories who just happen to be plugged into places I am not." Tristram also finds it helpful to talk with publicists and people in public relations, who after all are in the business of promoting their clients' ideas as well as their products and services. "I've found a few really good people who have interesting clients and who understand what makes a good feature," she observes. "They often will pitch me instead of an editor, because they see I can often bring a good idea more credibility when I pitch it myself."

Carol Milano, a health-care freelancer, gets most of her most salable ideas while interviewing sources for other assignments. "After we've been talking a while, someone will start telling me about another project he or she is involved in, and I jot down lots of notes," she says. While researching one recent assignment on wellness centers for seniors, several of her interviewees told interesting stories of how they had raised the money to fund their centers. Although finances weren't part of her original assignment, she pitched a follow-up story called "Fiscal Fitness: Innovative Ways to Raise the Money for Your Facility's Projects" to the magazine of a national association of senior centers, and the editor assigned the piece. Milano also keeps her ears open to the ideas and experiences of nonprofessional sources—otherwise known as friends and relatives. "My mother told me that she was so discouraged to see my ailing eighty-two-year-old father napping all day long, she'd decided to buy him a computer to try to perk him up," she says. "Their teenaged grandson set it all up and taught my dad the basics. And pretty soon he was eagerly spending his afternoons at a monitor instead of snoozing. I found a researcher at Duke University who had studied seniors and computers and sold an article on the topic to a health Web site—using my dad's experience to open both the query and the article."

Do not discount the ideas that come from some of your most valuable allies in the business of freelancing—editors themselves. Editors often feed promising story ideas to the writers they think can best develop them. My first assignment for the *Atlantic Monthly* was one such gift from heaven. I met one of the *Atlantic*'s senior editors at a writing conference and spent a few minutes chatting with him. When he found out I lived in Minneapolis, he said, "You know, there's a story in Minneapolis that I've been interested in for a long time, but I don't think I'll ever get around to it myself. Do you think you might be able to check up on it?" Dumbfounded, I said yes without even knowing what the story was about. The result was a piece that the *Atlantic* published about a year after my initial conversation with the editor. Remember, other people's ideas can be just as good or better than your own, and don't be afraid to consider someone else's twist or take on your idea. It may be an improvement.

Someone Else Got There First

Paying attention to your own experiences is very good. Listening to others is great. Most writers, however, find that stories that have already hit print or the airwaves are the best sources of ideas. "A writer must also read. Voraciously. The things others have done will serve as points of departure for his own work," advises William Ruehlmann in his book *Stalking the Feature Story* (Knopf). "He must read the classics and the daily newspaper, slick magazines and old yellowing pulps, handbills passed out by street partisans, the backs of cereal boxes." Yes, the publication or broadcast of a story means that someone else got there first. But where they went with the story may not be where you would go. Despite the recent prominence of narrative journalism in newspapers, for example, most papers still rely on telling the basics: describing what happened yesterday. A house burned down. A jury delivered its verdict. Somebody won an award. Each of these events can be the starting point or the conclusion of a compelling story, and any of them can ignite a great story idea if you just ask the right questions. What kinds of questions? Transport yourself into question-asking mode, and you'll find that most news accounts in print and on television raise more questions than they answer. When you read, hear, or watch a news story that interests you, you can capture a wealth of intriguing ideas by asking these questions:

* Who are the people most affected by this news? Who stands to gain and lose?

* What person or group is at the center of these events?

* How have the personal qualities of the people involved affected the outcome?

* How and why did this happen? What might these events lead to?

* Has this happened before?

* What's the problem here, what are some possible solutions, and who might be able to provide those solutions?

* How does this news make you feel? Why?

∗ Why should anyone care about this? Who *would* care about this?

∗ Is this news part of a trend?

In other words, let your curiosity (if it is truly aroused) run wild. Each question can suggest an idea for a new story, one that explores terrain that the original account probably only skirted. Here is the gist of a wire service story taken almost at random from a recent edition of my city's daily newspaper. On the surface, there is not much that is striking about it. Dozens of stories like it appear every week in newspapers and on the evening news. Even so, close examination shows that it suggests many unanswered questions, and behind each question lies a possible story idea. Look it over, and see what you find:

MOM TAKES AIM AT BOOSTER SEAT MAKER

The Texas mother of a toddler who died in an auto accident while strapped into a Cosco Explorer booster seat is targeting the seat's manufacturer in a campaign to prompt a recall of the model. Melanie Armstrong's 33-pound son was thrown from a minivan in the 1999 crash, and she says the Cosco seat, marketed for children as small as 30 pounds, is unsafe for kids under 40 pounds. A spokesperson for Cosco says the booster seat has an excellent safety record and meets all federal standards.

Just 87 words, and it raises so many questions. For example:

∗ Should parents be concerned about the safety of booster seats designed for children in the thirty- to forty-pound range? How are booster seats tested, and how adequate are the federal standards? Can parents do anything to make their toddlers safer in the car?

∗ How has Cosco handled Melanie Armstrong's campaign? Do the company's products have a good safety record? How have similar challenges from consumers been handled in the past?

- Who is Melanie Armstrong? How is she running her campaign? How is it affecting her family? What in her past has prepared her to undertake this?

- How exactly did Melanie Armstrong's son die, and could his death have been prevented?

- Is anyone else campaigning against booster seats? Who are the industry's defenders?

- Are any new booster seat laws or regulations on the horizon? Why or why not? What are manufacturers doing to make booster seats safer?

- Do you have a toddler? What does this news item make you want to do? Why?

Obviously, there's no shortage of questions. And questions lie at the heart of many of the best story ideas. Your job is to select the questions that intrigue you the most and run with them. Claire Tristram often cultivates ideas this way. "In my field, mostly writing 'think' pieces about technology, there's usually some sort of news announcement about a breakthrough technology. It gets reported in science magazines and maybe gets a very superficial treatment in newspapers," she says. "Then it's there for the picking for a more thoughtful analysis. So it's often a very straightforward process of picking up the business section or the technology section of the paper and seeing what's being covered, and in that act also discovering what they've missed." Many writers find that their local media offer the best story ideas, as opposed to publications and broadcasts with a national audience. For more than ten years, I read in my hometown newspaper about Max Weisberg, a mentally retarded sports bookmaker with a special gift for calculating game spreads and odds despite his other limitations. The newspaper articles focused on Max's frequent court trials, nearly all of which resulted in acquittals. One day it occurred to me that Max could be the subject of a magazine article that probed deeper than the newspaper's chronicles of his days in court, but instead examined his background and the innovative defense strategy his lawyer mounted. The story sold to the first magazine I proposed it to, the *Atlantic Monthly*.

Books can also serve up unusual story ideas. I have a particular fondness for the idea-stirring potential of footnotes. Footnotes often detail odd facts or events that authors can't find a place for in their narrative yet can't bring themselves to discard. Years ago, I read a book by Frederick Starr called *Red and Hot: The Fate of Jazz in the Soviet Union* (Limelight). One of Starr's footnotes mentioned that a group of twenty-two African-Americans visited Moscow in 1932 to make a movie, and that they met Paul Robeson and other musicians while in Russia. The footnote stopped me dead. I wondered why those Americans were in the USSR and what happened to them. I found the answers and published the story in *American Heritage*.

Identifying and Keeping Good Ideas

Not all ideas are created equal. The best ideas will carry an emotional wallop, be timely, hold your own interest, and directly affect the lives of your readers or pique their curiosity. "I distinguish good from bad ideas by how much they stay with me," says Kathryn Lance, the author of fifty books of nonfiction and fiction. "If I can't stop thinking of something, I know there is something to it." And they must be what professional writers call "sellable." That means they must compel an editor to make the assignment. A few otherwise good stories fail to do that, usually because the idea lacks emotion or the right slant. Good ideas are slippery and elusive—they want to escape from your grasp. You must record them or risk losing them. But after noting them, then what? Most writers have filing systems of one kind or another. My idea files, stored in a massive five-drawer cabinet, are organized by general topic ("Law" or "Psychology") or by specific story ("Weisberg, Max") once I have accumulated enough information. The problem is that months go by before I revisit many of these files, and I forget what's in them.

Ideas do us no good, and they certainly make us no money, if they are not developed and proposed, so some writers set aside time each day or week to hone their ideas and write proposals based on them. Many writers devote time to thinking about ideas, and some consider it an important part of their regular business planning. Some ideas quickly show themselves to be right or wrong for you, and some need time to ripen or sour. Virtually every writer who makes a living as a freelancer has a system for jotting down ideas, gathering more background information, and keeping track of ideas that have been pitched and the editors who have received them. The respective lists are fluid and ever-changing.

Carol Bly, one of America's best writers and teachers of fiction, once described a story as "a combination of what the writer supposed the story would be about—plus what actually turned up in the course of writing." Creating good and satisfying ideas for articles and books involves that same engrossing process of seizing your *donnée* and poking at it until you have something new and mysterious that's all your own. You start with something you saw or heard or read, and turn it like wet clay on a potter's wheel. The end product can surprise even you.

JACK EL-HAI (*www.el-hai.com*), who lives in Minneapolis, primarily writes about medicine and the law for such publications as the *Atlantic Monthly,* the *Washington Post Magazine, American Health,* and *American Heritage.* His biography of lobotomy developer and promoter Walter Freeman will be published in 2004.

5

Seven Secrets
of a Successful
Magazine Query

LISA COLLIER COOL

How would you like to make a $2,000, $5,000, or even $10,000 magazine sale, simply by investing the time it takes to write a letter? A query letter—a combination article proposal and sales pitch—is one of the experienced, professional writer's most effective ways of finding work and building up business. It is also the fastest and most efficient way for beginners to break into print. In the time it takes to research and write one story, you could craft several queries, greatly multiplying your odds of a sale. Using a proposal instead of a finished article also lets you get timely ideas out quickly, and reduces time wasted on unsalable projects. A query can also be personalized for many different magazines—or to sell the same story to several noncompetitive markets.

Most important, a good pitch letter sells an editor on *you*—not just that one article. Even if the editor doesn't want the idea you're pitching—perhaps because she already has a story on that topic in the works, or feels the subject isn't quite right for her magazine—an appealing proposal could still land you an assignment. I once sent a query about dream interpretation to several magazines and ended up selling two completely unrelated articles: *Cosmopolitan* gave me an assignment to write about modeling agencies, while *Playgirl* hired me to write about video dating services. Why? Although I was pitching the wrong project, I apparently did it well enough to convince these editors that I was the right person to handle *their* ideas. That's the true magic of a query. Using a few well-chosen paragraphs to showcase your talents, you can get your work into the hands of someone with the power to launch or upgrade your writing career: a buying editor.

How do you write a winning query? Here's the method I've used to sell more than 300 articles to such magazines as *Glamour, Good Housekeeping, Harper's, Marie Claire, Ladies Home Journal, Parents*, and *Penthouse*.

Step 1: It All Starts with an Idea

A few years ago, I got a letter from a woman who read my book *How to Write Irresistible Query Letters* saying that since she found it so hard to think of her own ideas, did I mind if she stole some of mine? Despite her promise to send me a copy of anything she sold by plagiarizing my work, I found her offer easy to refuse. What I'd like to tell her—and you—is that salable concepts are everywhere, if you know where to look. My colleague Jack El-Hai discusses finding and developing ideas in more depth (Chapter 4), and I'd like to reinforce his advice with my own experience. I get many of my ideas delivered right to my door in my morning paper. For example, I recently read a news story about a dog that saved a baby's life. I wrote a short query, sent it off to *Woman's Day,* and made a $2,500 sale.

Along with keeping an eye out for human-interest dramas like this, also watch for medical, scientific, or technological breakthroughs; stories about unusual people, services, or businesses; trends; and bizarre or sensational crimes. Also consider the larger implications of the news: After reading about various mishaps in clinical trials, I proposed an investigative article on why human experiments are becoming so dangerous—and promptly got an assignment from *Penthouse.* Remember that most national magazines take four to twelve months to publish an article, so it's important to go beyond the headlines, as I did with this story. After all, editors don't want to commission an article that will be out of date by the time it gets into print.

Get on as many media mailing lists as possible. Call or write organizations in your field of interest, requesting that they add your name, address, fax number, and e-mail address to their press list. Since I often write about health, I've done this with many medical groups—with very profitable results. When the American Diabetes Association sent me information on a new study showing that type-2 diabetes was on the rise, I immediately queried *Good Housekeeping*—and landed a $5,000 assignment. Since I'm also interested in medical dramas involving kids, I've asked a number of children's hospitals around the United States to e-mail me about any remarkable pediatric cases they get. So far, I've sold three "miracle baby" stories I found through hospital publicists.

Another good source of ideas is your personal experience. Research is minimal when you're writing about the subject you're most expert in— yourself. (And you're sure to have an exclusive, too!) When freelancer Kathy Sena decided to go to an in-line skating camp for women, she sent a pitch about her upcoming trip to *Shape* magazine—and snagged a dream assignment. Not only did she get paid for the article, but the publication picked up the tab for a fun-filled week at the camp. Another writer, Paula Dranov, used her own difficulties with fibroid tumors and migraine headaches as a springboard for useful stories for other women with these disorders. And on a sadder note, I was inspired to write an article about skin cancer for *Marie Claire* recently, hoping to help young women avoid the disease that killed my father a few years ago.

If there's nothing in your own life that sparks a story concept, ask experts you know—your doctor, lawyer, real estate agent, banker—what's going on in their fields. By talking to my brother-in-law, a psychiatrist, I learned that Ritalin was being overprescribed for adults. An editor at *Self* bought the story, which won the American Society of Journalists and Authors' 2001 Outstanding Article Award. And while I was interviewing a fetal surgeon for a *Good Housekeeping* article, the doctor happened to mention an amazing prenatal operation he'd done: removing a tumor that was actually bigger than the baby. That conversation sparked a $7,500 sale to another women's magazine. It pays to be a good listener.

Step 2: Find an Intriguing Slant

An idea alone isn't enough. To interest an editor, you also need a slant, your special spin on the subject that distinguishes it from what's already out there. If little or nothing has previously been written about the topic, novelty alone can be an angle: A few years ago, I received a report from the National Fire Protection Association showing that most fires in America are set by children—not only by little kids playing with matches, but also by delinquents who use arson as a form of vandalism. Since this was news to me, I sent out a query using scary statistics from the report, and sold the story to *Penthouse*. Focusing on a hidden danger is also a good angle for not-so-new subjects. Even though a lot has been written about hepatitis C, I successfully pitched an article focusing on an alarming study: Up to 250,000 American women may have contracted the disease through tainted blood they received during cesarean sections.

If your idea is neither new nor frightening, look for an aspect other writers have neglected. That's how freelancer Diane Benson Harrington managed to sell a toilet training story to *Parents:* "I suggested 'Potty Training for Late Bloomers'—and discussed how to deal with kids over age three who hadn't figured it out yet. That's a whole different set of frustrations than trying to teach a two-year-old," she explains. Or look for a way to turn the story inside out. A couple of months ago, I read a fascinating profile of a professor who studies skunks. That inspired me to pitch a story about his *wife,* who loves her man even when he comes home reeking after a run-in with one of his research subjects.

Still having trouble coming up with a slant? Linking your idea to an emotion, issue, or practical concern will enhance its sales prospects. As I was writing this, I was interrupted by a call from an editor from *Health* with an offer to buy a story of mine that contains all three elements. My query began with a tragic anecdote about a woman whose baby died of a serious but treatable disease because her state didn't offer a $25 test that could identify newborns with that disorder. I then discussed the issues involved—the equipment to do this test is costly; the disease is quite rare, so the price per life saved is relatively high—and offered moms-to-be important advice, including information on how they could arrange to have their babies tested privately. Similarly, as you develop *your* idea into a query, show how your story will make readers angry, amazed, alarmed, or amused; provide enticing food for thought; and give them some useful benefit or plan for action.

Step 3: Do Some Digging

The better your research, the easier it will be to sell your article. As Diane Harrington advises her writing students, "Never send a query until you're sure the story has legs. Do the research *first,* because if you don't know the basic information—enough to answer an editor's inevitable preassignment questions—then you could miss out on a sale." The bottom line, she adds, is that "if any part of your query contains the words, 'I'd like to find out more about (your basic premise),' then it's not ready to submit." Since a query is short, it's not necessary to chase down every last detail. Instead, the goal is to get some fast facts. Go online and do a Google search (*www.google.com*) to look for sites that deal with your topic. A word of caution, however: There's a lot of misinformation on the Net, so make sure to get your facts from a reputable source, such as the Centers for Disease Control Web site (*cdc.gov*) rather than Jimmy's Personal Homepage. Often you can find an organization with a fact sheet or report that gives all the background you need on your topic. You may want to call the group and get additional information from its press officer—or ask to be put in touch with an expert. For human interest stories, it's helpful to do a short phone interview to get an overview of the person's experiences, plus such basics as his or her age, marital status, number of children, occupation, and address.

Step 4: Target a Market

Identify magazines that might be interested in your idea, and why. Your query must emphasize the ingredients of your story that make it appropriate for that publication's audience. When I was pitching my juvenile arson article, I decided to aim it at *Penthouse* because almost all fires are set by boys or young men—an obvious male angle. If, on the other hand, I had wanted to pitch that story to a woman's magazine, I would have taken a dramatically different approach, such as advice for parents: "Fire-Proofing Your Kids." To find the best bets for your proposals, take a tip from freelancer Melba Newsome. Several times a year, she makes a research trip to her local library and spends the afternoon reading a wide variety of magazines. Not only has that helped her target her pitches more effectively, but she's also cracked several new markets.

Even if you already know something about a certain magazine, it pays to check out several recent back issues at the library. Not only does this spare you the embarrassment of learning that your topic already was addressed in last month's cover story, but it will alert you to any recent changes in format or direction.

Such research yields other dividends as well, adds Harrington. "You need to know what separates this magazine from its competitors in terms of content and style, and answer the question editors most want to know: Why is this idea perfect for *them*—and not another magazine? One of the most common complaints among editors is that they receive far too many queries from writers who obviously haven't read the magazine, and therefore pitch ideas that either already have appeared there or aren't appropriate for that magazine in the first place.

Use what you've gleaned from a close study of your target publication to whet an editor's appetite for your story. When editors go into assignment meetings to discuss what to buy, they have to envision where a piece might fit into the magazine, what its cover line might be, and potential sidebars (short, related articles) and boxes (super-short, related items, such as a list of sources of additional information). Get ahead of the game by doing the editor's work for her in your query. Offer a catchy title, intriguing sidebar ideas, and even suggest which department might run it. That will set off your query as the work of a true professional.

Step 5: Write a Powerhouse Lead

When I was a literary agent, one of my bestselling clients, William Hoffman, used to say that the way to get an editor's attention is to punch him in the nose—with your first paragraph. Make that lead a knockout and you're halfway to a sale. Freelancer Joan Price tries to write the opening sentence of the query as if it could be the first paragraph of the article: "Write to the magazine's audience, not the editor. That shows that (a) you can write in the style of the magazine, (b) you can hook the reader, and (c) you know your subject well enough to craft the opening. Many new writers mistakenly think they need to talk 'about' the article rather than let it speak for itself." Here's how Susanne Alexander uses this technique in a captivating query to *Reader's Digest* about kids from Belfast who are brought to the United States for a five-week program aimed at breaking the cycle of hatred and violence in Northern Ireland:

> Fear, excitement and shyness chase through their eyes, as fast as the clouds in windy Chicago where they've landed, or a stray bullet in their native Belfast, Northern Ireland. At eleven and twelve, they are wide-eyed and curious, but they also arrived with the baggage of all their country's conflicts and prejudices.

Dos and don'ts for your lead:

Do start with a dramatic anecdote, intriguing quote, vivid description, provocative questions, or compelling statistics and facts. All these can be a great way to hook an editor's interest. Or try a note of mystery; one of the most riveting first sentences I've ever read is, "When Joan Bardona went into labor shortly before 4:00 A.M., she had no idea she was about to make medical history." Who wouldn't read the second sentence?

Don't open with an extended list, a definition (unless very witty), lengthy geographical descriptions (opt for action instead), highly technical material or jargon, or an explanation of why you've chosen this particular topic. Editors want to know what's going to be in the article, and they want to know it right away.

Step 6: Add an Enticing Summary and Author's Bio

Now that you've gotten the editor interested, close the deal with an appetizing description of the article's key ingredients. As one editor puts it, "Show us you've already gone halfway down the road by including enough facts, figures, and details to prove that your story is real." Here's how Jim Morrison accomplished this in his query to *Smithsonian* about a group of people with an unusual hobby:

> Jenkins and his buddies are dedicated to nurturing tree climbing as a recreational sport like hiking or rock climbing. For the tallest trees, they use custom equipment, firing a guide line using a bow and arrow or a line gun and then climbing up the rope to a branch using mechanical ascenders, a ratchet device with a stirrup that allows them to move up the rope a few feet at a time. Several times a year, these modern-day Tarzans organize overnight stays, rigging sleeping hammocks called "treeboats" between branches as high as 100 feet from the forest floor.

If your lead hasn't made the focus of your proposed article crystal clear, then start the summary with a statement of purpose: "My article will focus on experimental surgery—and the shocking lack of regulation that's endangering patients." Then back up this assertion with some relevant facts and figures. You may want to mention some sources, such as respected experts, you plan to use; offer some additional anecdotes; suggest sidebars; cite studies or news events that show that your topic is hot right now. It's often helpful to include a short outline listing some interesting points you'll cover. A lively way to present these specifics is "bullet formation," as Timothy Harper does in this query to the *Atlantic Monthly*:

> Here's why Allan Dalton is the perfect pickup basketball player:
> - He's played plenty of organized ball: small college star, drafted by the Celtics (made it to the last cut), many company and Y and rec league teams over the years. But he's always played more in pickup games on playgrounds and in open gyms.
> - He plays a lot: once a day, usually, sometimes twice. If he didn't have a job that let him play for a couple of hours every day at lunchtime, he'd either change the job or find a new one.
> - Physically, he's not intimidating: 6-foot-1, about 185 pounds, a bit

of a belly, a thick knee brace (two operations) and a face that looks at least 52 years old.

* He can play virtually any position, depending on the talent on the court with him, but ordinarily plays point guard. He controls games. Sometimes if a teammate can only play the point, he slides over to a wing, but the offense still runs through him since the point inevitably turns it over as soon as the ball is across the ten-second line.

After summing up the story, include a short author's bio, listing your magazine, newspaper, or book credits and any other relevant credentials. If, for example, your topic is "Helping Your Child Ace Standardized Exams," mentioning that you're both a parent and high school teacher could help cinch the sale.

Step 7: Rejection-Proof Your Proposal

A number of common mistakes can sabotage your query. Here's a checklist of problems to avoid:

MANGLED MONIKERS: When I was a literary agent, I often received queries misaddressed to "Liza," "Leslie," or in one memorable case, "Shirley." Not only does getting an editor's name, title, or the address of the magazine wrong speak poorly of your research skills, but it annoys editors and may delay response to your query.

FAULTY FACTS: A writer I know lost a sale because he misidentified one of the personalities he mentioned in the query. The editor noticed the mistake and concluded that the writer was a sloppy researcher. Always double-check facts, even if you think you already know the correct information.

EXCESSIVE CAGINESS: Don't be afraid to give away the store. Many inexperienced writers are reluctant to include specifics in their pitches out of concern that the editor will steal their ideas, tips, or suggested sources. The more details you provide, the more likely you are to get the assignment. Reputable, ethical editors do not steal stories or ideas.

GUSHING OR GROVELING: Don't write, "I hope this idea works for your magazine" or "I'll welcome your editorial imput" or "I've always wanted to write for your magazine." Such remarks sound amateurish. Instead, close your query with a line such as, "I look forward to your reaction." As Harrington explains, "Ultimately, it's better to write queries from a position of strength and confidence. *Assume* that your idea is right for them (or else you wouldn't be sending it, right?) and *know* you're getting the assignment."

FUZZY THINKING: If an editor can't quickly grasp what you're talking about, your query won't sell. Check to make sure you've clearly explained your slant, organized your ideas to flow smoothly from point to point, and avoided jargon and technical terms.

STYLISTIC STUMBLES: Even the most meticulous writer can inadvertently compose a poorly worded sentence or spoil a well-crafted phrase with an unfortunate typo. One trick that helps you catch such errors is to read your query aloud before sending it out.

UNENTICING HEADERS: For e-mail queries, a catchy subject line will up the chances of a quick—and positive—response. If I'm submitting to an editor I haven't worked with before, I either use the name of someone she does know in the header, such as "Melba Newsome Thought You'd Like This," or an interest-grabbing phrase, like "Amazing Twin Medical Drama."

QUERIES THAT JUST WON'T QUIT: The longer your query, the greater the risk of losing the editor's interest. Try to limit your pitch to one typewritten page—two at the most. Remember that the ideal query has just enough information to spark a sale—and not one word more. As Stephen King puts it, "Leave out the boring parts."

SUBMISSION JITTERS: While it's crucial to polish your pitch, some writers get so anxious about the possibility of rejection that they nitpick endlessly. Even if you're querying for the very first time—or trying to break into a new or more important market—don't let nervousness keep you from getting your work out promptly. Every assignment begins with a submission, so the faster you get your work out, the sooner you'll achieve your ultimate goal—an assignment and a sale.

LISA COLLIER COOL, who can be reached at *lwcollier@aol.com*, is a best-selling author and winner of eleven journalism awards, including the 1999 National Magazine Award for Consumer Service. Her books include *How to Write Irresistible Query Letters* (Writer's Digest Books) and *Beware the Night: A New York City Cop Investigates the Supernatural* (with Ralph Sarchie, St. Martin's Press). She is president of the American Society of Journalists and Authors.

6

How to Sell
a Book

Sherry Suib Cohen

I t's pure grace to sell a book you care about. What a feel-ing! Whether a new, blossoming writer or a seasoned, published one, we all wonder exactly what publishers want. Of course, most publishers can't tell us what they want, either. They know it when they see it. Our job, and our challenge, is to show them what they want before they know they want it.

The good news is that you don't have to be a genius to

sell a book. I remember how the late Jacqueline Susann used to give endless and boring interviews on *how* she wrote—what color paper she wrote which draft on, and all about the tiny little blackboards she kept in her writing room and how writerly she was. It made the reader feel like the author had precious secrets known only to her. Well, there are no secrets here. You don't need blackboards, colored paper, or even a writing room. You need heart and passion—and a way with words. You need a point of view and the kind of patience great carpenters have that keeps them doing and doing and doing what they do until they get it just right.

So just how do you sell a book?

First, the Idea

My colleagues Jack El-Hai and Lisa Collier Cool have discussed ideas in general and ideas for magazine stories in the two previous chapters. So I'm not going to delve into how you might find ideas—beyond one personal tip for would-be authors searching for book ideas: Check out the magazine *American Demographics.* It's full of research and cutting-edge insights about coming trends. A study in the magazine on road rage, for example, led to my bestseller *Hot Buttons,* co-authored with Sybil Evans.

If you think you have a good idea for a book, take a few moments to check whether or not it's been done before. Research your idea at Amazon.com, BarnesandNoble.com or through *Books in Print,* either online or at the library. While there's nothing totally new under the sun, and your point of view can always skew an idea differently, if something too similar has already been written, toss the idea. There are about 70,000 books published yearly and most of them are nonfiction—pretty heavy competition. But if you've got an original idea for a book, if you're passionate about the subject and can live with it for a year or two, and if you can write an intriguing proposal, chances are you can land a good contract. Believe it.

Then, the Agent

Few sentient publishers will look at your book if it comes in "over the transom" and ends up in the slush pile with many other agentless books. It's a one-in-a-zillion chance that attention will be paid without an agent to run interference. There are some houses that may look at an agentless proposal, according to *Writer's Market,* including university presses and very small presses. Try them if you like. But frankly, I don't hold out much hope for success there—and this comes from someone who did sell her first book to a small press without an agent. I was extraordinarily lucky and it was a million years ago.

The good news is that you don't have to be rich, well-published, or even well-connected to get an agent to represent you. There are plenty of young, fairly new, but excellent agencies out there willing to take a chance with a novice, if they deem your work publishable. If you write well and you have a good book idea, you will find an agent. If you're new at the game, the best agent you can get is one who, like you, is new and hungry. She or he will return your phone calls. To approach an agent, write your best pitch letter. Knock that agent dead with your wonderful, clear style. Tell a little bit about yourself, your idea, and why you think his or her whole career rests on hooking up with you. This is no time to be shy, but keep the pitch to a page or two. If one agent turns you down, try another. If you pitch two or three agents at once—some agents don't mind multiple pitches, but some do—make sure you tell the agents that they're not the only ones you're approaching. It's the fair and right thing to do. When you have identified a particular agent you'd like to work with, either approach that agent exclusively or find out— from agent listings or by calling the agency directly—whether that agent will consider your pitch even if it is also being sent to other agents.

When you do find an agent who has agreed to take you on, expect this person to be your firmest advocate. If she or he has suggestions on how to improve your proposal (see next page), listen to that advice and follow it; the agent wants to sell your book to a publishing house almost as much as you do, and knows a lot more about how to sell it. Don't nag. Don't nudge. Don't expect your agent to be your parent, lend you money, or hold your hand in sad times. This is a business relationship. Your agent should guide you and be the one to make most of the decisions when it comes to selling the book. Listen and learn.

The Unforgettable Title

You'll need at least a working title, but a really strong title—one that everyone agrees is perfect from the outset—can help sell a book both to the editor and later, to the public. One of my books with a great title was *Decorating Rich*, which I co-authored with my college roommate, Teri Seidman. I'm convinced that the title—who doesn't want to create a rich-looking home for peanuts?—paved the way for the book to become a bestseller and a Book of the Month Club selection. On the strength of that book, we sold another book on the virtues of comfort in a home: *Decorating for Comfort*. It might even have been a better book, but it sold many fewer copies: I'm convinced that the relatively blah title was a big factor. The title has to tell what the book is about—but still be snappy and fresh.

The Proposal

Many otherwise brilliant people think that you write books before you sell them. Wrong. Unlike novels, nonfiction books are always sold on the basis of a proposal. Before you write a word of the real thing, you sell the book and get paid an advance against future royalties, all based on the proposal.

A proposal is simply a sales device explaining what you want to do in your book, how your book will be different and better than competing books, who will want to buy it, and why you're the best person in the universe to write it. Experienced writers and agents have their own pet formulas for putting together a proposal, but all proposals contain certain common elements, and they all try to achieve the same goal—to provide publishers enough information to commit their time and money to printing, distributing, and promoting the book.

All good book proposals contain a pitch, a marketing plan, a chapter outline, and one or more sample chapters. I combine my pitch and marketing plan into Part I of my proposals. I tell the publisher what the book is about and why it's a hot topic, who I am and why I'm qualified to write the book, what I can do to help sell the book, and my ideas for how the publishing house can help sell it. It sounds unfair—I mean, you're the writer, not the bookseller or the publicist. But in today's competitive marketplace you've got to sell your book twice, first to the publisher before you write it, and then to the rest of the world.

If your agent manages to get some interest from one or more editors at publishing houses, that doesn't mean your book is necessarily going to get published. Editors love books, and would publish many more if they could. But the typical editor is just one voice on a publishing committee that decides whether or not to buy your manuscript, and for how much money. Senior editors, marketing people, publicists, and the publisher can overrule the editor. They all sit down and listen to your would-be editor try to convince them to publish your book and give you the money you want. The editor's only ammunition is your proposal.

The second part of my proposal includes the chapter outline and the sample chapter. The chapter outline spells out, chapter by chapter, the material the book will cover. Most writers summarize each chapter in a few sentences to a few paragraphs. A full sample chapter is usually required, and some editors prefer that it be the first chapter. Sample chapters and chapter outlines aren't carved in stone, of course. You can always rewrite them, sometimes drastically, when you actually do the book. But they should give a flavor of how the book is going to read throughout.

Somewhere in the proposal, give an idea of about how many words your book will contain. There are about 250 words on a double-spaced page, so a 60,000-word book would run about 240 manuscript pages. Many publishers like books between 60,000 and 80,000 words; 100,000 words is a long book these days. If you pitch a book that will run 300,000 words, it is very unlikely that it will ever be published. Also give the publisher an expected delivery date for the manuscript, typically eight to twelve months after you sign the contract. Publishers also appreciate your ideas, if any, for illustrations. Having a well-known person write a foreword or introduction is a big plus for many publishers. Physical presentation counts in proposals. Your proposal must look gorgeous, with lots of white space. Subheadings are good, and make for easier reading. Use a good printer that gives sharp, dark copies. Ignore the million typefaces on your computer: Most experienced writers stick to 12-point Times New Roman.

Here are some of the key elements of my own proposals, which typically run thirty to fifty pages. These basic elements, which I developed under a formula devised by my late, great agent Connie Clausen, include the concept, the audience, the competition, the marketing/publicity, and relevant material about the author. These elements, along with an introductory letter from my agent, a few of my clips and reviews, and of course the chapter outline and sample chapter, have been part of every successful proposal I've ever written. I know that many other writers include virtually the same elements in their proposals, though we may not handle them in quite the same manner.

The Concept

This is the actual idea, the overview of the book. Your pitch should be strong, intriguing, and, in the very beginning, distilled down to a quick summary—some agents advise thirty words or less, some want to be able to say it all in thirty seconds or less. In publishing circles, the concept is sometimes known as "the hook." Here's a good one: *This is a self-*

help book on how to be expert at auto mechanics without blowing yourself up. And another: *This book is a skeptic's practical look at the paranormal.*

After the summary or hook, follow up with details. Start out with the seductive line: the great dramatic scene or the amazing, surprising, fantastic statistic right up front to catch the editor's attention. When describing the concept of the book, convey a bone-deep sense of your passion for this idea. At the same time, think of the sales representative who's eventually got to pitch your book to the manager of a bookstore; he's probably going to have about thirty seconds to make the sale.

If you begin with a great quote or anecdote, make sure it's interesting, irresistibly funny, or shocking. Long, boring, background anecdotes are lethal. Pay attention to tone; you want it immediate, heartfelt, and personal. When I was selling a book on the paranormal, I started by telling how I got the idea when my mother died. "My mother died a year ago," I wrote, "but I haven't finished looking for her." My concept section—summary or hook and then follow-up details—is usually three to six pages. Editors who read all the way to the end of the concept section are probably going to read the rest of the proposal, and if they read the entire proposal they're probably going to be interested in the book. An editor typically won't decide to try to acquire a book after reading only the concept. But many, many editors decide *not* to buy a book based on the concept. In fact, if a concept doesn't grab them, many editors stop reading.

The Audience

Who cares about your book—and who *will* care? This section of the proposal tells the publisher who will be interested in the book. The larger the market the better, but don't go wild in your projection because it will sound phony. Not everyone is interested. Even if everyone should be, don't say that. It sounds amateurish, and publishers care less about who will be interested than who will buy. You have to convince an editor that the book will appeal to a certain market—the larger the better, again—and that those people not only are book buyers, but that they will buy *your* book.

Interesting statistics are always good, if you can get them. If you're pitching a book on angels, it's useful to say that in a recent Harris poll one out of every four people said they believe in angels; that is, 25 percent of the population will be a possible audience for your book. A book on baby boomers? How many of them will there be, and how old will they be, in five years? Why will they care about your book? It's fine to draw conclusions, but don't oversell or make extravagant claims. Clearly identify the market for the book. Will the book appeal only to young mothers? For instance, don't pitch a book called *The Complete Book of Breastfeeding* and say that women of all ages will buy it. Instead, concentrate on young mothers-to-be, and focus on statistics such as how many young mothers there are in the country, and how through the years young mothers have proved to be reliable book buyers. (*American Demographics* is also a good source for this kind of background information.) Don't make defensive comments such as, "Of course, this is only a rough estimate." The editor will wonder why you didn't take the time to find out the exact numbers from a credible source. This section should also include something about what you bring to the table. What special audience markets can you yourself tap? What connections do you have with what group of people that might translate into sales? Do you have access and connections to hospitals, universities, social agencies, libraries, college bookstores? Why will they buy the book?

The Competition

You *must* do your homework here. Tell the publisher what books are out there that might compete with your book. Don't try to fool the editors by saying, "This book has never been done before," unless it really is true. Besides, there's a real danger in that: If no one has ever done it before, there must be a reason. Publishers take gambles, but calculated gambles. If other books on the subject do well, that's a plus for you; the fact that they exist won't kill your book. A publisher may feel that if no one has ever published a book on the history of pumpernickel bread, "Well, there must be a good reason and I'm not going to be a hero and buck the wisdom of the crowd." Build on your previous research by further exploring the Internet, online booksellers, bookstores, and publishing industry resources to find out what other books on the subject have been published.

Once you've surveyed the field, summarize it in this part of your proposal. Mention five to ten books on the subject (don't give the publisher fifty books to compare to yours) and tell why yours is different—and why it will be better. You're doing the work for the publisher and they love when you do it honestly and well. Give the title, author, and publishing information—publishing house and publication date—of each book. By the way, don't bother badmouthing bestsellers. Publishers rarely want to hear anything bad about a book that makes money, and it can hurt your credibility. And be careful that the books you choose to say are inferior haven't been published by houses receiving your proposal.

Marketing and Publicity

Can you help sell your book? Whom do you know personally who will give your book a leg up? What particular media would be interested in having you wax lyrical about the proposed book? When I was trying to sell my book on the paranormal, I found out how many TV shows in the last three months had psychics, mediums, or astrologers as guests. I cited polls describing how often the public bought books about the paranormal. Controversy is good. Will your book spark a debate? Will it be quoted in the local gossip columns? Does it have a hook for possible TV shows—or will the media think it's a yawn? Will the lifestyle columns of local newspapers be interested? Why? Explaining how your book evokes excitement one way or another helps a PR department think about it positively. Do you have a Web site? Will you create one to push your book? Will you spend time or money yourself on publicity? This isn't always necessary, but some houses like to know when an author is willing to share expenses on a book tour or willing to write personal letters and send them out to potential reviewers.

About the Author

You need to introduce yourself here, and show how you'll be valuable in marketing this book. First, your credentials. Do you have a degree, and what is your profession? If you have magazine clips, credits, or reviews from other books, talk about them, and perhaps include a few of the better ones. If you regularly lecture, present your lecture schedule for the year. If you have never written before but are a lawyer, doctor, or scientist, state your expertise and make it relate to the book. The publisher doesn't want to know that you're a skiing champion if you want to sell a book about marriage. Publishers never cared that I spent maybe one-fifth of my life fishing—until I tried to sell a book called *Secrets of a Very Good Marriage: Lessons from the Sea.* Then it was interesting to them, and I did sell the book.

What's your *platform?* Writers rarely use this term but editors use it all the time. "What's the author's platform?" the publisher will ask the agent who's trying to pitch your book. A platform is the author's ability to reach a large market. Do you have your own television or radio show? Do you write a newspaper column? Do you lead business seminars, or are you interviewed for your expertise on beekeeping? These are platforms. The first questions the salespeople will ask about your proposal will be about platform: They'll want to know if you lead workshops, appear at seminars, speak on the motivational circuit. Is she media savvy? (That generally means: Can you handle yourself on television?) Are you frequently tapped as a spokesperson for your subject? Do you write for a magazine that will showcase the book when it comes out? Will potential buyers interested in the topic of the book recognize your name?

TV is huge, so if you're a frequent TV guest, it's a good idea to send a tape showing your stuff. It could be you giving a lecture or appearing as a guest expert on a daytime TV show. Select clips carefully, and edit the tape down (there are companies that do this inexpensively) so that the whole thing is no longer than twelve minutes. Send only the portion where you sound good and look credible. The publisher wants to see you as a great salesperson on radio or television.

What if you're really new at the game and have no clips, no TV appearances, no lectures? You can still sell yourself on your expertise. Say, you've been a kindergarten teacher for twenty years and you want to write a book about children's values. You may not have been on TV, but who's a better expert than you? Also, if you have no platform to speak of, consider offering names of well-known people who might write blurbs about the book. Don't tell a publisher, "I live in Pasadena, I've never been published before, I'm not good at selling books—but I have a great book in me." To a publisher, you and your book are an investment, and you probably won't get published unless you can show that you and your book have the potential to make money for the publishing house.

SHERRY SUIB COHEN's nineteen books include *Cool Hair: A Teenager's Guide to the Best Beauty Secrets of Hair, Makeup, and Style* (St. Martins' Press). She is an award-winning writer for many magazines, a contributing editor to *Lifetime*, and is a former contributing editor to *New Woman, McCall's*, and *Rosie*. She lives in Westhampton Beach, New York, and New York City. She can be contacted at *suib@aol.com*.

7

Writing for the Web

LISA IANNUCCI

The World Wide Web hasn't come to dominate communications and the media in the way that early proponents once said it would, but professional writers still have many opportunities to write for Web sites—providing content, it's called. And while the demand for content diminished with the fading of the Internet boom in the early 2000s, when an estimated 900 commercial Web sites went out of business, there are still opportunities to write online for reasonable pay. Those opportunities can be especially appealing for beginning freelancers, who may find the bar to entry lower online than at traditional print publications. The opportunities are there if you're open to the experience and are willing to devote time and energy to marketing yourself.

Most freelancers, including me, still do more for print than online clients. But there are exceptions. In 1996, when financial writer Brian O'Connell began freelancing, he went the traditional route, mailing resumes and clips to prospective editors. However, he soon found it too cumbersome and expensive as he became more familiar with the Internet. Before long, O'Connell began experimenting with e-mailing cover letters with resumes and clips to prospective clients. It was much cheaper and faster. Online clients, of course, were more amenable to being approached via e-mail. Within a year, O'Connell was no longer sending out postal queries at all, and he was focusing his marketing efforts on online clients. Today he earns a six-figure annual income, including some print work—both articles and books—but the heart of his business is online writing for publications such as TheStreet.com and CBS MarketWatch.com.

Finding Online Work

The best place to find online work, naturally, is online. O'Connell spends a few hours each Tuesday scanning job boards such as *www.mediabistro.com, www.freelancewriting.com,* and *www.freelanceworkexchange.com.* When he sees a project that might be of interest, he fires off an e-mail and whatever else the prospective client wants, including a resume and writing samples. "I usually hear back on half and maybe get a job or two out of it; some are now regular," he says. Some job boards, such as those of the National Writers Union and the American Society of Journalists and Authors, require a fee and, in the case of ASJA, membership approval with published credits. O'Connell doesn't mind paying. "You can go onto some sites, but they aren't going to get you anywhere as a freelancer financially. You have to pay to get good leads," says O'Connell, who invests a few hundred dollars a year on such sites. Some Web sites also provide databases that editors scan for potential writers. Adding your name and uploading your work to libraries on these sites is another way to make your work visible. Linda Wasmer Andrews, a health and psychology writer, says, "The editor of FitDV.com contacted and hired me to write an article after seeing my listing on a freelance writing database."

Elizabeth Crane also spares a few hours each week to scan her so-called "job dump." She doesn't recall where she found one three-line ad, but it led to a steady gig writing for an educational magazine. She says that sending out postal queries isn't even worth her time now; answering an online ad only takes a minute. "As I continue, I'm also becoming a lot choosier; ... How successful you are at finding jobs depends on where you are at in your career and what you expect. If you expect to find a little more work if you do it this way, then you might find something. If you are already looking at it as your main source of revenue, you're probably not going to be happy yet."

Many writers parlay their relationships with print clients into online work for the same clients' Web sites. "I wrote patient education material for Sloan Kettering Cancer Center and they needed a writer for their new Web site," says science writer Catherine Dold, who does more than 50 percent of her writing for Web sites. "With that experience on hand, I've written for OnHealth.com, iVillage.com, Drugstore.com, and many others. Most jobs were word of mouth from editors I've worked for." Although Janine Latus checks some job boards, she has found most of her online work through her print editors. "A former editor of mine now works for MoneyCentral.com, and knowing we worked well together I starting writing for the site," says Latus, who cautions that not all assignments lead to regular work. "I wrote stories for start-up Web sites, but it didn't always work out." Many experienced writers can attest to the fickleness of the online market through the Internet boom and bust. Lisa Price was writing children's software reviews when a small retail Web site started by KB Toys, now known as KBKids.com, contacted her to add content. "I did a few pieces and became their features editor, but in the many redesigns, the company decided to drop content because it distracted customers from their real purpose, which is to buy, buy, buy."

"We had to fight pretty hard to get contracts out of some clients, and once we got them we had to keep pestering them to pay," says Jonathan Price, co-author with his wife Lisa of *Hot Text: Web Writing that Works.* "One company merged with another; one panicked when its stock prices declined and sales dried up. First, they told us we would have to wait for new assignments. Then we were told that articles would be done in-house, and finally, one day, the company dissolved." Freelance writer Joan Price (no relation to Jonathan and Lisa) cautions online writers to maintain the rights to their articles. "I worked with a fitness Web site, agreeing to one reprint article per month in exchange for hosting my Web site, but other writers signed all-rights contracts. At this point, I had no idea that this site wouldn't go on forever. After the deal was done, the owner used the content on other Web sites, but I had made this arrangement and knew they couldn't do anything with my stories."

Just as in traditional media, you are going to meet people on the Internet who are just looking to make a dollar at your expense—to offer you "exposure" but little or no money. Whether it's a start-up publication or an established one, treat it the same way you would treat clients who aren't online. Do not begin any work without a contract, and check out the company, publication, or Web site prior to signing anything. Ask for a phone number or address. If they hesitate, be concerned. You should want some way of contacting your client other than e-mail.

Online Pay

Obviously the pay depends on the client, but most experienced professional writers do not lower their rates for online work. Most of the writers interviewed for this chapter say they take online assignments for fifty cents or more a word, but they all say they know less-experienced writers who will take less. The consensus is that lower rates for online rights are acceptable only for the same reason as lower rates for traditional print rights—such as an assignment being especially quick or easy to do. That said, many online assignments are relatively short and generalized compared with print magazine stories, and can be done quickly. "The time required for research and rewrites usually is considerably less as well, so I think online work may be more profitable," says Linda Wasmer Andrews. "I've had the same experience as everyone else of seeing many markets die over the past few years. However, new ones keep springing up to take their place. Payment has generally been on time, and I've only been stiffed once."

Others, like Catherine Dold, have not seen any reduction in online work. "There is tons of health copy that needs to be done and I'm always busy," she says. "Pharmaceutical companies are creating Web sites for every drug they launch. Insurance companies are creating Web sites on how to manage your ailment. There's tons of patient education material to be written."

Reprints

Many smaller Webzines and other Web sites don't have large budgets for content but don't demand original work, so there are terrific opportunities to resell stories from your inventory. For example, if you live in Maine and have written an article on the latest arthritis remedies for your local newspaper, a publication in California may be interested. Sending an editor the original article by e-mail with a cover letter can lead to a sale. Editors might ask you to add quotes from their local sources, but the bulk of your research and story can remain the same. There are Web sites that can help you find regional publications. For example, *www.bizpubs.org* lists regional business magazines and *www.parentingpublications.org* gives a reasonably comprehensive list of parenting publications.

Look for opportunities everywhere to market yourself. When you join an online forum where you can post messages, introduce yourself. Leave a short paragraph about who you are and what you do, even if it's not a writer's site. For example, if you visit a comic-book Web site, post a message about how much you enjoy comic books and that you're a writer. It is possible that editors of collectibles magazines frequent sites to keep up on the interests of their audience and may spot your posting. When you get involved in any online conversations, sign your message with your name, a brief description of your business, and a business-only phone number, if possible. For example, "Cordially, Pam Smith, a freelance writer specializing in travel and health." It's like handing a business card to everyone you've talked to online. (For more on promoting your writing business and yourself as a writer, see Chapter 22.)

When you are answering ads or sending e-mail queries to magazines, be professional. Online chatting is very informal, but keep your tone respectful, as you would in a postal query. If an editor says, "E-mail queries accepted," send the queries privately and not through public messages in the forum. Send a paragraph or two on the topic of interest and a line about your credentials, just as you would with a postal query. When you get to know an editor better, your queries may be a little more informal. Online postings usually need fast responses, so I keep a bio and tearsheet file ready to e-mail at a moment's notice. However, read the ad carefully. Potential e-mail viruses prevent many editors from accepting attachments. Instead, paste the article into the body of the e-mail. Editors who post online requests are usually bombarded. Give them at least a week or two to respond and if you haven't heard from them, drop them a line and remind them about what you sent and who you are.

To become more successful at using online services to make money, Lisa and Jonathan Price suggest that you develop a specialty. "If possible, become what editors call an SME [subject matter expert]," says

Jonathan. "Focus on business sites these days, because they are the only ones with money to pay you decently." Dold suggests approaching corporations, large and small. "Every company is going to have an online presence of some sort, and they need writers desperately," she advises. "You should also learn some design ability and how sites are put together." If you're approaching a large company, sometimes a well-timed, professional cold call via e-mail to the corporate communications department can get your foot in the door for lucrative assignments. If it's a very small company, you might approach the owner and offer to beef up the Web site, or perhaps create the site in the first place.

LISA IANNUCCI, who lives in Poughkeepsie, New York, writes books and magazine articles and is a contributing writer for *www.cooperator.oag.com* and other Web sites. She also founded and supervises the site *www.youngwidowsandwidowers.com* for men and women who have lost spouses. Her books include *The Unofficial Guide to Minding Your Money* (Macmillan) and *Birth Defects* (Enslow).

8

Why Literary Agents Need You More Than Ever—And How to Get the Agent You Need

MICHAEL LARSEN, AAR

In Anne Lamott's wonderful book about writing, *Bird by Bird: Some Instructions on Writing and Life*, she describes an old cartoon. Two men are sitting on a couch at a cocktail party. One man has a beard and looks like a writer. The other seems like a normal person. The writer is saying to the other guy, "We're still pretty far apart. I'm looking for a six-figure advance, and they're refusing to read the manuscript."

If you find yourself pretty far apart from a publisher, maybe you need an agent. Here's how an agent can help you:

- An agent is a mediator between two realities: the writer and the marketplace.

- An agent is a scout who knows what publishers are looking for.

- An agent is a midwife who can provide the editorial guidance needed to help writers give birth to their ideas.

- An agent is a matchmaker who knows which editors and publishers to submit books to and, just as important, which to avoid. An agent continues to send out a manuscript until it is sold or until the agent has tried all likely publishers. It's taken my partner Elizabeth Pomada and me as few as four phone calls and as long as ten years to sell a book.

- When a publisher makes an offer, an agent is a negotiator who hammers out the most favorable possible contract for a working marriage between a writer and a publisher. Publishers offer an advance against royalties, traditionally based on their estimate of the author's first year's royalties. Large houses pay between $5,000 and $25,000 for most books, but they will pay whatever agents or competitive bidders convince them a book is worth. The contract, which is between the author and the publisher and which the writer must understand, approve, and sign, enables the agent to act on the writer's behalf and receive income earned through the contract. The agent then deducts a 15 percent commission and forwards the rest to the author.

- An agent serves as a buffer and liaison between the author and the publisher on editorial, financial, production, and promotional questions that arise throughout the publication process.

- An agent is the author's advocate in helping to solve problems such as a late or rejected manuscript, a bad jacket design, or an editor leaving the house.

- An agent follows up on subsidiary rights and may appoint co-agents for film and foreign rights.

- An agent is a mentor who is a source of advice about writing and a client's career.

- An agent can also be a rainmaker who can get ideas from editors or come up with ideas for clients.

- In a desert of rejection, an agent is an oasis of encouragement.

Agents reject more than 90 percent of the submissions they see, but they also receive far more rejections than writers. By absorbing rejections and being a focal point for their authors' business dealings, agents help free their clients to write. As a continuing source of manuscripts, agents have more clout with editors than writers. Here's another way of looking at agents: Have you ever heard an experienced professional author say he or she would have a better, more productive career without an agent? Writers who have agents believe they make more money because they have agents. Writers' shares of subsidiary-rights income is greater and they receive it sooner if their agents handle those rights and payments. Agents enable their clients to avoid haggling about rights and money with their editors so they can work together harmoniously to make their books successful.

Al Capone once said, "Anyone who sleeps in the trunk of a car deserves to be shot." A writer who approaches a multimedia, multinational conglomerate without help is asking for trouble. The selling of a book deserves the same level of skill, care, knowledge, and experience that writers lavish on writing them. Agents can't write books as well as authors can; but authors can't sell them as well as agents can. At a time when editors change jobs and publishers change hands unexpectedly, an agent may be the only stable element in a writer's career.

Like publishers, agents are motivated by love and money:

- They need big books to make big bucks.

- They love to get excited about their books and authors.

﹡ And they must do a good job on the first book if they expect to work on the author's next book.

Finding an Agent

Publishers and agents start working with a writer in the hope that they will establish a permanent relationship that will grow more profitable and creative as the writer's career develops. They both face the perpetual challenge of finding good books. It's been said that an agent is like a bank loan: You can only get one if you can prove that you don't need it. But there are more than 800 agents, and more than 90 percent of them must find new writers to make a living. So I think it's easy to get an agent in just three simple steps:

﹡ Write a salable novel or proposal for a nonfiction book. This is increasingly hard to do for new writers who want to be published by big houses. (More on that in a moment.)

﹡ Use the list that follows to research agents.

﹡ Contact as many agents as you want, letting them know if you are approaching other agents simultaneously.

Eleven Ways to Find an Agent (or Publisher)

1. NETWORK. Get to know all the professionals that you can in publishing and in your field.

2. WRITER'S ORGANIZATIONS. *Literary Market Place (LMP): The Directory of the American Book Publishing Industry with Industry Yellow Pages* (Bowker), which is in your library, has a list of them.

3. THE ASSOCIATION OF AUTHORS' REPRESENTATIVES (AAR). The 350 literary and play agents in AAR are experienced and reputable, and the organization continues to grow. The directories below indicate when an agent is a member of AAR. The organization's Web site is *www.aar-online.org.*

4. DIRECTORIES IN LIBRARIES AND BOOKSTORES. *Writer's Guide to Book Editors, Publishers and Literary Agents: Who They Are! What They Want! And How to Win Them Over* (Allworth) by Jeff Herman is an annual listing that includes more than 200 agents. *Writers' Market* (Writer's Digest Books) is another annual listing of 500 agents. *Literary Agents: A Writer's Guide* (Penguin USA) by Adam Begley is published in association with *Poets & Writers* and lists 200 agents. *Literary Market Place (LMP): The Directory of the American Book Publishing Industry with Industry Yellow Pages* (Bowker) includes basic information on about 500 agents. *The Writer's Handbook* (The Writer) by Sylvia Burack is an annual listing of more than 150 agents.

5. LITERARY EVENTS. Writing classes, seminars and conferences, readings, lectures, book signings, and book festivals all present opportunities to meet and learn about agents.

6. NEWSLETTERS. For example, *Talking Agents, The AR&E Newsletter*, a bimonthly newsletter about agents and their sales, available by subscription in print or online: Agent R & E, *www.agentresearch.com.*

7. MAGAZINES. *The Writer, Writer's Digest, Poets & Writers,* and other writing magazines sometimes have articles by and about agents. So does the trade magazine *Publishers Weekly,* which also has a "Hot-Deals" column that describes agents' sales.

8. PUBLISHERS' CATALOGS. These may include the names of the agents who control the rights on their clients' books. Catalogs are available in libraries, and you can request them from publishers.

9. BOOKS. Look at the dedications and acknowledgment pages of books, especially those in the field you are writing about. Contact agents who represent the kinds of books you want to write.

10. **THE INTERNET.** Click *www.literaryagent.com* and *www.publishers-lunch.com*. My agency's Web site, *www.larsen-pomada.com*, has helpful information.

11. **LET AGENTS FIND YOU** by giving talks and by getting publicity and getting published online or off.

Writing a Nonfiction Proposal That Creates a Career

Nonfiction writers are luckier than novelists. It's easier to write, sell, and promote nonfiction. First novels usually have to be finished, but 90 percent of nonfiction books are sold with proposals. What follows was written with large publishing houses in mind. Because of their lower overheads, small and medium-sized houses can prosper by selling fewer copies, so they don't require as much promotional ammunition as the big houses.

Sherry Suib Cohen (Chapter 6) describes how she as an author puts together a book proposal. Here's my take on what all agents look for in a proposal. You'll note that while my approach may be a little different, both descriptions of a proposal are aimed at doing the same thing: getting agents and publishers excited about your book. A book proposal provides the publisher and you with three road maps for the book you want to write:

* how you will write it;

* how you will promote it; and

* how you will create a career by writing other books, ideally on the same subject.

Introduction

A proposal usually runs from thirty-five to fifty pages and has three parts: an introduction, a chapter outline, and a sample chapter. The introduction has three sections: the Overview; Resources Needed to Complete the Book; and About the Author. In the Overview, you start with a subject "hook," the most exciting, compelling thing that you can say in as few words as possible to grab an agent's or editor's attention and justify the book. This may be a quote, an event, a statistic, a fact, a trend, or an anecdote that leads to a statistic. Here are the other elements of the Overview:

* The title: Unless it's a serious book or a reference book, the title must tell and sell.

* The book's "selling handle": a sentence that begins "[The title of the book] will be the first book to . . ." The selling handle can also be a Hollywood pitch: "It's *Robin Hood* meets *Anne of Green Gables.*"

* The estimated length of your book (and the number of illustrations).

* Your book's special features: tone, humor, structure, anecdotes, checklists, exercises, sidebars, and other elements that will give the text visual appeal. Use competitive books as models.

* The name of a well-known authority who will give your book credibility and salability and who has agreed to write a foreword: If you can't get a commitment, write, "The author will contact A, B, C, et cetera, for a foreword."

* What you have done to answer technical or legal questions (optional): If your book's on a specialized subject, name the expert who has reviewed it. If your book will present legal problems, name the intellectual property attorney who has reviewed it.

* Back matter, such as an appendix (optional): Use comparable books as a guide. Indicate how many manuscript pages each section will have.

* Markets for your book: List the groups of potential book buyers,

starting with the largest one. Then list the channels other than bookstores that can sell your book.

- Subsidiary-rights possibilities such as foreign, serial, audio, electronic, film, and book-club rights: Start with the most commercial one.

- Spin-offs: Make the proposal a road map for your publishing career by listing related books that you will write, in order of their commercial appeal.

- A mission statement (optional): If you feel a sense of mission about your book, write a paragraph in the first person describing your commitment to writing and promoting your book(s).

- Your platform (optional): If you will promote your book with talks around the country and you want to be published by a big house, you need to have continuing national visibility through talks or the media or both when you sell your book.

Having a national platform is essential to establish the credibility of your promotion plan. Writers have nothing more valuable than their credibility. That's why the Golden Rule of writing a proposal is "Never exaggerate."

Your promotion plan must be a believable expansion of what you are now doing. Editors will not believe that you will give fifty talks a year around the country if you have given only five locally. What you are already doing to build and sustain national visibility will be vital to convincing a big publisher that you have a national platform that you will continue to enlarge when your book is published. Write a list, in descending order of importance, of the most effective things you have done and are doing to promote your work and yourself nationally through speaking, the media, or both.

In addition to indicating how many talks you give a year, mention your fee and the number of people you speak before in a year, if the numbers will impress agents. If you are already doing back-of-room sales, include how much you average in sales at your talks or in a year's time.

* The promotion plan: In descending order of importance, list what you will do to promote your book on publication and after. This is your road map for your book's success. For most books aimed at a wide audience, this list is far more important than your book's content in determining the editor, publisher, and deal you will get. So make your plan as long and strong as you can. Ideally, writers should start with this sentence: "The author will match the publisher's consumer, out-of-pocket promotion budget up to X." Most writers can't afford an impressive promotion budget so they don't include one. That's okay.

But the following three numbers are essential for big houses:

* "When the book is published, the author will give presentations in the following X cities. . . ." List the cities you will get yourself to, starting with the major markets. Your publisher's publicist should be willing to piggyback on at least some of your appearances, the goal being to concentrate maximum impact during your book's one-to-three-month launch window.

* "The author will continue to do X talks a year. . . ." Give the number of events that you will continue to do a year.

* "The author will sell X books a year . . . ," assuming that one out of four listeners buys a book.

The greater the continuing national impact you can create for your book, the greater the commitment you have a right to expect for it from a publisher.

* A review of competitive and complementary books: A list of the six books that will be most competitive with yours, including the title,

author, publisher, year of publication, and price. Then in two phrases, starting with verbs, describe what each book does and fails to do. End with a list of the ways your book will be different and better than the competition.

In the second part of the introduction, "Resources Needed to Complete the Book," list out-of-pocket expenses of $500 or more, covering travel, illustrations, permissions, or a foreword, and a round figure for how much each will cost. Add them up and include the total. The last sentence: "The author will deliver the manuscript X months after the receipt of the advance." If time is the only resource you need, add this sentence to the end of your overview. Agents may not want you to include the costs in your proposal but they will need to know them to negotiate the deal.

In the last part of the introduction, "About the Author," the goal is to include everything not listed in your platform that you want agents and editors to know about you, in descending order of relevance and importance. Include media experience. If you have an audio- or video-cassette of yourself in action, mention it. If you will meet with interested editors at your expense, say so. If you have ideas for books that don't relate to the book you are proposing, mention up to three of them. Writing your bio in the third person will avoid a page full of "I's." After your bio, scan in or affix a five-by-seven or eight-by-ten photo that makes you look like a successful author and, if possible, relates to your book.

The Outline

The second part of your proposal must convince an editor that your idea will generate a book's worth of information and that you know the best structure for presenting it. Start with a page listing the chapters and the page of the proposal that each chapter outline begins on. Make chapter titles tell and sell. Use successful books as models. For an A-to-

Z reference book, your outline will be the list of entries. For a book with identically structured chapters—for example, a guidebook to ten great cities—just list the cities and what the book will cover in each city in the section about the book's special features.

For most books, start each chapter outline on a new page, and aim for one line of outline for every page of text you guesstimate. For example, nineteen lines of outline for a nineteen-page chapter. To help make chapter outlines enjoyable to read, start each one with the strongest anecdote or quote from the chapter, but don't repeat what's in the overview or sample chapter. A mistake many writers make in composing their outlines is that they write about their subject rather than about the chapters, so be sure to describe what each chapter will cover.

A Sample Chapter

Editors usually want to see one sample chapter, but experienced journalists looking to expand a magazine article into a book can substitute the article if it is long enough and strong enough. For most books from new writers, editors like to see the most exciting, representative twenty- to twenty-five-page chapter, or that much sample material. If more chapters will create more enthusiasm, send more. For a narrative book that should read like a novel and will have the greatest impact if the editor sees all of it, submit the first two chapters with an introduction and a two-page synopsis instead of an outline, and if you can finish the manuscript before you approach agents, be prepared to send the rest of it.

Remember that the tougher the book business gets, the more agents need new writers to make a living. If you are writing to meet the needs of the marketplace and you can promote your work, now is a great time to be a writer.

MICHAEL LARSEN, AAR, of the Michael Larsen–Elizabeth Pomada Literary Agents in San Francisco adapted this chapter from his books *How to Write a Book Proposal* (Writer's Digest Books) and *Literary Agents: What They Do, How They Do It, and How to Find and Work with the Right One for You* (Wiley). With Jay Conrad Levinson, author of *Guerilla Marketing*, and Rick Frishman, president of Planned Television Arts, he is co-author of *Guerrilla Marketing for Writers: 100 Weapons for Selling Your Work* (Writer's Digest). Reach him at *www.larsen-pomada.com*. If you have questions, please call (415) 673-0939 or e-mail *larsenpoma@aol.com*. Elizabeth has served on the board of ASJA.

9

Research:
Finding the Right
Stuff

MINDA ZETLIN AND STEVE WEINBERG

The technology boom of the past two decades—computers, e-mail, the World Wide Web—has had a tremendous impact on the business of freelance writing. Technology has helped us become more productive but, at the same time, it has forced us to become more focused on effective use of our time. Since nonfiction writers spend so much of their time on research, and technology offers so many opportunities to become more efficient and therefore more productive, writers must continually try to improve their research methods and techniques. Better research results in higher-quality work. More effective research saves time—and time is money for the freelance writer.

This chapter is in two parts. Minda Zetlin offers tips on online research, and then Steve Weinberg, recognizing that the Internet sometimes cannot replace old-fashioned shoe leather, phone calls, face-to-face interviews, and real-life paper documents, discusses traditional research and why freelancers need to be wary of becoming too reliant on their computers and the Web.

First, Minda Zetlin:

Down the road from my mother's house in northern Florida is a house that was accidentally built on one of the state's many sinkholes. Every year when I visit I drive by that house, and every year it's disappeared a bit further into the ground. Looking at that house reminds me how it feels to write a story without enough research. I feel as if my story, without a solid foundation, will sink into the ground. That's why I'm obsessive about research. I want to know everything about a topic before I sit down to write. A few years ago I mentioned this to an editor, who answered, "Of course you do. All the best writers over-research." On one hand, I was flattered. At the same time, I thought, "That's easy for you to say. After all, if I spend three days researching an article instead of three hours, you'll get a stronger piece and still pay me the same fee for it."

Therein lies the dilemma. Writing an article with insufficient information yields a product it's difficult to be proud of. But spend too many hours researching each piece and you'll never be able to pay the bills. The solution, for me at least, has a couple of answers. The first is to strike a balance between too much research and too little. I try to learn enough for each article (or book) to write with authority, but not so much that I'm compiling huge amounts of information I'll never have room to use. The second answer is to research smart, so I don't waste time getting the material I need.

Caveat Surfer

The Internet is the Great Equalizer (don't let anyone tell you it's golf!). One of the many ways it's leveled the playing field is by giving anyone—even a lone writer sitting at home with nothing more than an Internet connection and a Web browser—access some of the greatest stores of information the world has ever known. Also some of the greatest stores of *mis*information. Freelance writer Heather Millar made contact through the Internet with some miscreants who promised to tell her in detail how they were conducting a thriving online business in illegal drugs. She secured an assignment from *Wired* magazine and set out to meet them. That's when things got hinky. Every attempt she wisely made to verify what they were saying met with a stone wall. Soon enough, she discovered the truth: She'd been the victim of an elaborate hoax. Television journalist Pierre Salinger was not so lucky a few years ago after a jumbo jet crashed near New York under mysterious circumstances. A rumor immediately began making the rounds on the Internet claiming the plane had been shot down by the U.S. military. The FBI had already debunked that rumor when Salinger took it to the airwaves, claiming he had new information from the Internet. He wound up with egg on his face and an object lesson in the pitfalls of trusting the Web.

A healthy skepticism should also apply to more legitimate or official-looking information found on the Internet—just as it should with printed matter. If you received a glossy, well-produced brochure claiming that cigarette smoking was beneficial to one's health, you'd probably look for the fine print to determine the sources and who paid for it. The same should apply to Web sites: Before accepting a claim wholesale, find out who's making it. (The site *www.whois.net,* which gives information on domain name ownership, can help.) "Some commercial enterprises are growing quite savvy about designing sites that purport to offer unbiased information from professional organizations or average Joes, but that really are little more than promotional vehicles for their products or services," says health/psych writer Linda Wasmer Andrews. For more dependable medical and science info, she recommends *www.pubmed.gov* and *www.commons.cit.nih.gov/crisp,* both of which are sponsored by the federal government.

The Web is designed to be used in a meandering way. You find an interesting site, which includes links. You follow one of these to the next interesting site, and so on. Nevertheless, I spend my online time more efficiently if I know exactly what I'm trying to accomplish before I set out. Depending on what I'm looking for, I access different research tools in different ways. I've divided up information about these tools according to my own three preferred uses—finding facts, finding people, and gaining expertise. Please note that this is intended only as a guideline; every research situation is different, and so is every researcher. You may find that different tools work best for your own research projects.

Finding Facts

Most of the time, I avoid using already-published matter, whether in print or on the Internet, as a primary research tool. I like to depend on "fresh" research and quoting live people, both because I'm likelier to get an accurate quote if it's not filtered through someone else's reporting and because things change quickly (I'm primarily a business and technology writer). What was accurate a week ago may no longer be so today. But there are many times when the Internet is very handy for reporting. For instance, when I finish writing this chapter, I'll go back to one of my current assignments, writing 100-word descriptions of various companies for listings in a tech magazine. Since what's needed is a very brief overview, reading what others have written about these companies makes more sense than conducting a series of interviews.

For fact-finding, my preferred tool is databases of articles, usually those published in newspapers and magazines. For instance, for the descriptions of the tech companies, besides visiting the companies' own sites, I used three independent databases. The first was *www.elibrary.com*, which costs about $60 a year and lets users search hundreds of newspapers, magazines, and broadcast reports. Two similar databases are available free: *www.findarticles.com* and *www.northernlight.com*. My second source was *www.hoovers.com*, which provides information on most publicly traded companies. Individual subscriptions cost about $400 a year, but even without a subscription Hoover's offers lots of basic information about each of the companies it covers. My third source was *www.computerworld.com*, mainly because I'm a *Computerworld* magazine contributor and I know that the company has a huge searchable database and that its reporting is solid.

Another valuable source is LexisNexis, originally created as a database for legal documents, then expanded to include newspapers as well. LexisNexis has long been considered the top research site, but for many years it was unavailable to individuals. "I remember that when the New York University library first had access to it, you could only use LexisNexis at really inconvenient, off-peak hours. And you couldn't just sit at the keyboard and type in your query, but had to give a note to a technician who would fit it in at his convenience," recalls science writer Dan Drollette. "Even five years ago, libraries and research institutions made me go through this rigmarole—and charged one hundred dollars per search." These days, LexisNexis is much more affordable. In pay-as-you-go mode, you can search the database for free, and pay $3 apiece to access actual articles (more for legal documents). Or you can pay $30 to search the newspaper database for an entire day (again, legal documents cost more). Check it out at *http://Web.lexis.com/xchange/ccsubs/cc_prods.asp*.

Then there's the good old public library. You may be able to access your library's database without getting up from your desk. Offerings vary from state to state, so you'll have to check out your local library system to find out if you have this option. California-based business writer Christine Larson used to run into three common problems when doing research online: It was hard to find a central resource that could search multiple newspaper and magazine archives; the archives she did find often didn't have full text; and, in the end, she'd sometimes have to pay for what she wanted. When she moved to Sacramento, she signed up for a library card—and her research problems evaporated. Through the library's Web site and its links to InfoTrack Onefile, she could do massive full-text searches of newspapers, magazines, and academic journals from her home—for free. She could search for books in the library catalog, place a hold, and have the book delivered to her nearby library branch. For a recent story on salary negotiation, she ordered a book through Amazon.com, to be shipped second-day air. At the same time, she placed a hold on the book at the library. Two days later, the library sent her an e-mail saying the book had arrived at her local branch around the corner. When the Amazon book arrived later that day, she shipped it back. Besides InfoTrack, Larson used the library to explore other vast databases such as Dow Jones News Retrieval (*www.dowjones.com*) and Lexis-Nexis (*www.lexisnexis.com*).

Finding People

The Internet is especially useful as a preliminary research tool, both to become familiar with a subject and, more important, to help find sources to interview. In my work, most of these fit into one of three categories: subject matter experts, representatives of organizations (such as CEOs) or what I think of as "anecdotal" sources, and ordinary people who can speak to a topic from personal experience. For example, for a book about telecommuting, I used the Internet to find and communicate with about a dozen telecommuters who had agreed to share their thoughts and describe their experiences. When looking for representatives of organizations, or for background on a potential source, search engines are often the quickest way to find what I want. (For more on finding experts, see Chapter 10.)

Search engines come and go, and I've had different favorites. But in recent years my favorite, and the industry standard, has been *www.google.com*. Google's simple but brilliant concept is to prioritize sites according to how many other sites have links to them, reasoning that what site builders find useful, searchers will too. "In effect, all the people who create Web sites are 'voting' on Google's rankings," notes medical writer Sarah Wernick. This works surprisingly well, and Google search results are consistently more relevant than other engines'. (Even if it weren't the best, Google would still deserve support for its no-popup-ads policy.) Google is a great tool when I'm looking *for* something, as opposed to *for information about* something. On the other hand, if I were looking for something in a specific location, say a florist in DeLand, Florida, where my mother lives, I'd use Yahoo's yellow pages, which list businesses in specific locations.

When it comes to anecdotal research and looking for people to talk about their experiences, I often visit online communities (message boards, forums, listservs, etc.). In this case, you're interacting with other people, so rules of etiquette apply. It's considered bad form to just post a general request for interviews to a group of strangers—and you probably won't get much response, anyway. A better method is to read a few weeks' or months' worth of posts and then send a private e-mail to posters who may fit what you're writing, telling them you've read their posts and asking if they'd be willing to talk. The standard place to search through newsgroup postings used to be Deja News, but that was acquired by Google in 2001, so here I am recommending Google again. If you enter *www.deja.com* or *www.dejanews.com*, you'll be redirected to *http://groups.google.com*. There, you can search more than 500 million archived messages. In addition, all the large general-interest sites, including Yahoo, AOL, ATT.net, About.com, and others, have their own thriving communities centered on many topics. These are often good places to find communities discussing what you're interested in.

Gaining Expertise

The third way I use online research is to gain general expertise, the sort of background we need when starting off on a project, or to gain enough knowledge to write a magazine query or book proposal. There are three easy ways to do this. The first is to identify what I think of as "power sites" that address my topic in a profound way, with links to other sites and articles about the subject I need, in searchable form. When I was writing about the Y2K problem way back when, the greatest power site was *www.year2000.com.* Among other things, this site seemed to link to every news story on the subject, no mean feat in late 1999. For research on my telecommuting book, the power site was *www.telecommute.org,* which belongs to the International Telework Association and Council. Power sites make your life easier. Ask around, or use search engines as ways to start pinning them down.

The second way the Internet can help you gain expertise is "push"— that is, the automatic delivery of relevant news stories (or links to stories) to your mailbox. Or at least, news stories containing specific words or phrases that you select. Since I'm an AOL member, I have this set up through AOL, but there are many free places to get this service, including Yahoo (*www.yahoo.com*) and major newspapers. Another way you can sometimes get push is to sign up for free e-mail news or newsletter delivery with the subject matter sites for your topic.

The third way is to join online communities that focus on your topic. This time, instead of searching for specific messages that might help you, you sign up, read the posts regularly, and become an active member of the community in question. For instance, I spend a lot of my time reading message boards and listserv mail about freelance writing generated by ASJA's online community. In fact, that's how I hooked up with the other ASJA members who contributed their insights to this chapter.

Steve Weinberg Writes:

Individuals. Institutions. Issues. The three I's. Almost every freelance piece for a magazine or newspaper and almost every book focuses on an individual, an institution, an issue, or some combination of the three. Of course, lots of information about individuals, institutions, and issues can be found online. But much of the most revealing information about individuals, institutions, and issues cannot be found online. So-called "traditional" research is often the better answer, and freelance writers should not limit themselves to the research they can do on their computer screens. If they do, they may be limiting the scope—and the quality—of their work.

An example: I agreed to write an in-depth magazine profile of a federal government policymaker highly placed in the George W. Bush administration. I knew that his nomination had to have been approved in a public hearing by the Governmental Affairs Committee of the U.S. Senate, then by a majority vote of the full Senate after a debate. The committee hearing included a question-and-answer session involving the nominee and several U.S. senators, verbal testimony from the nominee's supporters and detractors, written support and opposition from individuals and organizations across the nation, and submission for the record of both academic and popular articles by the nominee himself, a long-time Harvard University professor who held a Ph.D. All that information ended up in a bound volume available at no cost to me by requesting it from the Senate committee or by checking it out of the government documents library (part of the state university library) in the city where I live.

Most of the invaluable information in that hearing volume was not available online. In a similar vein, most information that sheds light on criminal cases or civil actions filed in courthouses across the nation is not available online. Freelance journalists who mine the files at the local courthouse will find not only the complaint and the reply, but also related documents that might include income tax returns, bankruptcy filings, employment histories, insurance policies, campaign contributions, evidence of extramarital affairs, drunk-driving violations, and Social Security numbers, that open additional doors. Most government offices—city, county, state, federal—are staffed by clerks who know a lot about how to locate the information they collect. I first learned how to trace the ownership of land, starting with the home of an elected politician who allegedly lived outside the district he represented, by asking a clerk in the Recorder of Deeds office to walk me through the process. Within thirty minutes, I understood the system.

To this day, deeds and mortgage papers are rarely found online. Journalists with a documents state of mind can learn incrementally by visiting one government office per day, or week, or month. Ask for blank copies of all the forms they use to collect information from individuals and institutions. Study the forms. Notice, for example, that the voter registration form found at the county courthouse provides the previous home address of the applicant. That previous address might be just what is needed to link the individual to somebody he has denied knowing. It would be futile to attempt a discussion of every document of value to freelance journalists, and whether that document is available primarily online, in libraries, or at government agencies. The futility is related to the volume of material—there are so many documents obtainable so many different ways that a thorough discussion would cover thousands of book pages. Instead, it makes sense to devise a general strategy for research that takes in traditional methods and online skills.

The general strategy makes use of both paper trails and people trails. Good research always requires searching for documents that shed light on individuals, institutions, or issues. Then you need to find human beings who can illuminate what the documents mean. Let us explore the paper trail first. It has two forks—secondary documents and primary documents. A newspaper article about an individual, institution, or issue would be a secondary document. It should never be the stopping point. Instead, already-published information should be used as a map. For example, the newspaper article might mention a speech given by the Bush administration appointee who is the subject of my research. Without having found the newspaper article, I might never have known about the speech. (Not so incidentally, "traditional" books, rarely found online in their entirety, are the ultimate secondary source document. The footnotes and the endnotes almost always mention hundreds of obtainable primary source documents.) My next step is to find the actual speech. It is the primary document, the best evidence of what my subject actually said to his audience. The best evidence of a profile subject's date of birth would not be a newspaper article stating his age or even a mention of his age in a speech by the subject himself. Rather, the best evidence would be his birth certificate, a primary document.

On the people trail, there are also two forks—the "formers" and the "currents." The formers can tell me a great deal about my profile subject's past—his former teacher, his former minister, his former accountant, his former secretary, his former boss, his former neighbor, his former roommate, maybe a former spouse. Then there is the current teacher, minister, accountant, secretary, boss, neighbor, roommate, and maybe a current spouse. The combination of secondary and primary documents on the paper trail and former and current human sources on the people trail will almost always yield a compelling story.

Freelance journalists who lack confidence in finding and following paper and people trails can seek guides. My favorite is *The Investigative Reporter's Handbook: A Guide to Documents, Databases and Techniques.* The 600-page book is available through its publisher (Bedford/St. Martin's) or through Investigative Reporters and Editors (*www.ire.org* or 573-882-2042), the organization in Columbia, Missouri, that commissioned it. All the income from its sale goes to IRE, a not-for-profit organization that supports investigative reporting.

ASJA board member MINDA ZETLIN is an author and speaker specializing in business and technology. The author of *Telecommuting for Dummies* (Hungry Minds), she lives in Woodstock, New York, with her husband Bill Pfleging, a large number of computers, and four cats. She can be contacted through her Web site, *www.mindazetlin.com.*

STEVE WEINBERG is a freelance magazine writer, book reviewer, and author in Columbia, Missouri. From 1983 to 1990, he also served as executive director of the 5,000-member organization Investigative Reporters and Editors. He continues to write for IRE's magazine, the *IRE Journal,* along with many other publications.

10

How to Find Experts

ESTELLE SOBEL

Finding experts is a key to your ability to create a credible, newsworthy story. Of course, your first step toward finding a worthy expert is looking in your own backyard. Why not first check with your contacts and colleagues to see if they can point you in the right direction? This chapter also will cover the following places to get help finding experts:

- Online services such as ProfNet and MediaMap, search engines such as Google, and databases such as LexisNexis and FindArticles.

- Articles published in print media.

- Associations and groups devoted to professions, trades, hobbies, causes, and other special interests.

- Public-relations agencies.

- Publishers and agents.

- Universities, hospitals, and other venues on the cutting edge of research.

- Local continuing-education courses.

ProfNet was started in the early 1990s by Dan Forbush at the State University of New York at Stony Brook as a network of university information officers. Today it is part of the PR Newswire service that delivers press releases electronically. Go to *www.profnet.com* and e-mail your query asking for experts on a particular topic. Describe the publication you are writing for and the story you want to write. Specify how you want to be contacted (many writers prefer e-mail, since phone and fax replies can be intrusive and overwhelming). Your request is automatically sent out to thousands of public-relations professionals at colleges, universities, research organizations, nonprofit groups, government agencies, and corporations around the world. You have the option of narrowing the groups that receive your request. Once your query goes out (queries are distributed three times a day), you will start getting e-mails with the names of experts and their contact information. The user guide at ProfNet's Web page is a handy tool. Reporters working on a tight deadline can access ProfNet's experts database, with the names of more than 4,000 people with expertise in various areas and their contact information. You can find a name and contact the expert directly, rather than sending out a general query and waiting for replies.

A caution: Some journalists find ProfNet responses off target. Usually the fault lies in the journalist's query—unclear, vague, overly broad. Sometimes, though, the off-the-wall responses can help point out other angles to a story, or related stories. MediaMap.com and BusinessWire.com are similar services, offering journalists the opportunity to have their queries distributed to a wide network of people. AuthorsandExperts.com is a free service for producers and journalists to use when they need an expert. ReligionSource.org, a service of the American Academy of Religion at Emory University, helps journalists find sources on religion and ethics for stories on politics, education, the courts, health, science, art, lifestyle, international issues, and culture. You can search by topic to get contact information and credentials on some 5,000 scholars covering 1,400 topics. Experts.com assists attorneys, journalists, and researchers in locating experts. Guestfinder.com and Speakers.com are used by television producers to find talk show guests and speakers, but are also sources for print journalists looking for experts on a wide range of topics.

The Sources and Experts Web Page (*http://sunsite.unc.edu/slanews/ internet/experts.html*) has many links to Internet sites that list specialists on a wide variety of subjects. The National Press Club offers a Directory of News Sources at *http://npc.press.org/newssources/index.cfm*. The Foundation for American Communications, a nonprofit organization that sponsors educational programs and online resources for journalists, runs *www.facsnet.org*. FACSNET offers the Reporters Cardfile, a list of think tanks, advocacy groups, and special interest organizations. Another good resource is *www.journaliststoolbox.com*, with many helpful links.

Reading magazines is a great way to find the experts right for your story. After all, if they gave good quotes to another writer, they'll probably be just as interesting and candid for you. If you don't have access to many magazines, there are several ways you can locate articles. LexisNexis (*www.lexisnexis.com*) is a fee-based service that searches for articles from a wide variety of magazines and newspapers going as far back as ten years. FindArticles (*www.findarticles.com*) is a free way to do the same thing, though the article base is more limited and includes more trade publications. Newswise (*www.newswise.com*) maintains a comprehensive database of news releases from top institutions engaged in scientific, medical, liberal-arts, and business research. Once you have passed the credentials test, you will get a free press pass, which allows access to embargoed news releases, as well as the opportunity to subscribe to SciWire, MedWire, BizWire, or LifeWire. Press pass holders may scan these digests offline, then retrieve individual articles via on-demand e-mail service. You can also forward queries to hundreds of higher-education and research institutions.

Google (*www.google.com*) is the favorite search engine of many journalists. Depending on what you are looking for, you can plug in a name or a topic and get surprisingly accurate results. Some journalists swear by *www.dogpile.com,* which takes whatever you type in and runs it through at least nine other search engines, including Google, Look-Smart, AskJeeves, About, Overture, FindWhat, and FAST. You can also search for experts by going onto bulletin boards (such as the one at *www.mediabistro.com,* and several on Yahoo) that cover specific subjects. For example, if you are writing about breast cancer, you can access a wide range of survivors through the chat groups of the Susan G. Komen Foundation (*www.komen.org*).

Some print references are updated yearly, assuring you of a wide choice of experts. One such book is *The Yearbook of Experts, Authorities & Spokespersons (www.yearbook.com),* which highlights experts, authorities, and spokespeople who are available for media interviews. Experts listed in this directory have paid for their listings. Another book is *The Source Book of Multicultural Experts (www.multicultural.com),* a valuable free tool for journalists that lists more than 100 businesses and organizations owned by minorities and women, with full contact information and a description of services.

A great way to find an authority or specialist on a particular subject is to search out associations such as the National Cancer Institute, the

American Dietetics Association, the Arthritis Foundation, the Association for Research in International Adoption, the Association of National Advertisers, and the American Association of Retired Persons (AARP). Each association usually has a Web site with a media section that provides current and past press releases as well as contact information for association spokespeople. Most public libraries also have directories of associations representing thousands of groups and causes. "It may be a little time-consuming, and require some additional expense, but I find great experts through professional organizations," says Sharon Naylor, a freelancer who specializes in wedding planning. "For instance, the Association of Bridal Consultants and the International Special Events Society are filled with the kinds of experts I love to speak with to keep on top of the newest trends in weddings and special events. I go to their meetings and conferences, schmooze a little, make great contacts (when they hear I'm an author, they come running!), and wind up with tons of experts for current and future story ideas. It's the person-to-person meeting that makes a big difference, and I often go home with even more story ideas than I started with. This probably works best in a narrow field like mine, but it's the best way I've found to chance upon excellent resources and recommendations."

Whether it is the Food and Drug Administration (FDA) or the National Institutes of Health (NIH), government agencies are great places to locate experts. To make contact all you have to do is visit the agency's Web site and locate an e-mail list of its representatives, information officers, and analysts. Most government agency Web pages list their staff by area of expertise, and also include the phone numbers or e-mail addresses for their public-relations or press offices. In fact, while working on a book proposal, it was easy for me to contact an analyst at the U.S. Census Bureau to help me locate certain demographic data, because the Bureau has a subject contacts list that groups census analysts by their demographic specialties. "I look at the press releases on the subject from government agencies," freelance writer Irene Levine says. "They usually provide the name and phone number of a public information officer and identify the government expert on the subject. Since I often write about health and mental health, I try to find advocacy organizations involved with the topic or issue. They generally can put me in touch with consumers."

Most colleges, universities, and trade and professional institutions have a list of experts on staff who are available for journalists to interview. The best method for finding a professor to interview is to visit the institution's Web site and locate the corresponding department. Usually the Web site will offer a listing of faculty e-mail addresses. Simply send the professor an e-mail explaining who you are, what you are writing about, whom you are writing for, and how much time you'll need for an interview. Most professors are surprisingly accessible this way. "Almost every college and university maintains a speakers/experts file of their professors in almost all categories," notes Stevanne Auerbach, a freelancer known as Dr. Toy. "Some actually promote their expert faculty in press releases."

Besides universities and professional or trade schools, it is useful to check the catalogs put out by continuing-education programs, such as the Learning Annex in New York, to find experts. Many communities and school districts around the country offer such programs. Find the class or workshop relating to your topic and either contact the instructor directly or get the contact information from the program's headquarters. Most hospitals have Web sites, where contact information for a press person or media spokesperson is often listed. They also list directories of doctors and their specialties. Other great sources for doctors are the "Best Doctors in the Country" books and the annual *New York* magazine "Best Doctors in New York" issue. Another way to find a doctor is to locate a recent scientific study published in a peer-reviewed journal, such as the *Journal of the American Medical Association* or the *New England Journal of Medicine*. You can locate these studies by looking up the associations or journals on the Web or by doing a search on PubMed from the National Library of Medicine (*www.ncbi.nlm.nih.gov/entrez/query.fcgi*).

Public-relations professionals are hired to do a job—publicize their clients. This makes it very easy for you if you happen to be working on a story that can feature their clients. You can contact the Public Relations Society of America (*www.prsa.org*) to find out what agencies handle the type of experts you are looking for. Another helpful site is *www.odwyers.com,* where you can look up a company's public-relations firm.

Publishing houses such as Simon & Schuster, Broadway Books, St. Martin's Press, McGraw-Hill, and HarperCollins can be great resources for experts. Call or e-mail to ask for a recent catalog, or call the publicity department directly. You can find experts who have written or are writing books on your topic. You can also check out books that authors have written on *www.amazon.com* and *www.barnesandnoble.com.* Another way to find authors is through their literary agents. Katharine Sands of the Sarah Jane Freymann Literary Agency in New York City says this: "Literary agents not only represent experts on their published books, they are constantly hearing about up-to-the-minute experts through the buzz on other books, even ones they do not represent. Agents keep vast Rolodexes and are always aware of experts from reading articles, acknowledgment pages, and course catalogs. Literary agents traverse a plethora of professions and have a wide variety of clients and contacts. At my firm, we've represented everything from rabbis to rock stars. And doctors, rocket scientists, lawyers, chefs, ichthyologists, and other more esoteric experts are always contacting agents to discuss their potential books. When you are on deadline and need to find an expert, chances are a literary agent knows the right person. Need a shark expert for a quote on deadline? Chances are the agent you call has just read a manuscript by an ichthyologist who has an idea for a mystery series about a sexy ichthyologist who solves crimes."

Finally, one of the best ways to find experts and other good sources for your stories is through people you've already interviewed. For many journalists, the last question in any interview is always, "Who else should I talk to about this?"

ESTELLE SOBEL, who specializes in health writing and magazine launches, has been editor-in-chief of five national magazines, including *Body by Jake*. Her articles have appeared in *Biography, Let's Live, Successful Meetings, Energy, Oxygen, Nutritional Outlook,* and *Energy Times*. An adjunct professor at New York University, she is the co-author of *Beautiful Skin: Every Woman's Guide to Looking Her Best at Any Age* (Adams Media). She can be reached at estellewriter@aol.com and at her Web site, *www.geocities.com/chesolimini/evitas/Sobel*.

11

Writer-Editor Relations

Megan McMorris

In an office setting, the hierarchy is clear: bosses, co-workers, and assistants. Those lines are a tad fuzzy when you're a freelance writer. Suddenly, it's just you and your editor, who is kinda your boss, somewhat your co-worker, and sometimes even your friend. One thing is certain about editors, though: We can't live without 'em. After all, editors are the ones who polish and publish our work—and, of course, pay us. And just like any other relationship, we need to nurture it so it will thrive—and so they'll keep paying us for our words. We asked writers and editors for their do/don't lists, pet peeves and raves, mistakes and successes, all in the name of getting you in the door—and keeping the door from slamming shut—with an editor. Here are tips for establishing and maintaining good relationships with editors.

Let's start before the start of a relationship. You have your sights on breaking in with an editor, and have sparkling clips that prove you're ready for the job. How do you approach the editor? Back in the not-so-distant age before the Internet boom, this wasn't a quandary. You sent your queries (with the obligatory SASE—remember those?) in the mail, following the standard query-letter format. (See Chapter 5 on queries.) With e-mail, though, those rules are changing by the second. E-mail takes the formality out of everything, demands a faster response time, and makes it easier to send out your brilliant ideas. Before you hit the "send" button, though, realize one thing: Editors who haven't worked with you before may not appreciate your unknown name popping up in their inboxes. It puts pressure on them to get back to you ASAP; also, they'll need to see some clips if you're unknown to them, so it's best to pop those into the mail and follow the editor's lead about e-mail contacts from then on. To make matters confusing, however, e-mail has created new rules—and left others by the wayside. Some editors prefer e-mail queries because they cut down on the pile of papers on their desk, while others still prefer the snail-mail route. When in doubt, check with the assistant in the department and ask how an editor prefers queries.

More important than e-mail versus snail mail are your story ideas. "I've had many new writers just send clips and a letter saying 'I'd love to write for you—do you have any stories you want me to do?'" says Heather Gowen, news editor at *Parents* magazine. "I'd rather see five or six ideas—even if we don't use them, at least it gives me an idea of your style and where you're coming from." You don't need to spend days honing that perfect idea, either; rough sketches or a few ideas are better. "I think three is the magic number for ideas, with a paragraph for each," says James Vlahos, senior editor at *National Geographic Adventure* magazine. "Then there's more to work with, and I might say, 'I like the second idea. Can you come up with a full proposal on that?' It also saves the writer time, because then you don't have to spend two days on a fleshed-out idea only to have us say, 'We already did that.' Also, I'd tell writers to spend more time on your ideas, and don't tell me as much about who you are and why you're the best person to write this. I'm more likely to think, 'Oh, this is a great idea. I wonder if this writer is good enough,' versus 'Oh, these are great clips. I wonder what this writer can do for us.'"

The Waiting Game

You turn in your ideas, expecting an editor to jump at the bait and assign you a 2,000-word feature within the week. In an ideal world, things would happen that quickly. In the real world, it's rare. Between meetings, closing an issue, meetings, photo shoots—and did I mention meetings?—an editor's day entails much more than sitting in front of a computer. "People think editors are just sitting there and have all this time to carefully read all these ideas and clips," says Vlahos (who had to reschedule our interview three times because of, you guessed it, unexpected meetings). Bottom line: Editors are busy. They don't hate you. They may even like your idea, but it's probably just piled up on an editor's to-do pile. Of course, that doesn't mean you need to twiddle your thumbs for months if you're sitting on a timely pitch. If you haven't heard back from them after a considerable time, it's okay to follow up, but there's a fine line between a quick follow-up e-mail and pestering. "I get a little bit irritated when people inundate me with phone calls and follow-ups," says Alexa Sherman, senior associate editor at *Shape* magazine. "If they haven't heard from me in a month, they should definitely call or e-mail me and I will let them know if they should continue to follow up after that or not."

Once You've Got an Assignment

If your cat just had emergency surgery and you're going to miss your deadline, don't leap to call an editor and tell her this. Do everything you can, including working longer and harder, to meet your deadline. It's simple advice, but it's often overlooked. If you are certain you're going to have a problem, by all means, call the editor. When I was an editor, one writer missed her deadline without calling, and then went AWOL for two weeks after her deadline. I didn't care if she was the best writer in the world; my first trip was to the executive editor's office, where I vented my frustration at the writer. Even though my top editor was a personal friend of the writer, she took my frustration into consideration and I never had to work with that writer again.

If you get your revision notes back and your article is hacked to shreds, take a deep breath before you bring it up with your editor. "I've had a couple writers who have had fits when I change things," says freelancer Ann Monroe, who edits a business section for *Newsweek Japan*. "*Newsweek* has a very distinct voice which is hard to nail and it's heavily edited, and I don't have time to soothe writers' battered egos." That doesn't mean you have to hold your tongue and let your words get trampled on all the time. "I'm a really equal-opportunity editor, and I appreciate input," Vlahos says. "Just choose your battles. If it's a short piece, a lot of times it will be revised and rewritten, so don't bellyache or whine about it. If you're a more experienced writer and you really feel like your voice has been lost, you can tactfully bring it up, like 'I noticed you changed this around. How about saying this instead?'" Bottom line: It's all in your approach. Overall, editors are the ones who know their voice the best. You may choose not to work with a magazine that slashes your words to bits time and again, but it's best to hold your tongue unless you really feel as if they've crossed the line.

With money matters, too, it's all in the approach. If you just received an assignment from a magazine that you've never worked for before and the pay isn't quite what you were hoping for, it's okay to ask for more. Just remember: An editor isn't maniacally rubbing her hands together, pondering ways to get the most work out of you for the least amount of pay. She's working on a budget dictated by her higher-ups. While it's fine to ask for more money, be pleasant in your request. After you've accepted an assignment, make sure you do everything you can to turn in your best work—even if the paycheck isn't quite as fat as you'd like. You never know where your editor may land next, and she'll be more likely to bring you with her if you've turned in stellar work and been professional and easy to work with. The same goes for shorter articles. Your dream assignment may be a six-page narrative feature, but you get a three-hundred-word short. Don't short-shrift your work just because it's small. "Even if it's a three-hundred word item, take whatever you've been given and try to make it the best it can be," Vlahos says. "If someone really turns in solid work on a short piece, that's someone I'll try out for larger pieces along the way. If someone is uncooperative when you go back to them for changes, that's someone I don't want to work with again. My Rolodex is filled with solid, competent, cooperative, and friendly writers, and those are the people I'll give assignments to."

Nurturing the Relationship

The fastest route to an editor is through his or her assistant. I had a particularly good relationship with the assistant who answered my editor's phone. Rather than just briskly ask for the editor, I would address her by name and ask how she was doing. When my editor left, all it took was a simple e-mail to the assistant; she recommended me to her new boss, and I quickly became one of the new editor's regulars, too. "It's vital to treat assistants with respect. I had a story I wanted to pitch to *George* and I talked to the editorial assistant on the phone about who I should send it to," says freelancer W. Thomas Smith, Jr. "After talking to him for a while, I finally asked him if I could address the query to him. It gave him a reason to go to the boss with my idea, and it gave him a feeling of importance. They ended up running the story." Likewise with the fact-checker: No one likes calls from fact-checkers, but make sure to be as helpful and pleasant as possible. If you're not, your editor's desk is the first place they will go. As an editor, I found it an unwelcome surprise when a fact-checker would tell me that a writer—who was all smiles to me—had been rude to him. It turned me off to the writer. You may have thought the story was finished long ago and you may have moved on to other things, but it's vital to see an article through to its completion. Fact-checking is often the last impression your editor has of you, and you want to make it a good one.

You may think that you should never bug an editor, but there are times when you should pick up the phone—and it's better than e-mail. Freelance writer Jackie Dishner learned this the hard way. "I'd been writing for a business publication for several years. The pay was minimal, but the stories were fairly easy to research and write. The editor called with an assignment, but unlike previous times, she had no contacts for me. To make a long story short, the story was problematic: I didn't have enough information, couldn't really find the story within the assignment, people weren't returning my phone calls or following up with promised information, I didn't have enough sources to call, and I was getting frustrated. Finally, I threw my hands up in the air and rushed off an e-mail to the editor to let her know I was frustrated and that my time was too valuable, and that I couldn't finish the story. I've never heard from her since! I burned a bridge that day, and I know it. I realize I could have handled it better by calling the editor, describing the challenges I was facing, and asking her how she thought I might resolve them. Or perhaps I could have suggested the assignment be killed. But I should never have revealed all that frustration in an e-mail like that."

For Ann Monroe, who is both a writer and editor, the No. 1 rule for smooth editor-writer relations is never surprise an editor. "Nothing will wreck a relationship faster than turning in something an editor doesn't expect," she says. "Ask questions if you don't understand. People say not to bother editors too much, but I say that if you have any confusion, call an editor. Don't call them every time you get an interview, but if you have any major problems or questions, pick up the phone."

Beyond Business

You don't have to be friends with your editors. Many writers prefer to maintain strict business relationships. But many other successful freelancers naturally want to get to know the editors whose work and judgment they admire. Besides, even small personal gestures can help cement a business relationship. For example, many writers send holiday greeting cards, or let their editors know that they are making charitable contributions instead of sending cards. A few send gifts to their favorite editors. Many writers love to get together with their editors for drinks or a meal. They talk shop, of course, but also get to know each other personally. It's important, however, not to be too pushy. Start off on a professional note before you move on to small talk. Little bits of humor in conversation or e-mail often break the ice, but don't go so far as to forward those jokes that are always circulating on the Internet. Small talk can fall into a conversation—about other stories, families, travels, and so on—to help you and the editor get to know each other. If an editor is all business, even when you make a gingerly step or two toward extending the relationship onto a personal level, forget it.

Freelance writer W. Thomas Smith, Jr. tells how he targeted a national newspaper when he was starting out years ago. First he sent an idea to an editor. Then he began following up with persistent phone calls. The editor was always polite, but never gave him the answer he wanted. "Since she was so receptive to my calls, I failed to consider the fact that I was violating all the rules by continuing to call and check on the status of my idea," he says. "One morning, I reached her and said, 'Hi, I'm not trying to worry you with this but...' and she cut me off with, 'Well, then why are you?' I was floored, and thought I had ruined my chances with her. But then I remembered a book I had read which recalled a story about a female reporter who, knowing that Ronald Reagan's favorite color was red, intentionally wore a red dress and elbow-length red gloves to a White House press conference. When the president started fielding questions, the reporter in red gloves raised her hand and he called on her. The reporter was none other than the editor I had been calling! From that story, I knew she had to appreciate bold maneuvers, so I sent flowers to her with a note that said, 'In my quest to have my story published, I appeared overanxious and feel I may have become something of a nuisance. Please forgive my overzealous behavior.' Well, she called back and was laughing and telling me how thoughtful it was. I ended up writing for the paper for several years. Now, keep in mind that you have to read the editor pretty well to get away with something like this, but from the story I'd heard I thought she'd appreciate it. She's the only editor I've sent flowers to, and I'd never do it if I didn't think it would be received well."

Probably the best piece of advice is to remember that editors are human too. Don't forget to e-mail or call them with thanks for a job well done. Treat them as you would want to be treated, and you may find yourself at the beginning of a productive professional and personal relationship.

MEGAN MCMORRIS has worked on both sides of the editorial fence, as a magazine editor in New York City and now as a freelance writer in Portland, Oregon. She's written for *Self, Sports Illustrated Women, Fitness, Glamour,* and *Marie Claire,* among other magazines.

12

Collaborations:
The Pleasures and Perils
of Shared Bylines

SARAH WERNICK

I magine this:
Your book has just been published and the *Today Show* calls.

The book hits bestseller lists.

The publisher arranges a ten-city book tour.

The phone rings constantly with interview requests.

A glossy magazine features the book, with an author photo on the cover and a seven-page spread inside.

All this happened to me—sort of. The book was *Strong Women Stay Young;* the byline reads "Miriam Nelson, Ph.D., with Sarah Wernick." But I didn't chat with Katie Couric or rack up frequent flyer miles. Dr. Nelson, a fitness expert from Tufts University, appeared on network TV and did the book signings. She's the one whose phone rang constantly and who talked to reporters. My picture wasn't on that magazine cover and my name wasn't mentioned—not once!—in the seven-page story.

Did all this bother me? Not in the least. That's what I expect as a collaborative writer who writes with experts. But how would you feel? That's the first question to ponder if you're considering this kind of work. In this chapter, I'll discuss the pros and cons of collaborative writing. I'll give you some suggestions for finding a writing partner and establishing a working relationship. You'll also get tips—and hear some war stories—from other ASJA members who have shared a byline.

Is Collaborative Writing for You?

We write for many reasons. Think about yours. Are you writing to express yourself? To change the world? Or do you see this mostly as a way to earn a living? Consider your vision of the writing life. Do you relish your independence—or would you prefer to be part of a team? What about publicity: Would you get a kick out of an *Oprah* appearance, or does the thought make you cringe? Collaborative writing isn't a path to fame, but it can offer fortune. Five of my six co-authored books received six-figure advances, thanks to the marketing potential of my collaborators and their expertise.

Money isn't the only benefit. I'm not a qualified specialist, but I can write on any topic that interests me—provided I have an appropriate collaborator. Working with an expert expands my reach. Miriam Nelson and I received wonderful letters from our readers. I was thrilled to hear from a stroke survivor who returned to her teaching job, thanks to a book in which I had a part. I've also learned a great deal from the experts I've worked with. For example, when I collaborated on *The Emotional Problems of Normal Children* with Stanley Turecki, M.D., a child psychiatrist, his insights taught me to be a better parent.

> None of my books were ghostwritten; my name is on the cover. But I don't think of them as "my" books. They are primarily the collaborators' books, since the content is theirs. I write in their voices, not my own, and I don't expect reviewers and the press to pay attention to me. You have to take your ego out of the process to some extent. You need to inhabit the space between "just doing it for the money" and "getting too identified with it."
>
> —STEPHANIE GOLDEN

Collaborative writers often compare the relationship between coauthors to a marriage. Ideally, your collaborator is someone who shares the work, a person with whom you can brainstorm, a partner who rejoices with you when things go well and commiserates when they don't. Alas, collaborations, like marriages, aren't always ideal. You collaborate because you bring different assets to the project—yet because of these differences, you won't always see things the same way. A good collaboration agreement (more about that later) can help prevent problems. Still, painful difficulties may arise. Here's a small sample of the outpourings I received when I asked fellow ASJA members about their collaborations:

> I was hired by a publisher to co-author a book with a celebrity. He turned out to be a nightmare to work with. I would fax him questions and get back four pages of irrelevant ramblings. Eventually, my editor and I met with him together, to see if she could get him on track. After two and a half hours, she halted the meeting. She wrote up a memo

explaining exactly what I needed. Again, he produced a bunch of garbage. She fired him. There was no book. I wasted four months of my life.

—LESLIE PEPPER

I wrote a book with a married couple. The writing went well. Then, when the book was in production, the wife decided she wanted a divorce. Needless to say, they weren't speaking to each other and that affected promotion.

—RUTH WINTER

Steel yourself for the possibility of dealing with egomaniacal personality disorders. You might be lucky enough to team up with reasonable co-authors, as I have in some cases. However, many experts—particularly celebrities and the nouveau riche—treat you as though you were the hired help. They refer to you as "my writer," as in "my chauffeur" or "my cook."

Be prepared for periods of seething anger during which you flagellate yourself for squandering your time and talent by turning a member of the illiterati into a candidate for the bestseller list. And most of all, know in advance that once the manuscript is finished and accepted, the expert will almost certainly believe that he or she has actually written the book. You'll get your "with" or your "and" byline, and you'll get a teensy little bio blurb ("Carol Smith is a freelance writer living in New Jersey"), and you'll probably get a nod in the acknowledgments ("Carol Smith deserves my gratitude for helping me put this book together"). But most often, you won't get credit for your true contributions.

—SONDRA FORSYTH

Experts and collaborative writers connect in many different ways. Here's how it's happened for me:

- I interviewed Dr. Turecki for a magazine article about difficult children. When we were finished, I expressed interest in working with him. A year later, he called me.

- Miriam Nelson wrote an article for *JAMA*, the *Journal of the American Medical Association*, about the health benefits of weight lifting for middle-aged women. I thought her exercise program would make a good book. I wrote to ask if she'd like to collaborate.

- I interviewed Peggy McCarthy, a patient advocate, for a magazine article about lung cancer. Several years later, she told me that a prominent doctor had just published important findings about early detection of the disease. She brought the three of us together to write *Lung Cancer: Myths, Facts, Choices—and Hope*.

Lest this sound easy, I should add that experts frequently turn me down when I approach them. Some projects seem promising, then falter. As the saying goes, you must kiss many frogs before you find a prince.

Some writers wait for collaborative gigs to come to them. Or they count on their agents to find experts. But based on my experiences, as well as what I've heard from colleagues, I think it's much better (despite those frogs) for the writer to take the initiative. You'll learn that the world is full of potential co-authors. With so many attractive possibilities, you don't need to settle for a project that's merely so-so, or cave in when an expert demands unreasonable contract terms.

I'm always on the lookout for potential collaborators. I collect interesting articles and keep notes on ideas and contacts. When I'm ready for a new project, I go through the collection and prioritize. An appealing subject isn't enough. I also check bookstores to see what's available. Why squeeze into an overcrowded field if I can fill an unmet need? I send one propositioning letter at a time, waiting about three weeks for a response. If I'm turned down or receive no answer, the next expert gets a letter. I also write to agents and editors, asking them to keep my name on file for the next time a suitable project comes up.

> When I need a co-author expert, I immediately look at the *American Psychological Association Directory of Experts* (I write a lot about relationships) and *The Yearbook of Experts, Authorities, and Spokespersons*. If I needed a medical expert, I'd research who in the particular field has written related articles in journals like the *New England Journal of Medicine* or *JAMA*, and call the media-relations department of the American Medical Association and top hospitals for help.
>
> —FLORENCE ISAACS

Preliminaries

Before you and a potential collaborator decide to work together, you'll need to get acquainted. Unless you're paid for your time, keep this uncommitted period short. I'm willing to invest about a day—but no more—to talk and to prepare writing or editing samples. I make it clear, in a positive way, that this no-cost, no-obligations contact is limited. I might say: "I'd be delighted to meet with you on Friday afternoon, so we can decide if we want to move forward." Or: "I can't review your entire manuscript without a consulting contract, but I'd be glad to read and comment on the introductory chapter to give you a sense of how I work."

During our initial contact, I'm evaluating the expert, just as he or she is assessing me. Here are the key questions I ask myself:

* Does this person have material for a book? An idea isn't enough. A book requires at least 50,000 words of appropriate content, with a beginning, a middle, and an end. An example: A writer friend met with a young woman who hoped to publish a book about a year she'd spent working with abused children. But the would-be author lacked essential information. The youngsters' heartbreaking stories

ended without resolution, because she didn't know—and had no way to find out—what had happened to them since she left her job. My friend could see no way to turn her experience into a commercial book.

※ Will this person draw an attractive advance? A book advance is based in part on the size of your target audience and in part on what people in publishing call the *platform*: all the skills and connections the author brings to marketing. Platform is to publishing what location is to real estate. Outstanding professional credentials are a must. But I want the highest possible advance, so I also look for a platform. Does the expert give workshops or seminars? Speak at professional and popular conferences? Appear regularly on TV and radio or in print? Most of all, I'm hoping to find someone with star quality, which is difficult to describe but easy to spot.

※ Can this person understand and answer my questions? Dr. Big Shot (I'm disguising things a bit), a cardiologist with a prestigious medical-school appointment, approached me about writing a popular book on women's heart health. I said, "Several books have been published on this subject. What will be special about yours?" Dr. B. told me that her book would recommend good nutrition and exercise. I reworded the question, emphasizing the need for something different, such as new recommendations or an ingenious program that was particularly easy to follow. This prompted an incomprehensible monologue about enzymes. Clearly, we were not a good match.

※ Is this a person I want to work with for as long as it takes to write a book? First impressions could be wrong. But if warning flags start waving—for example, if the expert is inconsiderate during this "courtship" phase—pay attention.

I contacted an expert who had every qualification in spades. She was a physician, a professor, and an in-demand speaker. She had expertise, visibility, TV credentials, contacts, a wonderful platform, et cetera. All her references were five-star. The problem was that she overbooks herself and then doesn't deliver. After about the tenth promise that she would sign and return the collaboration agreement, I withdrew the offer.

—SANDRA LAMB

At the end of our initial contact—whether it's been a meeting, a phone conference, or a series of e-mails in which I offered comments on written material—I let the expert know what I'd like to do. If I'm not interested, I withdraw in a clear but uncritical way. Usually, I say something like: "I've enjoyed speaking with you, but I'm not the right writer for this book." If I think that a colleague might consider the gig, I offer to refer the expert to another writer. I conclude my farewell with friendly wishes for success with the book. If I'm interested, I express my enthusiasm and suggest that the expert get back to me when he or she has reached a decision. I explain that the next step would be for us to sign a collaboration agreement and offer to send the agreement I use.

What if the expert isn't ready to decide? I address any questions and, if it seems appropriate, suggest the option of my consulting on the project for a few days to a week. As with any consulting arrangement, I'd expect to sign an agreement before I start. For consulting services, a writer might charge anywhere from a few hundred dollars up to several thousand dollars per day, plus expenses, depending on experience. Unless there's a reason to do so, I don't give a deadline for a response. But in the absence of a commitment, I let the expert know that I'll continue looking. I might say: "I don't want to rush you. Both of us need to think about this and to explore our other options."

What about agents? Some books are sold without a literary agent. But that's increasingly difficult, especially if you're hoping for a sizable advance. An agent may be involved in a collaborative book from the outset: You or the expert may already have an agent to whom you're devoted. Or the agent may be the one who brings you together. Some collaborative writers prefer to work with their own agent, rather than using a single agent for the project. Their concern—and it's a valid one—is that a shared agent would favor the expert. My own view is that it's better to avoid the complications of having two agents on one book. And I never assume that an agent, who gets paid only if there's a sale, has interests identical to mine.

A number of resources for writers are helpful in the early stages of a collaboration. *The Writer's Legal Companion,* by Brad Bunnin and Peter Beren, in its third edition, contains a chapter on collaborations, which includes a model agreement. *The Writer's Legal Guide: An Authors Guild Desk Reference,* by Tad Crawford and Kay Murray, also in its third edition, has a chapter on collaborations. In addition, writer's organizations provide information and assistance for members; some, including ASJA, offer model collaboration agreements.

Put It in Writing

Here's the single most important point in this chapter:

> Don't start working with a collaborator until
> you have a signed written agreement.

No matter how carefully you select your co-author, problems may arise. Three anonymous real-life examples from ASJA members:

> After I put the whole deal together, including writing a lengthy book proposal (60 pages) and a sample chapter, the agent tossed me aside when the expert's former collaborator—who, I'd been assured, had retired—decided to do the rewrite.

I wrote a proposal for which an expert supplied some of the materials and ideas. Now the book project is scrapped. The expert may engage another writer; I want to pitch ideas from the proposal to magazines—but it's not clear who owns the proposal.

My co-author, without consulting me, hired a publicist—then asked me to share in paying for her. Though the publicist will be promoting my co-author, he says the publicity is for the book and since we will share in royalties we should share the costs. P.S.: The bill for the publicist was $25,000.

A written agreement can't prevent all difficulties. But it makes your understandings clearer and helps ensure that you'll be treated fairly—even if you need to go to court to make that happen. Consider getting advice from an attorney, an agent, or both before you sign. Here is a brief summary of the points that collaboration agreements should cover:

BASIC INFORMATION: Include the date, names of the collaborators, and a concise statement of the work you plan to do together (usually, to write a book proposal and a book on a subject that's described in a phrase).

RESPONSIBILITIES: Summarize each collaborator's responsibilities, including a work schedule. Specify who is responsible for the book's content and who has the final say over the manuscript. My agreements give the expert the final word about content—and the expert indemnifies me against claims by readers who feel they've been harmed by the book.

COMPENSATION: Arrangements vary considerably, though a 50/50 split of the advance and royalties is the single most common deal, according to reports from ASJA members. A celebrity expert whose platform will draw a significant advance may claim a larger share. On the other hand, the writer—who works full-time on the book—may receive more if the expert has substantial other income. Sometimes collaborators agree that the writer will receive all or most of the advance, but that the expert will collect the first royalties; once they're even, future royalties are divided 50/50.

CREDIT AND COPYRIGHT: If you want your name on the book cover and expect to share copyright, include these provisions in the agreement.

EXPENSES: List the types of expenses you'll share and how costs will be divided. It's helpful to agree that unlisted expenses above $25 will be mutually agreed upon before they are incurred.

THE UNEXPECTED AND THE UNPLEASANT: What if the book doesn't sell? Suppose the collaboration falls apart before the book is completed? The agreement should spell out what happens under these and other unfortunate circumstances. Who owns the jointly created material? What compensation will you receive for your efforts—including writing the proposal? Also decide how to handle disagreements that you can't resolve on your own. Arbitration is one possibility.

Making It Work

Once you and your new collaborator have signed an agreement, you can begin working together. Your first step with nonfiction is likely to be a book proposal. Consider this an engagement period: It will lay the foundation of your relationship when you write the book—and if things go badly, you can bail out before you sign a publishing contract.

Co-authors collaborate in many different ways. In my collaborations, I usually do all the writing. Depending on what's most convenient and productive, I obtain information from the expert via in-person meetings, telephone calls, e-mail, or a combination. I might attend a relevant seminar or speech by my co-author. Generally we work chapter by chapter. I start by presenting the expert with a chapter outline, which we discuss and flesh out. Then I write a rough draft, with many questions in the text, and we go through it together. I constantly ask for additional information that will make the material more lively. For instance, when Miriam Nelson told me about a study of strength training that was conducted at a nursing home, I asked how the staff had reacted when researchers recruited frail residents for a challenging weight-lifting program. Sometimes the expert helps me connect with other people, such as clients or research participants, who can supply anecdotes. By the time I write the next draft, there are fewer questions and comments. When we agree that the chapter is finished, we move on to the next. Here's how two other ASJA writers have managed their collaborations:

> I collaborate with co-authors via e-mail. We mail chapter sections back and forth, each writing a section or a chapter, and then editing the co-author's writing, and back and forth, until we're satisfied.
>
> —TINA B. TESSINA

> My first book, *Gut Reactions,* was written with Dr. David Taylor, then my family doc and a good friend. First, we agreed on a basic outline for the book and what would be in each chapter. David did a rough draft first (*very* rough) and I would rewrite in journalistic style. Then he'd check for accuracy. It worked very, very well.
>
> —MAXINE ROCK

As a writer, you have a great deal to offer an expert—even if you've never written a book before. You know how to reach an audience via the printed page; you can translate professional jargon into lively prose. You possess (or can acquire) the necessary expertise to shepherd a project through the proposal stage to publication. And you have valuable connections for publicity, thanks to your contacts with fellow writers. If you decide to share these assets with a collaborator, may both of you enjoy a productive and congenial partnership.

SARAH WERNICK is an award-winning freelance writer with a Ph.D. in sociology from Columbia University. She specializes in health, parenting, and self-help collaborations. Her books include the bestselling *Strong Women Stay Young* (Bantam), written with Miriam Nelson. Her next collaboration is *Quick Fit* (Atria). She also speaks on book proposals and collaborative writing. Visit her Web site at *www.sarahwernick.com*.

13

The Serendipity of Specialization

CLAIRE WALTER

This is an ode to specialization—to knowing a lot about a fairly narrow topic or two and writing about it or them again and again. It is an acknowledgment of the benefits of being an expert in a field or on a subject (or in a few select fields or a few subjects). Assignments on particular topics flow to those in the know, to those authorities whose words are trusted and whose bylines are recognized. It is also a very personal, subjective view, because the relationship between an authoritative writer and his or her subject is close.

I never set out to be an authority, but I became one. My last two staff editorial positions were both managing editor jobs—first of two ski trade publications and then of *Ski*, a major consumer ski publication. Those two jobs gave me insights, knowledge, and a reputation in that field, and created a passion for the sport. When I started freelancing, it seemed natural for me to identify myself as a ski writer. More than twenty years later, I still write a great deal about skiing—both downhill and cross-country. Research trips took me to the mountain regions where people ski, so I became knowledgeable about winter activities and destinations in New England, the Rockies, and the Alps. That broadened to writing about summer in those regions and also to major gateway cities to important ski resorts. I became a travel writer.

Like many freelancers, I had long felt that it was important to be in New York, the nation's magazine and book-publishing capital. There I was, in a city with hundreds of editors—and thousands of writers. In 1988, fed up with high-intensity urban living and longing to be closer to the mountains I wrote about, I moved to Colorado. I found mountains by the thousands but only a handful of writers covering them. Suddenly, magazines that I had never managed to break into when I was in New York were throwing assignments my way. After all, I was a Colorado-based ski writer—therefore not just an authority, but a well-placed one. No editor had to "send" me to the mountains because I was already in Boulder. Soon after moving West, I connected with Fulcrum Publishing, an important regional publisher. I wrote a book called *Rocky Mountain Skiing* for Fulcrum. It went into two editions and was the first of three books that I have done for them. The second was *Snowshoeing Colorado*, the first snowshoeing-specific trail guide to Colorado—not trivial, because snowshoeing is a fast-growing winter sport. That book helped stamp me as one of the first and foremost authorities writing on

showshoeing, and led to dozens of magazine, newspaper, and online feature and service articles.

Now, for a bigger leap. One of my avocations is cooking. When I
can, I am a volunteer assistant at the Cooking School of the Rockies. I
noticed the number of people who came to Boulder to take a series of
five-day, midweek cooking classes. Enchanting as my town may be, this
isn't Provence or Tuscany. But they came in a steady procession: dedicated home cooks spending a week refining their skills. Colorado
seemed ready for a guidebook and resource book for people interested
in food. Fulcrum is also the publisher of my latest book, *Culinary Colorado.*
It is a food-oriented travel guidebook to the state's best restaurants and
its cooking schools, fine bakeries, shops that sell cookware and accessories, wine and cheese specialty merchants, and more, and is being
copyedited as I write this. So, yes, I became a food writer. I have now
done food stories for a handful of major national magazines and food
Web sites, and eventually I hope to do more.

I am not the only writer who went from editing a special-interest
magazine to freelance writing in that field, nor the only writer who
turned a personal interest into a journalistic specialty. In 1956, David
Miller was an out-of-work trade magazine editor. He was sent by the
New York State unemployment office to an interview at *Industrial Photography,* where he worked for two years. He was hired away by *Modern
Photography,* a leading consumer magazine where he became managing
editor. "I figured it would be another two-year job," he says, "but it
turned out to be thirty."

Over three decades, he had built a powerful network of colleagues
who knew and respected him, so when that magazine folded Miller
called on his friends and contacts. The network proved invaluable, and
Miller has written about photography for the *New York Times, Resorts
& Incentives, Penthouse,* and others. Even in semi-retirement, he has
found work and work has found him. "When I retired, it wasn't crucial
to keep going for economic reasons, but for psychological ones," Miller

says. He is an authority on photography, and as long as he wants to write there will be markets for him.

Other writers find an interest, a passion, and write about that. Suzy Gershman is known for her successful *Born to Shop* books and for feature articles on shopping in major magazines. Her business card reads "Author, Journalist & Shopping Goddess." (Shopping goddess *does* sound even better than shopping authority, doesn't it?) She recalls, "The shopping thing—like most things in life—happened by accident. I was a real journalist at Time, Inc., and sold *Born to Shop* as a series in 1984. It was immediately a hit and has grown to sixteen different titles and one hundred revisions. I have had a shopping column in the big travel magazines like *Travel & Leisure* and *Travel/Holiday,* and I have done reporting for *National Geographic Traveler*." Gershman moved to France to rebuild her life after her husband's death—and in fact, she has a new book for Viking on moving to Paris as a widow and starting over. "I just finished that book," she says, "and am now revising *Born to Shop: China,* and then go into the regular rotations of revisions. I think the whole thing to having a specialty is the opportunity to work at it and revise things."

Still others put their education into the equation, but serendipity still seems to play the biggest role. Catherine Dold describes her discovery of science writing as a "haphazard" career path. After earning a degree in environmental biology, she went to New York for an entry-level job with the National Resources Defense Council. "I volunteered to help write the newsletter. It was a small organization, and if you had an idea, you could implement it," she notes. She "fell into the writing end" and discovered an aptitude for it. "I hadn't thought about writing as a career, but discovered that there was an actual profession of science writing," she recalls. Dold enrolled in a master's degree program in environmental journalism at New York University. After seven years at the NRDC, she became an editor at *Audubon* magazine, and two years later began freelancing. Freelancing is portable, and so are her specialties of medicine, health, and the environment, which fall under the umbrella category of science writing. She has written for major magazines and medical institutions. Her articles have appeared in such publications as the *New York Times, Smithsonian*, and *Cosmopolitan. Cosmo?* The ultimate girl-talk magazine covers health issues, and Dold has written about such varied topics as headaches and genetic testing.

Not everyone is a staff writer or editor before becoming a freelance writer. Washington, D.C.–based Candyce Stapen was an academician, with a Ph.D. in English literature and a position at the University of Maryland at Towson. She also had two children, eleven years apart in age. "It was hard to pick a movie, let alone a vacation or even a day outing, for a three-year-old and a fourteen-year-old," she recalls. "When I'd call a destination and ask if they had a children's program, they'd say 'yes,' and when we got there, it was a video arcade. That's not what we were looking for. There was a need for information on family travel." She has helped answer that need since 1983. She says that her husband's idea of weekend recreation was "puttering around the garden" or watching television sports, so she packed up the children and went about exploring the area. "I started writing for the *Washington Post* weekend section," she says. She would come home and write about their experiences and send the piece to the paper. "They'd call and ask a couple of questions, and then put the piece on the cover," she adds. "I didn't realize until later how difficult freelancing would be."

It took her two years to convince her book publisher, Globe Pequot, to put out a book on family travel. Now it is an acknowledged subspecialty of the guidebook genre. Stapen's most recent book, *The National Geographic Guide to Caribbean Family Vacations*, is her twenty-third. In those early freelancing years, Stapen decided that the demands of two jobs—teaching and writing—plus being a parent were too much. Put off by university politics as well, she gave up teaching to become a full-time freelancer. Later, when her older child was negotiating the minefield of his teen years, she began writing about that too, mainly for the *Post* and *USA Today*. "There was a market for those stories, and I found it personally interesting, too. I always figure that if I find something interesting, someone else will, too," she says. "That's the important thing. Your subject shouldn't be artificial. You've got to love it."

What Miller, Gershman, Stapen, Dold, and I—and many others—have discovered is the sheer efficiency in writing on topics we know well. We can write for top publications because we *are* authoritative. High-paying markets seeking cutting-edge stories compensate writers well for articles that require extensive research, and as specialists we can fill in with assignments from lower-paying markets because we know the topic intimately and can write quickly and easily. The "easy" way to make yourself known in a particular field is to find a staff position with a special-interest publication, striking out on your own to freelance when the time is right. If you don't have a true passion or a profession, and yet are attracted by the thought of specializing as a writer, a special-interest publication can introduce you to a field you end up loving, as I found while working at *Ski*. You will get to know people in the field, as David Miller did in photography, who will be invaluable in launching your freelance career. Don't expect big bucks for entry-level work, but do expect to find a niche and work up, sometimes surprisingly quickly.

Once you begin freelancing, you can use your passion—scuba diving, bird-watching, automobiles, mountain biking, sailing, rock climbing, gardening, traveling in Mexico, whatever—as a focus for your writing. Remember to emphasize your knowledge on your resume and in your query letters. If you are in a profession that people turn to for help, you can begin querying and writing on those topics. Psychologists, doctors, exercise physiologists, nutritionists, and other professionals have become well-published authors in their fields.

If there is a writers' organization in your field, whether you are a freelancer or a staffer, join as soon as you have credentials. Networking with other writers and editors in your specialty pays off big-time. When you begin to freelance, you might have to start with modest publications, but persist, collect clips, and "trade up" to better-paying markets. Once you are known, you too can spin the reputation that you make as, say, a magazine writer into books or online publications on your specialty. If you start with a book, you can write for magazines and other media on that topic, as I did with snowshoeing and food. After a time, editors come to you, and you will get referrals from people you know in your area of expertise. You will get calls from other writers looking for quotes on topics that you know well, which enhances your reputation as a specialist. Sometimes groups will ask you to come and speak about your specialty, and pay you for your time.

Remember, you can't spell authority without *author*.

CLAIRE WALTER is an award-winning, nationally published magazine writer and author or co-author of more than a dozen books, including *Culinary Colorado* and *Rocky Mountain Skiing* (Fulcrum Publishing). Her specialties are snow sports, travel, food, and fitness. Her Web site is *www.claire-walter.com*. She writes from Boulder, Colorado.

14

Self-Publishing: Alternatives for Getting Books into Print

MARILYN AND TOM ROSS

In yesteryear, Mark Twain, Virginia Woolf, and Ben Franklin privately published their work. Today the ranks of self-publishers have swollen like a raging river preparing to overtake its banks. Richard Paul Evans successfully dipped his toe in the self-publishing waters with a little book titled *The Christmas Box*—and subsequently scooped up a $4.125-million contract from Simon & Schuster. James Redfield, who self-published *The Celestine Prophecy,* garnered an $800,000 advance from Warner Books. This spiritual adventure parable resided on the *New York Times* bestseller list for more than three years. And Louise Hay's self-published book *You Can Heal Your Life* led her to establish a publishing house that has put out more than 150 books and 350 audiotapes. Hay House quintupled its sales over an eight-year period.

Why is self-publishing attracting so many qualified authors today? Even more important, how can you take advantage of this phenomenon to boost your career and your income? This chapter addresses the subject from a two-pronged approach: self-publishing your own book, and developing a freelance-paid project for a private client.

Why Self-Publish?

Self-publishing is shaping your own writing destiny, investing in your future. The reasons this approach makes sense today are manifold. First and foremost, you can make money. Why settle for a paltry royalty of 10 percent of net when you can have *all* the profits? Nine of ten books put out by traditional publishing houses never earn out their advances. Why consign yourself to that group? (Especially since many publishers want you to do the majority of the promotional work.)

In self-publishing you really begin to make big bucks when you go back to press after the first print run. Then the costs of editing, cover design, and typesetting are behind you. All you pay for is the printing. Let's say you have a 224-page paperback book that costs you about $1.90 to print traditionally and ship. You sell it for $14.95. Subtract the $5.68 discounts for wholesalers and bookstores (the average discount is 38 percent because you'll also sell many books at full retail price), and you are likely to make $7.37 per book: $14.95 minus $1.90 minus $5.68. That's almost 50 percent profit—certainly lucrative compared to normal New York publishing standards.

Another benefit of do-it-yourself publishing is control. No one will change your title, dress the book in a cover that embarrasses you, or edit out your favorite phrases. You call the shots. You also control how the book is promoted and sold. Timing is another advantage. Once a manuscript is accepted by a major house, it typically takes eighteen months before the book is available. And don't forget, it will take time to find an agent or publisher before that clock even starts. When you're the publisher, you can have a book out in three to six months. If the subject is time-sensitive, the faster turnaround gives you a huge edge.

Also, you can afford to give your books away when you self-publish. Sound like a strange statement? Who wants to give books away? You do! Offering complimentary copies to reviewers, reporters, radio and TV producers, Web sites, independent booksellers, and the like is the cheapest advertising you can find. And you can't do it if you're with a traditional publisher. We have walked both sides of this street: trade publishing and self-publishing. We once turned down a contract from a major house because it wanted to sell us copies at a 40 percent discount—but only if we used the books for the house's PR purposes. Using that same $14.95 book, can you really afford to give them away when you have to pay $8.97 each? No way.

Another intriguing reason to consider self-publishing is that it can be a practical and prosperous path into big trade houses. We have self-published twelve books, five of which we've also sold to trade publishers. They love to pick up successful self-published books because you've removed all the risk. You've already produced an attractive product (forgive us for calling your "baby" a product, but this is a business, and if you want to be successful you must think like a businessperson). You've proven there is a market for the title. Now they can pick up where you left off and get wider distribution into the trade. Properly negotiated, this is often a win/win alliance. You have fresh leverage because you own the rights to a validated book and can thus negotiate a larger advance. It's also important to ensure that you can continue selling the book into noncompetitive markets. They will want bookstores, wholesalers/distributors, and perhaps libraries. Yet there is a whole world of other opportunities to capitalize on. (More about that later.)

Freelancer Bonanza: Self-Publishing for Others

Savvy freelancers are also writing and producing books for others. When you consider this potential pool of prospects, there are many ways to go. Through our company, About Books, Inc., we've been publishing books for authors and companies for more than twenty-five years. Many of our recent clients are professionals who want to get their specialized knowledge between book covers. They realize that authoring a book gives them new visibility and credibility. It positions them ahead of the pack. When seeking freelance projects, look especially at the healing professions. We've done many books for M.D.'s, dentists, psychotherapists, alternative medicine experts, and the like. Also, forward-thinking entrepreneurs sometimes see the value in doing a book. And corporations might want a book or booklet to celebrate a key anniversary or to give away to push a new product or service. Churches often need help with histories and cookbooks.

How might your project shape up? In many cases you will be ghostwriting the entire book. In others, editing a manuscript. Often you will shepherd the venture through the entire production phase, serving as a book packager or book producer. Be sure to have a written agreement outlining specifically what you will do, what is expected of the other party, deadlines, and so on. We suggest a partial payment up front, another payment when you go to press, and the remainder upon delivery.

Educate Yourself for Success

It's vital to educate yourself. If you're responsible for another's project, you owe your client a quality product at a fair price. If you're doing your own book, a high-caliber job that's also affordable is your top concern. Book manufacturing, for instance, can cost double what it should if you don't know where to go. Is this project a candidate for traditional printing, or will Print on Demand (POD) be best?

In traditional printing, many copies of a book are printed at once; this is expensive, of course, and the books must be warehoused. POD is a high-tech, low-cost alternative; books are printed and shipped as they are ordered.

Let's explore these two options. POD has been ballyhooed by many as the solution of solutions. Not necessarily so. Many who have tried it are disillusioned. For certain jobs, where no more than a few hundred copies are needed, it's ideal. But you have to buy every copy at list price or at a modest discount, so this is not a viable approach if you're serious about self-publishing and want trade distribution. In that case you need an inexpensive book you can give away and sell at a steep discount to bookstores on a returnable basis; you'll probably want to print 3,000 to 5,000 copies. POD also would not be appropriate if you have a client corporation that wants several thousand copies; with that kind of volume, you can get a much cheaper per-copy print run from a private publishing house. POD makes absolute sense when only a few dozen or several hundred copies are needed for:

- Creating a short run of customized books for a specific market (for example, family genealogies or church histories).

- Early copies of a book (galleys) that are needed to solicit advance blurbs, first serial/excerpt rights, et cetera.

- Authors seeking a conventional trade publisher who needs a "sample."

- When the budget is minuscule and market testing is needed to determine the best title/cover design/selling strategy.

- Selling slow-moving backlist books that only move a few hundred copies each year.

- ✳ Established authors who want to break out of a genre and try a new passion.

- ✳ Authors with a loyal following who need some copies of their out-of-print books.

- ✳ Speakers and teachers who require customized workbooks for seminars or classes.

- ✳ Those wanting a few luxury hardcover first editions to be numbered and autographed.

Book Design 101

From a business perspective, the look of a book can be almost as important as its message. Of course, you will see that your book has a "Wow!" cover. In bookstores the small slice seen on the shelf, the spine, is your book's salesperson. If you don't catch customers' eyes with that, all is lost. Be sure it is colorful and the title is in large bold letters. A dramatic front cover is paramount. Study other books, either in bookstores or online at Amazon.com, to get ideas. The interior design needs to be reader-friendly. Remember that baby boomers' eyes are starting to rebel, so use at least 11-point type. Make the design open and inviting. Read to understand the nuances of this business. Surf the Internet. Attend conferences. Network with colleagues in similar circumstances. We'd suggest you start by reading our book *The Complete Guide to Self-Publishing.* We can modestly say that others have called it "the bible" of self-publishing.

Promotion and PR: The Great Equalizers

Marketing is a mind-set. It impacts virtually everything you do. And it should begin way before you have finished a book. Ideally, it starts when you first get a concept. You need to know exactly who your target readers are—and how to reach that market. Then you can write the book to directly meet their needs. Do some research and find out what is already available. Armed with that ammunition you can wage a campaign to provide a book that is better in some way: shorter, more complete, funnier, illustrated, indexed, more logically arranged, easier to use . . . you get the idea. Often the most thriving self-publishers have niche books, titles that appeal mainly to a select group of people. Why? Because then you can be a big fish in a little pond. When launching your marketing you can reach those people through associations they belong to, in newsletters and specialized magazines they read, and via conventions they attend. It's virtually impossible for a self-publisher to influence everyone. No one has that kind of marketing budget. But by doing books that appeal to a select audience you can find and motivate potential customers.

How best to do that? Blessed free publicity is the writer/publisher's best friend and the great equalizer. News releases are your primary workhorses, a mock review (favorable, of course, because you write and typeset it) is your second-best tool. Visit your local library or the Internet to locate current names and contact information for the associations, specialized publications, and other sources that might review, mention, or sell your book. Take some extra time to customize your pitch to them so it fits perfectly with their style and needs.

We're great believers in print publicity. It has staying power. We had a person call eight years after a piece about us appeared in the *New York Times*. Another perk with print is that it is recyclable. It's not just the initial appearance, but what you do with it. When you've got it, flaunt it. Put it in your media kit. Send it to buyers who have so far avoided you. Put it on your Web site. Include it when you send invoices or statements. Look for every conceivable way to circulate it again and again.

The media likes to climb on a moving bandwagon. If an editor or reporter sees a nice story featuring you as an expert, or a favorable review of your book, he or she is more inclined to give you more exposure. When thinking of print, don't overlook newspapers, and not necessarily just the review sections. Try for publicity off the book pages. Have a book on investing or entrepreneurship? Go for the business section. A how-to or self-help title stands a good chance in the lifestyle section. A book about baseball or football is a natural for the sports section. And so on. Also, consider smaller weekly newspapers. They are usually short-staffed and welcome interesting free material. You might write a special brief "tips" article where you list five, seven, or ten bits of advice related to your topic, and then provide info on ordering the book at the end. Editors love these because they offer value to their readers.

For certain titles, radio interviews are another smashing way to move books. You can do what is called "phoners" all across the country from your home or office—even in your bathrobe. Radio hosts will call and interview you for fifteen, thirty, even sixty minutes. Here you need a book that has wide general interest and costs less than $20. Or if you've published something that has regional appeal, such as *The Children's Guide to San Diego,* you can sell a lot of books by getting on stations in that metropolitan area. To support this effort, be sure books are available in at least one bookstore in the area and mention that store. Also give your phone number several times (assuming you accept credit cards). One final tip about radio: Don't talk about "my book." Repeat the title! Listeners tune in and out and need to know the name of the book you're discussing.

Selling Books in Nontraditional Ways

The fact is, 52 percent of all books are *not* sold in bookstores. They are sold by direct mail, in other retail outlets, as premiums, in catalogs, and on the Web. Though our space here is limited, and we cover this extensively in *Jump Start Your Book Sales,* let's explore a few of these alternative venues. Catalogs are wonderful places to sell books. There are some 15,000 different ones in existence covering more than 800 distinct categories. Revisit the library or Internet and research the ones that specialize in your subject area. Study their merchandise. They may not carry books. Yet. Call to find out who the buyer is and get any submission guidelines, then woo the heck out of them. Catalogs typically order books by case lots or more, pay promptly, reorder for months or years, and don't return books.

To a publisher, selling a book as a premium is what honey is to a bee. Companies, associations, and nonprofit organizations often buy books in large quantities. They use them as giveaways to build goodwill, to augment a product or service, or perhaps for internal training purposes. Churches and other groups might also be convinced to use your book as a fundraiser. The nectar from premiums ranges greatly. One publisher might sell 500 books to a company for a 50-percent discount; another could strike a deal with a corporation for 10,000 books at a 65-percent discount. There are no set rules. Your job is to be a creative, out-of-the-box thinker and identify potential partners. Who already serves your customer base? If you have a book on parenting, for instance, think toy companies and children's-wear manufacturers as a start.

Similarly, what retail stores might carry your books? Gourmet shops are a natural for cookbooks; a book on how to have younger-looking skin might fly in beauty shops and beauty-supply stores, an art book in museums and galleries. Have a gardening guide? Try nurseries, garden centers, home improvement stores, florists, and botanical gardens. We know of a novelist whose main character drove a Volvo. Would you believe that novel sold in Volvo showrooms?

Being an assertive promoter is not easy for many writers. Yet it can be done with grace and effectiveness once a marketing mind-set is in place. That, plus educating yourself about the entire process, will provide the keys to the kingdom. Self-publishing—taking charge of your own writing career, or performing the tasks as a freelancer—can be fun and lucrative. Why not dip your toes in the water?

MARILYN AND TOM ROSS of Buena Vista, Colorado, are gurus of self-publishing. Over twenty-five years they have helped thousands of authors and publishers produce and sell millions of books through consulting and through their books *The Complete Guide to Self-Publishing* (Writer's Digest Books) and *Jump Start Your Book Sales* (Communications Creativity). Marilyn also does private coaching via phone. Contact them through *www.SelfPublishingResources.com*.

15

Networking

Sandra E. Lamb

It's easy to lament that you aren't as wired for instant success as, say, a writer who has a New York City address, or who happens to be the sister of the editor-in-chief of the magazine you are querying. Truth is, you already have more potential networking connections than you can reap in your entire lifetime. So flip the switch on yourself, and realize that you can be well-connected by simply launching your own effective networking program.

Networking is the process of making and using contacts. It can be your secret weapon for success; and it's your first course of action before you launch a public-relations campaign or publicity blitz. First, identify who you are, and whom you know. And, more important, identify whom you want to get to know. Filling out the St. Martin's Press Author's Questionnaire for my book *Personal Notes: How to Write from the Heart for Any Occasion,* I realized that every book publisher, from the smallest to the largest, starts in exactly the same way to build an effective marketing plan: by determining the networking possibilities of the author. (It can work equally as well for the magazine writer, with a few thoughtful modifications.)

Getting Started

Start with a detailed self-analysis:

Who do you know?

Where did you grow up?

Where did you go to school?

Where do you live now?

What are your personal interests?

Which clubs and organizations do you belong to?

Who is going to be interested in your book?

What are your local media outlets?

What are you willing to do to promote yourself?

That's where everything must begin. And that's what makes all kinds of networking possible. Start thinking about these categories, and start creating special lists based on your background.

Make a General List of people you know who will be interested in your publishing news. To this list you'll send postcards about your new book, or a notice of your next feature article or speaking engagement. A Media Contacts list, which you'll want to further divide by radio, television, magazines, and so on, will be divided into those you have a connection to and those you want to contact for the first time. Organization Contacts will be a listing of people who are members of groups you participate in. This is where you'll send regular press releases and "good publishing news" items. Your Contacts Wish List may be a column on your other lists, or a separate listing of people you target—those you want to get to know. (You'll use all the names on all your lists to contact with personal notes and communications.)

Decide how you're going to store key information, and what you want to establish to trigger your follow-up. Create a media contact notebook; or, as Susanne Alexander, a business journalist and regular contributor to *Newsweek*, does, use a computerized approach like the one available from Microsoft Office Suite. Alexander even records notes and cues for herself about people she meets in social situations. These allow her to remember details to refer to later, like "friend of Susan Dibs," or "tall, blonde, Chamber of Commerce entrepreneur who has a beagle named Sophie." She enters the data using her contact management software, which automatically categorizes entries into subcategories for marketing follow-up and/or to receive her newsletter.

The key to networking is in the follow-up. And it's in the timing. It's safe to say that you can easily distinguish yourself after meeting a new person by sending a personal note (with a business card) within forty-eight hours of an initial meeting. If you have been fortunate and wise enough to establish another reason to contact the person again during that initial meeting, follow the Golden Rule of networking: Deliver what you promised, when you promised. Or before.

Take Personal Stock

Speaking of the Golden Rule, the Dale Carnegie tenets still work as keys to making your first impression a very good one. Ask yourself if you need to tune up your internal personal networking tools before you actually make that first contact:

1. ARE YOU GENUINELY INTERESTED IN OTHER PEOPLE? It's a necessary tool in your networking arsenal, and it will be quickly reflected in your approach and everything that comes after that first "Hello."

2. DO YOU HAVE A SMILE IN YOUR VOICE AND ON YOUR FACE? Even if you make telephone contact, it will come across. And it's energizing, to both you and the person to whom you're talking.

3. CAN YOU COMFORTABLY USE THE NAME OF THE PERSON YOU'RE ADDRESSING IN CONVERSATION? Using the person's preferred name and title, without undue familiarity, is key in making a solid connection.

4. ARE YOU A GOOD LISTENER? You'll want to maintain a balance of receiving much more information than you give in networking conversations (possibly 75 to 80 percent). That's the true sign of a good listener.

5. CAN YOU FRAME THE CONVERSATION IN TERMS OF THE OTHER PERSON'S INTERESTS AND GENUINELY MEAN IT? This can also take the form of "your readers," in talking to editors; "your listeners," for radio; and "your viewers," in talking to television producers.

6. CAN YOU SINCERELY MAKE THE OTHER PERSON FEEL IMPORTANT? This, of course, can't bear the ring of patronization. You can do this—and very effectively—if you remember three important keys: *empathy, optimism,* and maintaining and displaying *a sense of humor.*

Casting a Wide Net

Networking is an everyday, anywhere business. Standing in line at the post office or grocery store, attending a spa or restaurant grand opening, or even hanging out in the bleachers at a sporting event can produce lifelong connection results. So be outgoing wherever you are, talk to the person next to you, and share what you do. It worked for freelancer Sally Stich at a wedding dinner where she knew no one at her table. Talking to the woman seated next to her, Stich mentioned that she's a magazine writer. The woman replied, "Oh, my sister is an editor at a magazine. You should call her." Within a couple of days Stich sent this editor a note telling her she had met her sister, and asked the editor if she used freelance writers. The editor called a few days later and said that while she didn't use a lot of freelance material, she would give Sally an assignment because Sally "knew" her sister. That initial contact resulted in regular assignments for years.

Join the best and brightest writer, author, and speaker organizations you can qualify for, as well as other associations related to your writing areas. Look for those that are local, regional, and national in scope, and then decide which are the best fit and offer the most advantages. Be farsighted. Look for local organizations such as press clubs or media clubs. On a regional level, look for organizations such as the California Writers Club, the Colorado Authors' League, the Newswomen's Club of New York, the Connecticut Press Club, South West Writers, Midwest Writers. And take a look at national organizations such as the American Society of Journalists and Authors, PEN, the National Writers' Union, the Authors' Guild, the National Association of Science Writers, the Society of Environmental Journalists, the Society of American Travel Writers, the Garden Writers Association of America, Sisters in Crime, the National Federation of Press Women, Women in Communication, the Public Relations Society of America, the American Association of University Women, and the International Food, Wine and Travel Writers Association. These may have local and regional chapters, besides offering many, many networking opportunities at the national level. Be sure to ask, too, about the online benefits to members. ASJA, for example, creates a number of "online communities" where members with similar interests offer help, advice, and contact information to each other. Such memberships can be worth their weight in gold. To find them, do an Internet search, and double-check with your local reference librarian.

A number of writers' groups offer virtual professional and personal support, along with occasional job opportunities, through online forums, bulletin boards, and listservs. A couple of your first stops should be, of course, *www.asja.org* (American Society of Journalists and Authors) and *www.nwu.org* (National Writers Union). Look into some of the subscription Web sites that relate to your area of writing interest or specialty. Local and regional groups have Web sites, too, that can easily be located through Google (*www.google.com*) and other search engines. Then tune into one of the numerous subscription locations such as *www.freelancesuccess.com, www.hotjobs.com,* and *www.publisherslunch.com,* for all kinds of up-to-the-minute networking possibilities. (See Chapter 7 about writing for the Web.)

Meeting and Greeting

Merely joining a writers' organization isn't enough, of course. To network effectively you must get involved. Start small. Volunteer, as Sarah Wernick did, for something as simple as serving cookies and lemonade at a local National Writers Union chapter meeting. That's where Jim Doherty, then editor at *Smithsonian,* was speaking. "Thanks to this small extra effort, I was invited to join a group of volunteers who had dinner with Jim," Wernick recalls. "This gave me the opportunity to speak with him more personally. I sent him a query a few days later, referring to something relevant in our conversation—and soon had my first assignment from *Smithsonian.*" Don't despair if there isn't a local chapter to meet with. Create one, as Wernick and a few other local ASJA members did in Boston. "Two of us decided to contact all the members in this area and try to get together. About twelve people showed up at that first meeting. We've been meeting nearly every month since." This group, Wernick says, meets in different members' homes and brings potluck snacks. They invite lawyers, editors, and agents as guest speakers, and have turned these monthly meetings into a wealth of networking contacts.

Be sure to attend as many national association meetings as you can afford, and serve on panels if you can. "I try to be a panelist or speaker because I think editors pay attention to the writers who speak. Not only is that beneficial, but I have gotten other [paying] speaking gigs by being on a panel," says Sally Stich. Tina Tessina, author of *The 10 Smartest Decisions a Woman Can Make Before 40,* found her co-author and her agent for that book while serving on a panel at a writers' conference. When attending a meeting, always introduce yourself, describe what you do, and show interest in the other person. Many writers and authors have helped themselves out in the introduction department by creating their own oversized name tag with not only their name, but also a picture of their latest book cover, newsletter, or other defining title. This works both to help launch your introduction and to give others a reason to talk to you.

Here are a few other guidelines that will help you make the maximum number of networking contacts during these get-togethers:

BE PREPARED. If possible, know who will attend by getting a copy of the registration list beforehand. Target the people you want to be sure to meet. Use the opportunity to exchange business cards if that is a natural part of the exchange. Remember, you'll be upset with yourself if you later learn that half a dozen people you were dying to meet were actually at the meeting, but you didn't know they were there; or if you became involved in a lengthy discussion with friends and didn't make a single new contact.

BE ON TIME, OR EARLY. This will allow you to feel more relaxed and confident. You will also be able to position yourself so you can see people arriving; you'll be amazed at how many more people's names you'll remember because you've met them one at a time.

COURT THE COMPANY OF STRANGERS. Remember, your objective is to meet people. You're not there to promote or sell, at least not directly.

WEAR SOMETHING THAT MAKES YOU STAND OUT. For men this may be an interesting "conversation-starting" tie. For women, perhaps something in red, bright-colored eyeglass frames, an interesting pin or necklace, or the like.

BE APPROACHABLE. Smile and take the initiative of introducing yourself. Definitely send the message that you are interested in the other person, and that you have something to offer.

MINGLE. Circulate toward the center of things. Don't become sidelined. If possible, ask a friend or colleague to introduce you to those you want to meet. Sometimes the best thing for those of us who are shy is to be in charge of something, so we have a reason to circulate and be noticed.

HAVE SOMETHING OF VALUE TO ADD. That will allow you to exude the confidence you want to display.

Following Up

Follow up with the people you've met within forty-eight hours, if possible. And make it personal. A handwritten note on your monogrammed note card is perfect when writing something like, "It was so nice to meet you at the Press Club last night. As you suggested, I'll be in touch in the next several days with some ideas on the labor piece we discussed. . . ." If you made a promise to get in touch or pass something along, do it. Nothing kills the effectiveness of a wonderful first impression like a second bad one. (Use e-mail if you've learned that's the best way to pass along requested information to a particular contact.)

Use your networking currency in the best way possible by making your first telephone contact—and every one thereafter—in the most gracious way possible. It goes back to the essential principle of focusing on the other person and his or her needs and desires. Be considerate of her time, and this can be done best if you make the effort to learn her editorial schedule and habits. Before contacting a senior editor I've worked with over quite a number of years, I did essential research to find out (1) how she wanted to be contacted: telephone, e-mail, fax, or snail mail; (2) when she wanted to be contacted: on a certain day of the week and/or at a certain time of the day; (3) in what form and style she preferred to have queries submitted: first "pitched" by telephone, then "fleshed out" in written form by e-mail; or completely written out with the first paragraph that could become the opening of the magazine article; or submitted in hard copy by fax or snail mail; (4) when and how she preferred that I follow up on my queries. Being sensitive to this editor's preferences created the kind of connection I wanted in order to continue to work with her. But I'm also interested in her as a person, and from that first encounter we've built a friendship.

Building Networks

Nurturing relationships with editors, in addition to cementing their belief that you are a consummate professional who delivers what and when promised, will almost always result in connections to other editors. Freelancer Irene Levine notes, "Some of my most successful networking efforts have come from my relationships with editors who introduced me to other editors. For example, I wrote for a health dot-com that became defunct. The editor I worked with introduced me to the health editor of a major newspaper with whom I continue to work. When I worked with a newspaper syndicate, the editor there introduced me to a health Web site editor for whom I continue to work. In essence, editors have become mentors to me—leading me to new opportunities."

An increasing number of editors require networking to prequalify writers for an initial assignment. One New York editor recently told a writer, "If you can't network your way to someone who knows me, I won't read what you've sent. I'm too busy." But be careful networking from one editor to another within the same magazine. Some editors regard writers as part of their personal "stable," and will be upset if a writer contacts another editor at the same publication. It's best, if possible, to first discuss your idea with your primary editor.

Networking to new and better jobs without offending her primary editor is exactly what freelancer Carol Milano did when she noticed that a medical association magazine she'd been writing for had purchased a consumer Web site. "I wondered if the Web site would be using freelancers," she says. "I e-mailed the editorial assistant in 'my' department to ask, and she offered to go and ask at the office that would be handling the Web site. I realized it would also be courteous to check with my original editor at the magazine. She sent me a lovely note that said, 'I have no problem with that, and I really appreciate your being thoughtful enough to ask.'" You might ask your editor to give you the proper introduction and a reference to the other editor. Many freelancers regard it as a blessing, not a curse, when a favorite editor leaves a publication. Through good networking, the freelancer can often keep the existing gig with the editor's former publication, and then open up a new market by getting assignments from the editor's new publication.

Finally, if you remember that the best principle of networking is to give better than you get, you will always have a wealth of connections. We should be asking, "What can I do for you?" and "What can we do for each other?" rather than "What can you do for me?" And if someone helps you, do your best to help someone else. It's a law in the freelance universe, and it's the secret to prosperous networking.

SANDRA E. LAMB, author of *How to Write It: A Complete Guide to Everything You'll Ever Write* (Ten Speed Press) and *Personal Notes: How to Write from the Heart for Any Occasion* (St. Martin's Press), writes regularly for *Family Circle, Woman's Day, Parents*, and other magazines. A Denver-based newspaper columnist and speaker, she offers more tips for writers at *www.sandralamb.com.*

16

This Pen for Hire: Leveraging Your Skills

ANITA BARTHOLOMEW

Nothing beats the lifestyle of a freelance writer. You get paid for doing what you love. You can show up for work in your pajamas. You're your own boss. And in what other profession can you take off a whole afternoon whenever the mood strikes you? But you give up predictability and security to enjoy this lifestyle. When a magazine folds, an expected book deal fizzles, or a new editor with her own "stable" of writers takes over a publication, you can find yourself paying the mortgage with MasterCard (and the MasterCard bill with Visa).

To cushion yourself against an occasional drop in income, you may want to consider diversifying into nonjournalism assignments. Having an alternate means of supporting yourself also allows you to be more selective about the magazine and book deals you accept. Fawn Fitter, a writer with solid freelance credentials, does corporate writing on the side—mostly press releases and ghostwriting for executives—to round out her publishing income. Fitter has discovered that not only do corporate clients usually pay more than publishers, they typically pay more promptly. "In a perfect world, I would make a lot of money writing books," says Fitter. But until one of her books makes it onto the best-seller lists, Fitter has found a comfortable niche. Meanwhile, her corporate clients are wildly impressed by reliable, competent writers—and that, she says, is "seriously good for the ego."

Corporate writing isn't the only opportunity for freelance diversification. Many freelancers branch out into teaching, coaching, and editorial consulting. Some have sidelines as seminar leaders and public speakers. Sometimes, the sidelines become so lucrative—and so enjoyable—that writing takes a backseat. But what if you've never dabbled in other fields? Why would someone pick you for such an assignment? You may be surprised at how many skills you've developed as a freelance author or journalist—and how well these fit the "skill sets" needed for other types of work. Take a few moments to take inventory of your abilities:

- You're adept at using the written word to sell—you do it every time you write a query or proposal. This skill is essential for writing anything designed to influence opinion in any way, whether a story query or a product brochure.

- You can make your point quickly and with punch. This is essential for writing advertising copy with catchy headlines.

* You know what helps your peers in the media do their job and what just wastes their time. You can freelance at public-relations agencies, pitching story ideas to writers and editors.

* You're an expert on writing for publication and an authority on how the publishing business works. You can teach classes for aspiring writers—or hire yourself out as a publishing consultant to would-be authors.

* You have expertise in the subjects you've written about and have promoted your own books on radio and TV. You can get paid bookings as a public speaker or corporate spokesperson.

Writing for Nonpublishers

Virtually every organization or business uses promotional literature, much of it written by freelancers. Businesspeople and executives need writers to pen speeches and ghostwrite articles for trade magazines. Charitable organizations need people to tug at contributors' hearts in fundraising letters. Advertising and PR agencies use freelance writers and media-relations people to round out their staff. Below, I've sketched some broad categories to give you a sense of the kinds of opportunities you can look for—and where to look for them.

ADVERTISING: This is a fun, fast, intense field where creative people are highly valued. Ad agencies often need freelancers to help with print ads and brochures. Creative directors and copy chiefs will expect to see samples of your advertising work. These can be "spec" ads that you have written just for your portfolio—a few clever headlines on a mock-up ad will do the trick.

PUBLIC RELATIONS, MARKETING COMMUNICATIONS: Corporations, institutions, and the public-relations firms that represent them have an almost bottomless need for writers to create "collateral" materials: brochures, pamphlets, letters, white papers, press kits, and other printed documents. PR agency executives are often thrilled to get freelance help from professional journalists because you know what makes a good story. You know how a journalist thinks and works. You know not to waste the time of a fashion writer with a pitch to write an article about industrial plastics.

NEWSLETTERS, CASE HISTORIES, GHOSTWRITTEN ARTICLES: These gigs may come to you directly from corporations or through ad agencies or PR firms. Ghosted articles (your words, somebody else's byline) usually have to satisfy a dual purpose—provide valuable information to a trade or other publication's readership while advancing the agenda of a client.

BOOK-LENGTH PROJECTS: Nonpublishers sometimes sponsor book-length manuscripts. While these are not as ubiquitous as brochures, sell sheets, and catalogs, they have been around for quite a while—at least since 1904, when Jell-O sponsored a cookbook full of recipes that could be made with its products. Product-specific cookbooks and how-to books are designed to boost the usage of that product. Other books chart the histories of corporations and nonprofit organizations. Still others are privately published biographies of individuals.

What all these diverse projects have in common is the need for authors to write them. Pat McNees has enjoyed a long, successful career in traditional publishing, both on staff as an editor at major book publishers and as a freelancer. Several years ago, through ASJA's Writer Referral Service, she was offered a handsome sum by a retired Ohio businessman to help write his biography. It turned out to be a fascinating assignment. "I feel just as proud of that first commissioned biography as I do of anything I did for any traditional publisher," McNees says. "And I was given more freedom to do what I felt was right—with no commercial considerations [to make it sexier, more sensational, more marketable, and so on]." That book led to numerous others, commissioned by private, corporate, and institutional clients. Having found this special niche, McNees enjoys a measure of security rare among writers. "I have not spent a moment looking for work in the last twelve years."

Where do you begin to look for nonpublishing writing opportunities? Call or write advertising agencies, public-relations firms, and graphic designers. Check the classified ads. Network: at chambers of commerce, Toastmasters, and other business-oriented clubs. Join any writers' organizations for which you qualify and network within your profession. Share with colleagues: Ask your writer friends to refer any work that comes their way that they can't or don't want to do. (And refer any work you can't do to them.) Advertise your skills with a Web page. Check out the job-postings bulletin boards of the writers' groups you belong to. Send a press release to your local newspaper when major local businesses and institutions hire you for major projects.

Getting Paid in the Corporate World

Okay, the calls are coming in. XYZ Corporation needs a brochure. The university needs a fundraising letter. What do you charge? And how? First, let's look at how. One of the greatest mistakes journalists make when negotiating with corporate clients is to apply arcane publishing norms to nonpublishing contracts and fees.

Freelance journalists are accustomed to pay-per-word. But this isn't how the nonpublishing business world bills and pays for work. All the writers interviewed for this chapter indicated that the money a writer can make doing nonpublishing writing is significantly better. One of the reasons is that business writers are paid just like any other business-people. Corporate and institutional clients are paying for your time, talent, thought, expertise. No pay-per-word formula you can come up with is likely to compensate you as well as more-traditional-business fee arrangements. Pat McNees points out that another payment mistake writers make is underpricing. "Many writers who take on writing projects think that they will be more marketable if they come cheap. But a low price tag makes corporate people wonder how professional you are. If you have a track record and something to show a potential client, sometimes being expensive is a better strategy." Just as you had to adjust to the quirky norms of publishing fees when you took your first freelance newspaper or magazine writing assignment, so you need to adjust to the norms of the rest of the business world. For the most part, this adjustment should be a pleasant one.

Now let's deal with the question of how much. There is no set answer to this question. But we can ballpark fees, based on several factors:

WHERE IS THE CLIENT? A client in a major metropolitan area, as a general rule, is accustomed to paying more. If your client is based in a smaller, less affluent community, you might have to adjust your fees downward somewhat.

ARE YOU WRITING DIRECTLY FOR THE END-USER OR THROUGH A MIDDLEMAN? Agencies will pay you less than you are likely to get working directly for the client.

HOW LONG WILL THIS ASSIGNMENT LAST? If you're writing a single piece, expect to get paid more. If you're on a long-term assignment, however, you may set a daily or weekly rate that is somewhat less than you would get by the hour.

DOES THE ASSIGNMENT REQUIRE TECHNICAL KNOWLEDGE, EXPERTISE IN A PARTICULAR FIELD, OR SPECIAL TALENTS? Charge more for an assignment that requires you to know—or learn about—a specialized field or technology. You can also ask for more if the client has special requirements, for instance, if he wants a writer who can make people laugh—or cry.

HOW QUICKLY DO THEY NEED IT? Ask for more if it's a rush job. (Even if it's not really a rush job for you but it seems like the client thinks it is, ask for more.) How will the work be used? Advertising typically pays better than corporate communications. Writing for a major national corporation or product warrants a rate that's higher than what you'd charge the local auto mechanic.

With the above in mind, at today's rates, you might base a quote for writing done directly for a client (no middleman) at $125 to $250 per hour for a large corporation in a major metropolitan area and $75 to $150 per hour for a smaller company or one that is not in a major urban area. Adjust downward somewhat if you're writing through an ad agency, public-relations firm, graphic designer, or other middleman. Adjust upward if the assignment requires special skills or knowledge or if the client expects to get a lot of mileage out of the work. Again, these are very rough numbers; you'll have to negotiate and reach an agreement that works for you and the client. But remember: You can always drop your price; you won't be able to raise it if you begin too low.

For a longer-term assignment, set a day rate. If you've figured your hourly rate at $150 and the assignment will last ten days, you might charge just $1,000 per day, saving the client $200 per day compared to your hourly rate (make sure the client knows she's getting a break and that shorter assignments are charged at the hourly rate). Using the same logic, on a project that lasts for six weeks, you might offer your services at $4,500 per week, saving the client $500 per week when compared to your day rate. Not only does the average corporate client pay writers better, he probably has never heard the term "kill fee." And you should forget you ever heard the term. You're agreeing to set aside a certain amount of your valuable time to do work that you won't be able to sell elsewhere. Once the client contracts for the work, the client owes you for it. All of it.

Contracts, Estimates, Letters of Agreement

It's essential that you have a written contract with any client. This can make the difference between getting paid and not getting paid if, say, your contact is let go while you're in the middle of a project, or your client remembers your verbal agreement differently than you do, or he decides that he no longer needs the twenty-four-page manuscript you've handed him because he's discontinuing the product for which you wrote it. Contracts with nonpublishing clients are usually generated by you, the independent consultant. When I wrote corporate materials, I always had a lengthy discussion with the client first to determine what the client's expectations were in terms of copy, interviews, meetings, travel, and revisions. I'd also insist that all revisions come through one "point person"—otherwise you're likely end up with conflicting directions from ten different people. After roughing out the parameters, I'd estimate the hours necessary to complete the assignment and multiply that by an hourly rate that seemed appropriate. I'd then add 25 percent for the unexpected. For a finite project, my practice was to charge a set fee based on an estimate of the time I'd have to devote to it. That way, the client knew in advance that my fee would fit her budget. And I didn't have to watch the clock every minute. Present a contract bid that leaves as little room for ambiguity as possible. The client's signature at the bottom indicates acceptance. Often, writers ask for a deposit of one-quarter to one-third before beginning work. Consider the deposit essential the first few times you deal with a new client.

Conflicts of Interest

A journalist typically reports without a vested interest in how favorably the reader perceives the topic of his writing. A corporate writer is expected to shape the perception of the reader in the client's favor. So you should be certain that you feel comfortable with a client's product or point of view before accepting assignments. For example, many writers won't work for tobacco companies. And you need to be aware that real or perceived conflicts of interest might have an effect on your journalism career. "You're spending all this time becoming an expert in a field that ethically you can't turn around and write good journalism about," writer Claire Tristram says.

This is an important consideration when reviewing opportunities. You may think that your background as a reporter specializing in a particular topic would be a perfect fit for corporate or institutional clients in similar fields. But if you're wise, you'll look outside the field that you cover. Even if you believe that you can later report without bias on a topic that affects an industry for which you have written ghosted articles, brochures, or other such work, you'll have trouble convincing others. Your corporate or institutional clients may wonder if you'll use what you've learned against them. Your editors could be concerned that your loyalties are with the company whose product figures in your story. It's not an unreasonable concern.

Nonwriting Gigs for Writers

Think of the writer as publishing expert—teaching, coaching, and consulting: A 2002 survey found that 81 percent of American adults believe they have a book in them. At least some of those would-be authors will go out of their way to sign up for writing classes given by published authors who can pass along tips and tricks of the trade. Check for teaching opportunities at colleges and universities or in local adult education programs. And if there are no formal programs? Create your own. ASJA member Tim Perrin began teaching fledgling writers at almost the same time he began his own professional freelance-writing career. He finds teaching rewarding in ways that can't be measured in dollars alone. "I like working with people learning new skills, watching them 'get it' and improve," says Perrin. And because most of his students now take his classes online, it's easy to fit this sideline into a writing schedule.

Remember, the work doesn't begin and end in the classroom. Figure on spending at least as much time before and after classes; first to prepare the coursework and then to read and grade your students' papers. You may also find opportunities to teach, train, and coach that don't involve schools or classrooms. Often, it's a matter of recognizing a need and filling it. For instance, when the head of a public-relations firm complained to Tim Harper about her staffers' inability to pitch the agency's clients effectively, Harper saw an opportunity. "I offered to come in as a consultant. I worked with small groups and coached individuals—which in turn led to a number of similar coaching jobs over the years."

Harper also acts as a publishing consultant, sharing the knowledge and expertise he's gained during a long career as a journalist, author, and editor. For $1,000 to $3,000 he'll evaluate a manuscript. For additional fees based on an hourly rate Harper helps authors get their work into the best possible shape and steers manuscripts and proposals that he believes have commercial potential to agents and editors. He also guides new writers through self-publishing if traditional publishing channels aren't an option or don't pan out. For those who merely want advice, he will spend an hour on the phone, answering every possible publishing-related question the caller may have for $200. A few times, Harper says, novices have balked at the rate. "I've said, 'Look, we'll talk for an hour, if it's worth it, you send me a check for $200. If not, you're done with me.' And every time, they've sent the check." How can you get into this business? You might, like Harper, advertise yourself as a publishing consultant on your Web site. He also occasionally gets referrals from Columbia University, where he teaches writing, and through ASJA's Writer Referral Service.

The Writer as Speaker, Spokesperson, and Expert

If you have written a book or two showing expertise in a particular subject and you feel comfortable speaking to large groups, public speaking may make sense as a sideline. Those who go this route say it takes quite a bit of work to get started. But it's worth it. ASJA member Jan Jasper is both a freelance writer and a time-management consultant. So when efficient Jasper promoted her book on time management, *Take Back Your Time*, she promoted herself as well, as a seminar speaker on all matters related to time management and technology. All this effort has paid off nicely. Jasper has gotten gigs that take her around the country as a corporate spokesperson. What do such assignments entail? Companies enlist spokespersons to give talks—to groups of customers, prospective customers, and broadcasters—that tie their products in with positive themes. In Jasper's case, the theme is enhanced productivity. Jasper says that a beginning spokesperson can expect to make about $1,500 per day. But she knows a number of people who earn twice that. Spokespeople may also be hired to do television (or sometimes, radio) satellite "tours," for which rates are higher. For satellite tours, the spokesperson spends the day in a studio while broadcasters from various other locations call in to conduct interviews via remote connection. How well do satellite tours pay? Jasper says she hasn't yet discovered the upper limit. "I recently quoted someone $6,000 for a day. And she said, 'Oh, that's very reasonable.' And I thought, 'Damn, I should have quoted more.'"

Charlotte Libov, an author who writes about women and heart disease—and has lived through cardiac problems herself—has also successfully branched out into public speaking. But Libov's engagements are usually for conferences and meetings. Like corporate spokespersons, sought-after conference speakers can garner substantial fees. "A mid-list author can make three thousand to five thousand dollars," Libov says. What do you have to do to earn such a fee? "It can be a one-hour speech. Sometimes you negotiate packages. For instance, maybe I'll do a one-hour keynote and a workshop later in the day." She's also booked longer "speaking tours" through an agent. Longer engagements may pay less per speech but the fees still aren't bad. "I did a three-week tour through Minnesota and Wisconsin," says Libov. "That ended up paying about fifteen thousand dollars." She offers several tips for authors interested in developing their own public-speaking businesses:

- Make yourself as visible as possible. One ASJA member promotes her public-speaking business with full-page ads in airline magazines. But you can start right where you are with a minimal investment: Network, go to conferences, spread your business cards around, and join relevant organizations.

- Send a short video to anyone who expresses an interest in booking you. It need not show you doing public speaking; Libov sends clips of TV appearances instead.

- Do everything you can to get yourself identified with your topic— announce your appearances with press releases, publish a newsletter, invest in a professional-looking Web site.

- Ask for a testimonial each time you speak. You can even offer to write a draft for the person who booked you, which he or she can then read and sign.

There's a fringe benefit, of course, for writers who venture into public speaking. As an established speaker, you'll have a "platform," something that can boost the dollar amount of the advance on your next book—provided, of course, you write about the same subject matter.

When you think of the opportunities available to you, remember that you have a world of options, not just in but also outside traditional publishing. Some may bring satisfaction and financial rewards that are rarely available to the average freelance journalist. Some may let you explore entirely different avenues. And some may lead you to greater success in your publishing career.

ANITA BARTHOLOMEW has freelanced for numerous major magazines, including *Reader's Digest,* for which she is a contributing editor. Her specialties include narrative nonfiction, health, science, and social issues. She began her writing career as a print- and broadcast-advertising copywriter, winning awards for her humorous radio ads. She can be contacted through *www.anitabartholomew.com.*

17

Op-Eds and Essays: Leveraging Your Knowledge

LARRY ATKINS

Ten thousand pennies for your thoughts?

There are many newspapers and magazines that pay freelance writers to express their opinions in Op-Eds and personal essays. Through Op-Eds and essays, writers can share their personal experiences, inspire readers, or state a strong opinion that inspires change. Sometimes it's a way to use what you've learned in your reporting but couldn't use in a news story. It's a way of leveraging what you know or what you think.

Newspapers are the biggest market for Op-Eds and essays, but many magazines also accept opinion pieces or "personal" articles. Most literary magazines run personal essays, and programs on National Public Radio often carry commentaries by freelancers; I have done commentaries for *Morning Edition* and *Only a Game,* and I know a number of other freelancers who have been on other NPR programs. While it's flattering to get paid for your opinion, don't quit your day job for this type of writing; it doesn't pay as much as journalism. Most major regional newspapers pay between $75 and $150 for an Op-Ed piece, though some papers occasionally may go as high as $500. Major magazines pay more for personal essays. For instance, *Smithsonian* pays $1,000 to $1,500 for its back-page humor essays. Most newsmagazines and women's magazines pay comparable rates, but sometimes more or less than that.

Most newspapers encourage Op-Ed submissions of 700 to 800 words. The longest Op-Ed I've written was around 1,000 words, and the shortest was 400 words. Sometimes it's easier to break into a paper with a shorter article. Some papers are very strict about their word-count requirements. If a newspaper wants 700 words and you file 1,200, there's a good chance the editor won't even read it. Length is also important to magazine editors. "When you're writing Op-Eds and essays for magazines, have a specific market in mind," says Stephanie Abarbanel, senior articles editor at *Woman's Day.* "Notice the length of the articles. You would be surprised how many essays I get that are twice the length that we're looking for."

Despite the seemingly low rates, Op-Eds and essays can be attractive for freelancers since they don't take as much research and reporting as other types of articles. They can also raise your profile both among readers and editors, and they can help you to become established as an expert in your field. If you want to establish yourself as a financial writer, you might want to write Op-Eds when the market is in the news, such as during a boom or bust. If you want to focus on sports, write Op-Eds linked to major sports stories. Doing this type of writing can also help you sell a book by generating publicity, discussion, and controversy.

One advantage of submitting Op-Eds to newspapers as opposed to magazines is that decisions are often made right away. You don't have to wait two months to have someone read your manuscript. In July 2002, I wrote an Op-Ed criticizing the Bush administration's proposed Operation TIPS, which encouraged certain workers to report suspicious information to the government. I researched the article on a Saturday, wrote it on Sunday, submitted it on Monday, and saw it in print in the *Chicago Tribune* on Tuesday.

Supply and Demand

Competition for the Op-Ed page can be fierce. In Philadelphia, the *Inquirer* Commentary Page receives approximately 1,200 freelance Op-Ed submissions a week that compete for ten slots. However, persistence pays off. For five years I tried breaking into the *Baltimore Sun* Commentary page. I would send an Op-Ed at least once a month, to no avail. However, in 1999, the Commentary page editor left the paper. The interim editor accepted the first Op-Ed that I sent to her. Then she accepted my next two Op-Eds. She sent an e-mail praising my versatility. When a new permanent editor took over, the friendly interim editor put in a good word for me. I continued to place articles, and occasionally even got assignments to do Op-Eds. Similarly, it took me four years to break into the *Chicago Tribune* and *Newsday,* and six years to break into the *Atlanta Journal-Constitution.* Sometimes constant rejections might be an indication that you need to work at your craft and improve. As Stephanie Abarbanel of *Woman's Day* says, "Some writers just aren't ready for a national magazine—the style and content just aren't there yet. But all hope isn't lost; you can work at it and hone your skills. There is one freelance writer who I rejected a number of times during a five-year period. However, she continued to work at it and built up her writing clips by writing for other magazines. This year we published three of her essays."

Timing is critical for newspaper Op-Eds. In 1993, I sent the *Inquirer* an Op-Ed on the future of Temple University's declining football program from the perspective of a longtime fan. The *Inquirer* wasn't interested, so I sold the piece to a Philadelphia weekly. The day before it was scheduled to run, I got a call from the *Inquirer.* The editors had received an article calling for Temple to drop football, and they wanted to run it with my piece, side by side. I called the weekly paper to see if they could cancel my article, but it was too late. The article ran in the weekly. But the story had a happy ending. The following day, Temple's public-relations people called and told me that the *Inquirer* had contacted them to try to generate a positive Temple football article. The public-relations department asked me to write another positive Temple article, but with a different slant. A week later, my revised Temple football article ran in the *Inquirer.* "Newsworthiness sells," says Philadelphia *Inquirer* Commentary Page Editor John Timpane. "If you write about timely and hot topics, you will find your way into an editor's heart."

Exclusivity may or may not be an issue. Major national newspapers such as the *New York Times,* the *Washington Post* and the *Los Angeles Times* require that your submission be exclusive. Most national papers advise that if you haven't heard from them in two weeks, you're free to assume that the article has been rejected and you can submit it elsewhere. Ann Brenoff, assistant Op-Ed Page editor of the *Los Angeles Times,* recommends, "Do not submit simultaneously to other newspapers. Send to one paper at a time and wait for a response. We ask for five days to consider pieces, but generally respond sooner. I know that when you are writing about something in the news, this may mean you diminish your chances of getting published elsewhere. But we all want to publish material exclusively and violating this rule will mean the major papers won't consider your work in the future."

If you happen to submit articles to a daily in a city with more than one major regional newspaper, submit to only one paper at a time. For instance, do not simultaneously submit Op-Eds to the *New York Post* and the *New York Daily News*. Most major regional newspapers, such as the *Baltimore Sun*, the *Cleveland Plain Dealer*, the *Dallas Morning News*, and *Newsday*, allow simultaneous submissions to other regional newspapers in other cities that do not overlap with their circulation areas. To cover yourself, you should inform each publication that you are submitting your article to other major regional papers in other cities, but that your submission to the paper is exclusive to that paper's circulation area. On several occasions, I have sold the same article to several newspapers in different cities. Be aware, however, that you will have to overcome a huge home-court advantage in many situations. Many, if not most, newspapers prefer Op-Eds by local writers and about local issues.

Sometimes it helps to tailor the article to different markets, as I did in selling Op-Eds on youth volunteerism to four different newspapers— the *Baltimore Sun*, the *Cleveland Plain Dealer*, *Newsday*, and the *Los Angeles Daily News*. I used different examples of youth volunteer programs in each city for the respective papers. "One way to turn off an Op-Ed editor is to send a piece with an introduction that begins, 'Dear Editor,'" says Richard Gross, Commentary page editor at the *Baltimore Sun*. "That's an immediate move to the delete button because the editor knows immediately that the piece has been sent everywhere. Newspapers generally like some exclusivity, especially in their own market."

Placement Strategies

You must decide whether you want to place your article with a national publication such as the *New York Times* or the *Washington Post*, or whether you want to simultaneously submit your article to regional newspapers across the country. If you have written an article in anticipation of a major event or holiday, or if you've written an article about a subject that you are confident will be timely for a while (corporate responsibility, church sex abuse, terrorism), you might have the time and luxury to submit to the *New York Times*, wait for two weeks, and then send your article elsewhere if it is rejected. In 1999, after the Mars Polar Lander crashed on Mars, I wrote an Op-Ed expressing my hope that NASA would dedicate itself to sending humans to Mars by 2015. Then I had to decide where to send my article. If I sent the piece to the *New York Times*, it would have been tied up for two weeks. If the *Times* had rejected it, the article would have been too stale to send elsewhere. I decided to send it to many regional newspapers across the country, and it was printed in the *Dallas Morning News*, the *Indianapolis Star*, and elsewhere. In retrospect, it was a good move, because the *New York Times* ran two Op-Eds on the same subject by space experts during the same week.

You don't have to be a doctor, lawyer, or Harvard professor to write for the Op-Ed page. Everyone is an expert in something. If you have kids, you're an expert in parenting who can talk about homework or corporal punishment. If you're a teacher, you're an expert in education and can write about violence in schools. If you're Jewish, you're an expert on Jewish issues. In many cases, it is helpful to set forth personal experiences in your Op-Eds. "We look for people who have a personal connection with the news," says the Philadelphia *Inquirer*'s John Timpane. "If you have visited the Middle East on a recent trip or have family members there, that might give you personal standing to talk about it." However, make sure that your personal experience has a connection to the news. "Personal memories that mean nothing to anyone else is a no-no, unless the writer is trying to make a larger point that must be apparent immediately," says Richard Gross of the *Baltimore Sun*.

When Chris Cardone came off the bench to hit two home runs for Toms River, New Jersey, in the 1998 Little League World Series, I wrote that he had struck a blow for benchwarmers across the country, and I related my experiences as a benchwarmer for my high school soccer team. When my father had difficulty with the Philadelphia paratransit system, some research uncovered that it was a citywide problem; I wrote an article based on my father's experiences. Even when my articles get rejected, I keep them on file in case an issue becomes timely again, or I can rework some of the text into a future article. For instance, during the 1992 presidential election, I attempted to sell an Op-Ed on my distaste for hecklers at political rallies. Unfortunately, there were no takers. I tried again in 1996, to no avail. In 2000, I updated the piece and the *Christian Science Monitor* accepted it. Using statistics and getting quotes from experts in the field can also improve your Op-Eds. Anticipate events such as the Super Bowl, a political convention, the opening of baseball season, or the start of a new school year. Newspapers like to run Op-Eds with holiday themes such as Mother's Day, Thanksgiving, and Valentine's Day.

Unlike with newspapers, timeliness is not as essential when it comes to writing for magazines. For one thing, it takes most major magazines at least one month to get a chance to read your essay, and the lead time—from when the story is accepted until it runs—is often three months or more. Therefore, it is helpful to choose a topic or issue that will stay viable for a while. Unlike newspapers, many magazines don't want to consider articles that have been submitted to other publications. Look at *Writer's Market* or check the magazine's Web site to see whether such submissions are permissible or whether it requires exclusive submissions. For the most part, there is no need to query when you send a short essay to a magazine; just send the entire text.

The editing process can be frustrating for freelancers. Editors for most newspapers make changes on their own without consulting the writer. They almost always delete text for space and they occasionally will add their own phrases, sentences, or even a paragraph. I think it's reasonable to ask an editor to be consulted about substantive changes or to see the final edited version, but I wouldn't be adamant about it. Many times, editors like to edit articles the day before they run, and it isn't practical to get the author's final approval, especially if it's late in the day. It's not such a problem for magazines, which are under less time pressure.

Generating Ideas

Ideas for Op-Eds are all around you, but you have to be alert. It's as though you're watching a meteor shower in the middle of an empty field. If you turn your head for a second you might miss one, while someone next to you might see it. Many ideas are sparked by daily interactions with friends and family. It also helps to have strong opinions. Don't be wishy-washy. Have something original to say. As Ann Brenoff puts it, "Say something that hasn't been said before. The goal of a Commentary page is to affect outcome, to convince someone to see things your way. Hence we prefer pieces that call for a specific action rather than just comment after the fact on something that has occurred. We are drawn to pieces that have a literary flavor to them, that suggest fresh thinking and new ideas. Stating the obvious won't get you published."

For personal essays, editors like a personal story woven into a universal subject. The essay must have a point. Unless you extract a bigger truth in your article, you're merely relating an anecdote. The reader should be able to relate to the emotion that you're conveying. Write from the heart and try to make readers feel that they are not alone. Some personal essay markets for magazines include columns such as "Lives" in the *New York Times Magazine*, "Back Page" in *Smithsonian*, and "My Turn" in *Newsweek*. Other essay markets include the *Atlantic Monthly*, *Hope*, *Walking*, *Family Circle*, *Woman's Day*, *Conde Nast Bride's*, *Ladies' Home Journal*, *Ms.*, *Modern Maturity*, and *Glamour*. "Magazine Op-Eds and essays differ from newspapers in that newspapers are often more topical," says Stephanie Abarbanel of *Woman's Day*. "Newspapers and magazines both focus on important issues, but many magazines do it in a more personal way. Our essays at *Woman's Day* take a more personal perspective. They show that 'I did this' and describe 'My odyssey.' As a national magazine with 20 million readers, our essays have to resonate with a majority of our readers." Another editor who handles essays, Nancy Clark of *Family Circle,* looks for 750-word pieces that deal with everyday topics and "make me laugh out loud." "To break into the market," she suggests, "writers simply have to write what they know and keep submitting to a broad range of publications until they find one that is compatible with their voice."

There's nothing worse than spending time and effort in researching and writing an Op-Ed and having no one run it. I sell 90 percent of my Op-Eds to at least one publication. If I didn't have such a high success rate, I probably wouldn't write them as often. Although Op-Ed and essay writing doesn't pay as much as other types of writing, the intangible benefits are enormous. Chances are that your Op-Ed or essay won't change the world, but it might influence local government officials to take action on an issue, make someone laugh, or cause a reader to change the way he or she perceives life. Ten thousand pennies for your thoughts might not seem like much, but if one of your Op-Eds or essays can influence someone or something, the rewards are priceless.

LARRY ATKINS, a lawyer and writer in Philadelphia, has written more than 150 Op-Eds, articles, and essays for many publications, including the *Atlanta Journal-Constitution,* the *Baltimore Sun,* the *Chicago Tribune,* the *Christian Science Monitor,* the *Cleveland Plain Dealer,* the *Dallas Morning News*, National Public Radio (*Morning Edition, Only a Game*), *Newsday,* the *Philadelphia Inquirer,* and the *San Francisco Chronicle.* He can be contacted at *larryLTatkins@aol.com.*

18

Reprints, Re-Slants, and Other Ways to Resell Your Work

KELLY JAMES-ENGER

There are two ways to sell a story idea more than once: You can come up with a new slant on an article you've already written, or you can license, or sell, reprint rights once an article has appeared in a publication. With the latter, in some cases you may offer what I call a "tweak"—editing or revising the original story to better complement the reprint market. (Technically, I still consider this a reprint, *not* an original piece.) Too often, writers think up a story idea, pitch it to a market, receive an assignment, research and write the piece, turn it in, and receive a check. Then it's on to the next idea, the next query, and the next assignment. You'll get more from your research if you take advantage of what I call "re-slants."

Re-slants are different from reprints. A reprint is when you offer a market "second rights" (or "reprint rights") to a piece that's already been published. A re-slant is a whole new story—different angle, different approach, and possibly different experts, anecdotes, and research. However, you optimize your time because you're already familiar with the topic and you're able to recycle some of your research. If you're interested in developing re-slants, take a look at your initial story idea and think about other angles and other possible markets for it. If you're pitching a piece on aromatherapy to a general-interest magazine, for example, you might focus on how aromatherapy reduces stress. If you're pitching a fitness magazine, the story might examine how certain scents can improve athletic performance. You can gain additional mileage from your research by pitching a small business magazine a story on which scents consumers find most compelling; a women's publication might be interested in a short piece on using scented oils for massage.

Re-slanting ideas can pay big dividends. For example, I wrote a piece several years ago about how to determine your "money personality" for a bridal magazine. A few months later, I pitched and wrote a story on the same topic for a general-interest publication. I used the same expert, but interviewed her again for fresh quotes, and found anecdotes from different people to use as examples. Because I had done most of my background research, however, the second story took less time to write.

Spin Off New Ideas

Even if you can't think up a slew of different angles at the outset, watch for possible ideas during the research process. You may find unexpected story ideas popping up. Freelancer and ASJA member Kristin Baird Rattini wrote a feature for *People* about a twenty-five-year-old who had cleared 1 million pounds of trash from the Mississippi River, but the story didn't mention his "Adopt a Mississippi River Mile" program. Rattini pitched a story about that specific program to *Field & Stream,* and an editor assigned the piece. The number of ideas you can spin out of one basic concept is as unlimited as your imagination—and the number of interested markets you can find. And the more you know about a particular subject, the easier it is to develop different angles.

Take the numerous stories I've written about birth control. In 1998, I saw a press release about the "morning-after pill." I pitched it to *Fit,* which purchased a 1,500-word story on emergency contraception and how it works.

As I was researching the story for *Fit,* I pitched a related idea to *Marie Claire.* My editor there wanted to cover emergency contraception, but as part of a larger story on oral contraceptives. I wound up writing a 2,500-word feature on oral contraceptives. It included sidebars on emergency contraception, the pros and cons of different birth control methods, and new birth control developments. I then pitched a short piece on "the latest in birth control" to *Shape.* While researching the story for *Marie Claire,* I'd found some interesting studies that suggested that it might be healthier to take the pill continuously and avoid having monthly periods. That concept led to articles for both *Redbook* and *Oxygen.* I wrote "Cancer Prevention Breakthrough," a 2,000-word feature for *Redbook,* and "Your Monthly Period: Necessity or Nuisance?" for *Oxygen.* And because I had so much background material on different birth control methods for that sidebar for *Marie Claire,* I could query *Parents* with "The Mom's Guide to Birth Control" and pitch *For the Bride by Demetrios* with "The Bride's Guide to Birth Control." I used a similar query, but wrote two different articles for these markets. A few months later, I revisited the latest in birth control for a story called "Contraceptive Breakthroughs" for *Complete Woman.* All told, these stories have netted me more than $12,000 worth of work—from the same small kernel of an idea.

While it's not possible to spin off every idea into multiple markets, the key is to think creatively when pitching and researching stories. Breaking free from the "one-idea, one-story" philosophy is the first step. Ask yourself how many other angles you can find for a given story. A travel piece on Las Vegas could cover places to get married for a bridal magazine, or how to get the most for your money for a retirement magazine. Pitch the locale as a family destination for a regional newspaper, or highlight nearby activities like visiting the Hoover Dam. As you research your current story, watch for possible spin-off ideas, especially if you won't cover the topics in the article you're writing. Again, look for potential markets and pitch a new angle on the material to those publications.

Even after the story is completed, watch for other ways to rework your idea. Perhaps recent events have made your topic timely again, or you can tie in new research with your original idea. By making the most of the information you already have—whether on your hard drive or in your story files—you can save time and make more from your initial idea and your research.

One Story, Multiple Paychecks: Licensing Reprints

While spinning off more than one story from the same basic idea will net you more income for almost the same amount of work, there's an even easier way to get paid twice for the same work. License reprints and you can collect paychecks two or three times, or more, for the same article. While reprint markets may not offer as much as you were paid for the original piece, selling the same story more than once is like finding free money in your mailbox. Of course, you must *own* reprint rights in order to license them. If you sign work-for-hire or all-rights agreements, you're giving up your right to resell the same work in the future.

Think twice before you hand over your rights, and read publishing contracts carefully before signing them. Some magazines demand ninety-day or six-month exclusivity that precludes you from reprinting the story in any media during that time frame; others may expressly prohibit you from reprinting the story in competing publications. (See Chapter 21 on contracts.)

When marketing any work, remember that the more rights you hold on to, the better your odds of profiting from your writing. For print magazines, the best you can do is license one-time rights (although magazines often want *first* serial rights); for Web publications, non-exclusive online rights for a limited period of time. Invest in your future income by negotiating contracts today. You never know when you may find a reprint market for that seemingly obscure story you wrote ten years ago. Here are other tips for successful recycling:

REVIEW YOUR WORK. Look at your inventory, and consider any and all stories to which you own the rights. Do you have a lot of parenting pieces? Travel stories? Business articles? Make a list of all available stories, their titles, subject area, word count, and special features like sidebars and quizzes. Write down when reprint rights will be available for stories you're currently working on, and review and update your possible reprint list every three to six months. Although you may find it time-consuming to develop a list or database of stories, particularly at the outset, doing so will make it easier for you to earn income from reprints in the future. It's also more efficient to offer a potential market a batch of articles on the same subject rather than to market individual stories to different publications. Once you know what types of stories you have, you can start looking for potential markets for your work.

SCOUT FOR MARKETS. If you want to license reprints, plan to spend some time finding interested markets for your work. Because

I write mostly health and fitness, diet/nutrition, and bridal and relationship stories, I'm always on the lookout for smaller magazines that cover those subject areas. Annual market guides like *Writer's Market* and the *Writer's Handbook* include listings of magazines that buy reprints. Smaller-circulation publications, regional magazines and newspapers, and trade publications all may be interested in previously published material. Check their guidelines to see if they purchase reprinted stories. The more potential markets you find for your work, the better.

Kathy Sena, a freelancer and ASJA member in Los Angeles, has developed a network of regional parenting publications for her parenting and health stories and resells most of the articles she writes. When a story comes out, she offers it to markets throughout the country. While most of the markets want exclusive rights in their geographical area, she can sell the same story five, six, or more times by offering it to these regional magazines. "About 40 percent of my income comes from reprints," says Sena. "The checks aren't that big—maybe fifty or seventy-five dollars a story—but they add up quickly!"

Finding these markets takes some time and effort. Pick up regional publications when you travel. Ask friends to save magazines for you. Check newsstands frequently for markets you may have overlooked, and don't forget newspapers. By calling major newspapers in neighboring states, Melanie McManus, a Madison, Wisconsin, freelancer, has found new markets for her regional travel stories. She often resells stories to noncompeting publications and has seen one travel piece reprinted five times. Don't overlook the Internet—Web sites looking for content may be interested in electronic reprint rights to stories, especially if you have a lot of articles available in a particular subject area. I've sold non-exclusive Web rights to fitness, health, and business stories that originally appeared in print publications. Make sure you ask how long the site wants to retain rights to your work. Is it for six months? A year? Or indefinitely? The longer the site wants to retain the rights, the more money you should request.

MAKE YOUR PITCH. When you've found a potential reprint market, make your pitch. If I'm sending along only one story, I write the editor a short letter describing the article and why it will appeal to readers; I also note where and when it was published. I close the letter by asking if the editor is interested in purchasing reprint rights to the story, and I include a copy of the article. If I think that the market may be interested in more than one article, I send a letter that includes a story list describing relevant articles by topic and word count along with several clips. I then follow up by telephone in four to eight weeks to determine if the editor is interested in any of the stories I pitched.

You can make your reprint stories more attractive to editors by turning them into "tweaks." A tweak is when you take a story that's already been published and modify it slightly to fit a new market. While you may add some material, the majority of content has already been published, so I still consider this a reprint of sorts and market it accordingly. For instance, I sold a diet story that had originally appeared in a women's magazine to a bridal magazine. I changed the lead to target brides rather than working moms and deleted some material on exercising with children, but the majority of the article was identical to the original piece. By revising it to better fit the market, however, I increased my chance of reselling it.

NAME YOUR PRICE. In some cases, magazines or Web sites will offer a set amount for reprint rights; other publications will ask what your usual reprint fee is. Don't set your rates too low but keep in mind that regional publications usually have smaller budgets and will offer less than national magazines or well-funded Web sites. What you're willing to take for stories will depend on your own standards, but because reprint sales amount to "found money," I'm flexible on what I'll accept. I've sold reprint rights for as little as $20 and for as much as $500, depending on the size of the market and what I thought they would pay. When asked how much money you want for a particular story, request more than you'll settle for so there's some room for negotiation. If you're dealing with regional publications, editors may also request exclusivity within their area for a certain time period. Whether or not there is a formal contract, ask the editor if she'd like you to send an invoice or if she'll simply cut you a check.

CONSIDER SYNDICATION. Working with a syndicate—an individual or organization that offers reprint rights to your work to various media—is another way to net additional income from previously published work. Syndicates often pay a flat fee for rights to your work for a fixed time period; less frequently, they share any sales proceeds with you, usually a 50/50 split. While syndicate rates vary, I've received $100 to $125 for exclusive worldwide rights for one year to several bridal stories from one syndicate. After a year, though, I decided I could probably make more money on those pieces if I handled the marketing myself. I've also worked with two representatives who specialize in marketing articles overseas. Using this approach, I've made as little as $50 and as much as $250 for reprint rights to a single story. The one-person syndicate I currently use has placed my articles at publications in Denmark, Malaysia, Singapore, and Australia—and I've made about $1,500 in two years from these stories. If you want to find a syndicate, check *Writers' Market* or ask for recommendations from other writers. *Editor & Publisher* also publishes an annual syndicate directory.

KEEP IT UP. Continue to develop your list of reprint markets and consider those potential sales when you accept assignments. For example, I may accept work that pays less than my usual rate if I think I'll be able to license reprint rights to the story at least once or twice. And don't forget to offer new stories to your current reprint markets as they become available. If you want to make the most of your time, break free from the one-idea/one-story mind-set. Take an idea and see how many different angles you can pitch and sell to editors—and then how many additional markets you can find for your already-published work. You'll work more efficiently and, better yet, earn more money from your freelance career.

Freelancer KELLY JAMES-ENGER writes about health, fitness, and nutrition for more than forty national magazines, including *Redbook, Woman's Day, Family Circle*, and *Self*. She is the author of *Ready, Aim, Specialize! How to Create Your Own Writing Speciality and Make More Money* (The Writer). She lives in Downer Grove, Illinois. Her Web site is *www.kellyjamesenger.com.*

19

Making Pictures

BARBARA DeMARCO-BARRETT

When you've been snapping pictures most of your life, it can be hard to think about photography in a new way. Too often writers assume they know all they need to know about photography. But learning even a little more about making pictures can help a writer's business. For example, travel editors are often willing to buy your photos to go with your story. Even editors who are going to send their own photographers—whether for travel or any other kind of stories—often welcome writers' snapshots; your pictures may help them see the graphics potential of a story, and that might help them decide to buy the piece.

First, some basics. Often writers overemphasize the importance of hardware. While having excellent-quality photographic equipment is a plus, it's more important to know how to take a good picture. A top-of-the-line camera may help you take technically perfect pictures, but it's not going to take great pictures for you. *You* have to do that. That comes from learning to see the way a camera sees.

"Seeing" is major. Learning how to "see" in photo terms means understanding the way a camera sees as opposed to how your eyes see.

For instance, look at a window across the room. When you focus on the window, most likely that's all you see. You may not notice the chairs or other furniture between you and the window, or those toys trailing across the floor, or even the magazine overturned on the coffee table. But the camera notices. If you took a picture of the window from where you were sitting, everything in the room between you and the window would find its way into the photograph, making it look cluttered. A camera doesn't discriminate. It will record whatever is in its field of vision.

Therefore, you've got to tell the camera what to record. If you want a photo of the window, and nothing else, then you need to frame it in such a way that you capture the window and avoid the furnishings in the room. That may mean stepping closer to the window, sitting on the floor, and shooting upward, or standing on a chair and shooting downward. Once you understand that the camera lens is indiscriminate, you'll begin to shoot the images you want, and you'll learn to compose in the viewfinder rather than hoping for the best and correcting mistakes by cropping later. Try to create pictures that tell a story, especially in travel photography. Show the culture through how people dress, what they eat, how they interact. Here are things to keep in mind when composing a picture:

BACKGROUND. When you photograph a person, or a group of people, make sure there are no extraneous objects like telephone poles, trees, or other people's heads emerging from the back of your subject(s). Whatever surrounds your subject(s) will be in your picture, and don't rely on a software program like Adobe Photoshop to remove unwanted clutter that can mar an otherwise perfect picture. Better to compose in the camera. Shift positions, shoot the picture from another vantage point, or move your subject if you can.

RULE OF THIRDS. Centering your subject can often make for a static and dull picture. Instead, use the rule of thirds to make composition more compelling. This is a technique artists have used for hundreds of years. Mentally divide the viewfinder frame into thirds, horizontally and vertically, then use these four lines and four intersections as invisible guidelines to help you place your subject. By positioning your subject at one of these four intersecting points, you add a dynamic quality to your photograph. This works especially well with a small subject surrounded by a large, plain background. The rule of thirds can also help you to balance subjects with one another and help you decide where to place the horizon.

SHOOT LOOSE. If you want to increase your chances that an editor will choose your piece for the first page of a Sunday travel section or use an image as a double-truck (two-page spread), provide loose shots with great color and composition. Shooting loose means having uncluttered space, like sky or trees, in your picture and not focusing tightly on your subject. Give the editor a place for headlines. On a trip to India, I shot a series of pictures that ended up being used by various publications as a cover shot and a double-truck because I shot loose and allowed lots of sky where the editor could place the headline.

NO POSING. Editors like the people in your pictures to look natural. But what if the only people you see are tourists? Not a problem.

Just have the people you're with put down their cameras and look unposed; have them look away from the camera or busy themselves doing something. Since my eight-year-old son Travis began to walk and talk, he's accompanied me on shoots and has learned that unlike what most parents want, I don't want him to smile or look at the camera.

PHOTOGRAPHING CHILDREN. Rather than pose kids, let them do what they do and shoot them as they do it, keeping your shutter speed to 1/250 or faster. Rather than guide the child, let the child guide you, and you may find wonderful photo opportunities right in front of you.

FRAME IT. A doorway, window, or outcropping of large rocks or boulders can create a frame through which to shoot a picture. Keep your frame, and your subject, in focus by using a small aperture (the size of the lens opening, or f-stop) so there is sufficient depth of field (the area around the subject on which the lens is focused). Your foreground frame (between camera and subject) will draw attention to your subject, and if you can, expose for the subject so your frame goes dark.

SILHOUETTES. Silhouettes always make for interesting pictures and can dramatize your subjects when shape and design are important. Sunsets, for instance, can be all the more interesting if you feature a shape in the foreground, such as a lifeguard tower, a boat, or children playing along the shoreline.

What to Shoot For

There are good times—and not-so-good times—to shoot pictures. Ideally, get out there early in the day—or late. Once the sun rises high in the sky, after 10:30 or 11:00 A.M. and until 2:00 P.M., you might as well put your camera away. When the sun is directly overhead, it throws harsh shadows down on your subject, dispersing rays of color. Without a lot of finagling, your pictures will look washed out. I like to go out with my camera just after sunrise. I watch for changes I want in shadow and light, and then begin shooting. I've shot some of my best pictures before eight in the morning, when the light is rich with color. Sunsets can be tricky. The sky may look perfectly wondrous to you as the sun goes down, but if you wait until the actual sunset the image will look too dark. On my town's scenic beach, with rocks, cliffs, and outcroppings, photographers arrive two hours or more before sunset to start shooting, and by the time the sun actually sets, they are either trudging up the hill toward their cars or using their flashes. The sky may not be too dark for the eyes, but it's too dark for the camera.

Is it necessary to shoot on sunny days? Unless there's a point to shooting on an overcast day, the answer is a resounding yes. Most magazines, especially travel magazines, love sunny days and detest overcast, gray days. There are, of course, exceptions. The sky may be dramatic, full of thunderheads, or it may be raining. During or just after a rainstorm is a great time to shoot. Wet surfaces look wonderfully reflective in pictures. Or if it's a snowy day with an overcast sky, the ambient light and white earth may be just what you need to make a great photo. Ambient light and overcast days help to make color look more saturated and rich.

Shoot lots of film. Use transparency (slide) film when you're shooting with film, and shoot lots of it. It may seem wasteful or you may fear you're spending too much on film, but when you get back home you'll wish you'd shot more. Film is your most expendable commodity. Spend the extra dough. It's worth ensuring that you have the pictures you need. Bracket your more important shots by shooting with different exposures. Adjust the aperture, allowing more or less light in, and shoot again. Keep bracketing and shooting until you're satisfied that you've shot the scene in many different ways. One day, shooting in India, I bracketed through a couple of rolls of film and ended up with ten shots

I sold and resold to an in-flight magazine and several newspapers. The editors didn't buy the same exact exposure, but they all bought the same image. This was a great lesson in how bracketing and shooting lots can result in a sale—or lots of sales.

Take three steps closer. One of the biggest problems with pictures is that the photographer was too far away. Even when you think you're close enough, move in closer.

Learn about lighting and which film to use for which lighting. A low ASA-rated film is excellent for daylight and a high ASA film is good for low-light situations and flash photography.

Film or Digital?

Art directors at magazines still, for the most part, prefer freelancers to submit images in the form of transparencies—unless you shoot with a high-end digital camera capable of rendering a high-resolution image no smaller than 10 to 12 megabytes. "Film still has depth, color-saturation quality, and sharpness digital does not have," says Tammy Lechner, photo editor for *OCR Magazines* in Orange County, California. "But with the very high-end cameras, I'd say we are right at the point where there is basically no difference here. The advantages to digital are great. The immediacy of seeing the image during a shoot, the ability to immediately transfer the image through upload and download on the computer, and the storage capability of disks for the digital cameras have become greater and greater."

But most freelance writers don't necessarily want to spring for a high-end digital camera. "For a magazine photo that is going to run a full page, the image would have to be about twenty to twenty-five megabytes," says Lechner, "and for a double-truck [across two pages] it would have to be about fifty megabytes. Only the high-end digital cameras produced by Nikon and Canon can accomplish this—and these cameras cost in the area of eight thousand dollars. There are some very-good-quality cameras by Nikon and Canon in the range of two thousand dollars that can do ninety percent of what's needed for magazine work. The medium-range cameras are fine for Internet use, of course, and can get you a decent image for small reproduction, say a mug shot to a two-column image."

Liza Samala, art director for *Bella and Nails* magazine in Los Angeles, says, "A high-end digital camera is expensive and a lot of photographers can't afford the price. Most of my digital photo shoots are for products, whereas lifestyles and fashion—and especially the cover—are with film. I'm not one-hundred-percent convinced digital is better." Photos in newspapers are printed at a lower resolution; therefore a mid-range digital camera can work just fine. In any case, check first with the editor to make sure what format is preferred.

Other Considerations

Don't draw attention to the fact that you're carrying around expensive camera equipment. Use an innocuous bag, like a scruffy old duffel bag. Most airport X-ray machines in the past would not fog your film unless it is a high ASA, more than 1000. But it never hurts to ask an airline before you pack. Some new high-tech scanners, including those used on checked baggage, may indeed damage film. X-ray equipment doesn't affect digital images.

When you shoot slides—and if you're shooting color, unless the editor asks you for print film, you had better be shooting slides—don't send your editor the originals. Instead, bring your original to a professional photo shop and have dupes made. In my town, they're a dollar a dupe and well worth the cost. If the art director feels the color isn't saturated enough, he'll request the original, in which case, when you mail it, insure it for at least as much as you would be paid for the picture—and you might even consider how much you'd make over the lifetime of the photo, reselling it to different publications. "Please don't send us anything you can't bear to lose," says Belinda Hulin, an ASJA member and features editor at the *Florida Times-Union*. "Daily newspaper offices are riddled with black holes and we don't have time to keep tabs on things beyond getting them into the paper." It's a little more organized at magazines since they're on monthly, not daily, deadlines. Still, better safe than sorry.

If you mail transparencies, at your photo shop you can buy plastic sheets that hold up to a couple of dozen slides. Number these images and make sure your name is on each one. You can have a rubber stamp made with the copyright symbol and your name, or print out labels on your computer. The numbers should correspond to descriptions on your caption sheet. Editors love caption sheets that detail what the photo is about. "Please clearly caption the pictures," says Hulin. "We'd rather edit down too much information than have to track you down for clarifications."

Learn how to work with art directors and ask what they want from each assignment. Art directors—staffers who manage photo shoots and the visual end of magazines—work a bit differently than editors. "Part of being a successful photographer means having good customer service," says Samala. "You need to be able to work under pressure. Sometimes you only have thirty minutes to shoot someone, and photographers need to be able to work under pressure and be able to submit artwork that's acceptable to the art director's needs."

Basic accessories include a tripod, a flash, a cable release, and different lenses and filters. A tripod will help you keep your camera steady in low-light situations when you don't want to use a flash, and a cable release, which comes in many different lengths and attaches to the shutter release, can help you avoid jiggling the camera, causing the image to blur. A flash is a necessity, especially one with a 360-degree swivel head that allows you to bounce the flash off the ceiling or the wall. As for lenses, I have two: one 35/70 mm and a telephoto. You don't need more than that. I use a polarizing filter that helps reduce the sun's glare.

If you need a photo to illustrate an article but don't have the photo and you can't travel to shoot it yourself, contact the chamber of commerce, historical society, tourist bureau, United Nations, public-relations firms, hotels, travel agencies, airlines, and railroads, or go on the Internet and search it out. You can often borrow a photo for editorial use at no charge. If you want to shoot on location at a museum or another public place, contact the administrative staff and explain that you're shooting for editorial and not advertising, or you may pay dearly for permission to do so.

Some photographers routinely use model releases. If you're in a public place and the photo is for editorial purposes, it's your right to shoot it. On the other hand, I know some photographers who play it safe by making sure anyone recognizable in their pictures has signed a model release. You can purchase pads of release forms at photo shops, or go to *www.dpcorner.com/all_about/releases.shtml* and download them.

Finally, it's best to sell "one-time rights," but if you decide to sell "all rights" or "exclusive rights," be sure you're paid well—at least three or four times what you'd be paid for one-time rights. Check out Editorial Photographers at *www.editorialphoto.com* for information on rights, pay rates, and more. Also, for more on rights, go to *www.ppa.com/public/articles/index.htm.* Who knows? If you remember that good photos are made by you, not by the camera, you might discover that a picture really can be worth 1,000 words—and maybe more.

BARBARA DeMARCO-BARRETT is a freelancer and editor of *The ASJA Monthly.* She is a writing and photography instructor and host of *Writers on Writing,* a weekly radio show on KUCI in Orange County, California, and has sold photos to in-flight magazines, the *Los Angeles Times,* the *San Jose Mercury News,* the *Toronto Sun,* and more. She can be reached at *www.writersonwriting.com.*

20

Employing a Writing Assistant

LESTER A. PICKER

Let's face it. Life as a freelance writer can be challenging. We constantly juggle multiple assignments, research one article while interviewing for another, transcribe interview tapes, and talk to editors ... and that's before lunch. Don't get me wrong, though. Despite the challenges, the bottom line for me is that writing for a living sure beats a day job. Unfortunately, writing for a living is a bit less lucrative than, say, being the CEO of a Fortune 500 company. In fact, few freelancers earn as much as a neophyte elementary school teacher, minus the benefits package. Over the years, I've found that the most successful freelancers, those who are lucky enough to support themselves—let alone a family—treat their writing as a business. They are serious enough about their craft to creatively boost revenues, doggedly decrease expenses, and ceaselessly market their work. And sometimes they employ assistants to help achieve those goals.

The Road to Financial Security

My personal journey to financial self-sufficiency began with the realization that, no matter how hard I worked, it would be difficult to support my family on the strength of my writing alone. There just aren't enough hours in a day to develop pithy queries to editors, do the b-o-r-i-n-g research, churn out lively prose, send invoices, and threaten to send my bat-wielding cousin Vinnie after slow-paying editors. It finally dawned on me that if I could focus more on my writing and less on background research and paperwork, I'd be way ahead of the game. The strategy I developed was to employ a writing assistant to handle all—well, most— of the busywork, thereby freeing me up to churn out prose. So, over a period of several weeks, I developed a sketchy business plan that made more sense with each iteration.

When I felt the plan was ready, I put out the word to friends and business associates that I was looking for a part-time writing assistant. The rest, as they say, is history. I was lucky in initially finding a capable research assistant, an experience that taught me a lot about how to work as part of a writing team. I learned to give up some control of the creative process, that there was more than one way to uncover background information, and that the time invested in solid planning pays dividends in the long run. By the time I was ready to hire my second assistant, the writing muses smiled down on me and sent me a woman who was herself an aspiring writer. That made for a win-win situation where she was able to learn the business of freelancing while earning a paycheck. I got to focus on my writing, period. The other distractions I handed off to her.

Nuts and Bolts

Once I land an assignment, my assistant and I carefully plan how to execute it. We literally step away from our desks to a "meeting area" in my home office, pads in hand. We make certain that we each understand the assignment, then brainstorm reference sources. We develop a preliminary outline of how the article might flow. Typically, my assistant hits the Web and does some research. Within a day or two, she presents me with an overview of the topic to help me climb the learning curve quickly, along with key issues, contacts, highlighted printouts from the Web, and other supporting information. With a better grasp of the topic, I now have a good idea how I want the piece to proceed. The value added in her doing the initial research is that she is now familiar enough with the topic to identify other markets to approach for follow-up sales. Once I am done with my interviews, she transcribes them—thanks be to the Universal Forces of Goodness and Righteousness. I hate, hate, hate transcribing. Not having to face this dreaded task has increased my productivity beyond belief.

With my first draft completed, I hand it off to her. We discuss the slant I've taken and what other ways there might be to spin the topic. Once we're finished brainstorming, she is ready to research other markets for that topic. While I'm polishing the draft, she is already marketing new angles to other publications. This approach to writing makes the difference between surviving and thriving. Any freelancer knows that 80 percent of the effort it takes to write an article goes into landing the assignment in the first place, then climbing the steep learning curve needed to explain the content to readers. Once that is done, it is much easier to weave the content threads into many different tapestries, without having to start from scratch each time. Another value that my assistant brings to my writing is that she is able to develop sidebars, even if it is one as simple as compiling a comprehensive list of Web sites for readers, a task she has already completed through her initial research. On occasion I will offer her full authorship for the sidebar. That gives her an opportunity to get a published credit, which is a great motivation.

The down side to this arrangement is that you may also be creating your future competition. Once your assistant learns the ropes, you may lose her. In my case, my first two assistants each lasted about two years before launching their own part-time writing careers. But even so I have to admit to a certain degree of satisfaction in their subsequent efforts.

Once you hire an assistant, you also step into the thorny area of personnel issues. The day you most depend on your assistant, he or she will inevitably lose a dental filling or need to nurse a sick kid. On other days, you may find your coffee break stretching into an invigorating conversation that eats up a good chunk of your morning. However, I've come to believe that the advantages to having an assistant far outweigh the disadvantages, at least as far as the pocketbook goes. But an assistant is not for every writer. Some of us are more protective of our caves than others. Sharing yours with an assistant may not work for you. I've outlined a few alternatives below.

The Intern Connection

On many occasions I have used interns from local colleges who want to apprentice with a working writer. Many of my colleagues who teach writing at colleges and universities have done the same. I have to be honest; the results with interns are mixed. Perhaps I'm too cynical, but taking on the responsibility of an intern is more like donating time to your local charity than realizing any business advantage. It is a wonderful thing to do and it is a contribution toward our field. I still take on an intern periodically, but I'm much more selective about the process, and here's why: Interns are usually young, not quite a tumultuous teen but definitely not yet an adult, and that raises issues related to the professional image you want to project. It takes countless hours to train interns and, just when you expect the payoff, they're gone! Most come laden with transportation problems, exams, and enough creative excuses for not showing up to fill a book.

On the other hand, interns are enthusiastic and can give your writing an energy boost. Some are quite creative and a few even think out of the box, a real advantage when seeking new markets. One of my interns turned me on to a youth-market sports writing assignment. Unfortunately, when the assignment letter arrived in the mail along with a copy of the magazine, I realized that I couldn't understand the short-snippet, hip-jargon writing that the readership apparently favored. I turned down the assignment.

If you do decide to use an intern, make sure that you understand the requirements of the college. How many hours is the intern expected to work? If it's a summer program, exactly when does it start and end? Does the program have specific expectations regarding skills the intern is expected to learn? How much latitude do you have as far as assigning grunt work to the intern? To whom can you turn if you have a problem with the intern?

Off-Site Assistants

I've known some writers who work better with off-site assistants, delegating specific tasks, like transcription or research. I've done that, too, on occasion. There is one researcher I have used for years for particularly thorny topics. My suggestion is that you pay off-site people by the job, not the hour, at least until you develop a comfortable working relationship. In the case of my off-site researcher, I typically call him and discuss my specific need. He immediately gives me an estimate of how long he thinks he will need to do an initial line of inquiry, rarely more than an hour since he's a pro. He gets back to me, usually within twenty-four hours, with a not-to-exceed estimate of either the total job or the number of hours. If he runs into a problem, he calls me right away and we discuss alternatives. Having your off-site assistant check in with you regularly is a must, especially when you're working on deadline.

Rules for Being a Boss

If you are considering using an assistant, here are some tips that may ease the transition, gleaned from my own experience and that of several colleagues.

DEFINE THE JOB. Describe on paper exactly what you want from your assistant. Is this person responsible only for background research? Does the position include marketing to editors? How will you train your assistant to resell your work? Aspiring writers who serve as assistants often try to do too much, too quickly. In my case, I need someone to transcribe interviews (that alone is worth every penny to me!), do basic background article research on the Internet, photocopy materials, uncover new markets, and organize my files when I have a large writing project. Anything more than that is gravy, but comes only after the grunt work is done.

HIRE SMART. Spread the word among friends and colleagues that you're hiring and specify the traits and qualifications you are looking for in an assistant. You'll be amazed at how many people will jump at the chance to work with an experienced writer. Check references carefully. I once told a couple at a cocktail party that I was looking for an assistant. They turned to each other with a knowing smile and suggested that the woman standing behind me, whom they personally recommended, would be perfect. She turned out to be the best assistant I ever had. Hiring smart also means not financially strapping yourself to a concept that may not gel for you. Hire one day a week at first. If your income rises and your stress level goes down, then you've got a winning formula. But be sure that your assistant is okay with that plan.

OFFER FAIR PAY AND INCENTIVES. In the long run, a writing assistant will be worth the expense only if she eases the stress in your professional life and increases your revenues. I start my assistants at a training wage for three months. If it seems as if they'll work out, I up the wage considerably, then give raises every six months. If your assistant will be reselling your articles, build in incentives to motivate sales. For example, I offer 10 percent of resale fees, over and above her hourly wage, for every article she resells. Incentives can also be creative. For example, consider celebrating a major writing contract that the two of you landed by rewarding your assistant with a pair of tickets to a concert or dinner for two at a good restaurant.

OFFER CAREER ENHANCEMENT. Consider offering your assistant the opportunity to write a sidebar now and then, on his or her own time. When my assistant does that, she gets a byline, a published credit, and a cut of my fee for her contribution, again in addition to her base salary. For an aspiring writer, there is no better motivator. Some writers may disagree, but I have always felt comfortable in these instances paying my assistant from one-quarter to one-half of the sidebar fee and no more. You are running a business, right?

TRAIN, TRAIN, TRAIN. No assistant will be productive right out of the box. Take lots of time to properly train your assistant. Teach him the fine art of querying. Show him how fickle editors are so he learns that rejection slips are a writer's badge of honor. Help him understand that the key to successful reselling is solid market research. Give him examples of good query letters, whether your own or someone else's. Allow him to listen in on your informal telephone queries to editors with whom you have a strong relationship. Solid training leads to increased sales.

CRITIQUE CONSTRUCTIVELY. Investing your time to critique your assistant's early efforts will pay dividends down the road. Discuss strategies you would use to handle obstacles, particularly query rejections. Confront behaviors he may have that reduce your efficiency as a writer. If you aren't being "assisted," there is no point in paying for an assistant. But also ask for feedback. So what if your assistant is not a published writer? She is no doubt an avid reader. Ask her to read your first draft, checking for logical flow and ease of comprehension. Also request feedback on your business performance, on ways to cut expenses or increase revenues, for example.

SET PERSONAL AND BUSINESS GOALS. If you don't know where you are going, every road will get you there, an old proverb reminds us. One of the most efficient and effective ways to work as a team is to know each other's life goals. Don't keep your business goals a secret, either. Once you know that your assistant will work out, ask for her input on your business goals, and seek ways to integrate your assistant's life goals into the business. You'll be surprised at how deeply she will then buy into the success of the business. On the flip side, be sure to set performance goals. How many articles will be resold in what period of time? How many thirty-minute interviews do you expect her to transcribe each week? These goals will form the basis for the job-effectiveness reviews that lead to pay raises.

PLAN TOGETHER. One of the advantages of an assistant is having another couple of pounds of cerebral matter to help boost sales and revenues. Take fifteen minutes each day to brainstorm. How should we execute this assignment? Are there any angles in this article we can use to develop other queries?

SHARE YOUR PASSION. If you're not passionate about your work, who will be? There are two lessons I've learned about passion. Well, maybe more than two, but this article is about writing. The first lesson is that people thrive on passion. Writing assistants, in particular, feed off it. The second lesson is that passion is contagious. Pretty soon, your assistant will be selling more of your articles because, as the top salespeople will tell you, passion sells.

KNOW THYSELF. More than anything else, the kind of person you are may be the best predictor of whether, or how, an assistant will work out for you. In my case, I thoroughly enjoy the interpersonal interactions with my assistant. But I also need "cave time," blocks of uninterrupted time when I can write or twiddle my thumbs waiting for my muse, without worrying about what an employee might think. For me, that translates into an assistant who works only three days a week.

LESTER A. PICKER has more than 500 writing credits in publications such as *Forbes, Money, Bloomberg Personal Finance, Better Homes & Gardens,* and many others. He was a weekly columnist for the *Baltimore Sun* and a regular commentator on NPR's *Marketplace.* He can be reached at *lpicker@comcast.net.*

21

Contracts:
Protecting Writers' Rights

RICHARD A. MARINI

Once upon a time—actually not that long ago—most freelance writing assignments were made on a hand-shake or, at most, via a single-page assignment letter. The agreement was usually a simple one: The writer would license what are called First North American Serial Rights, or First North American Print Rights, to the publication. This gave the publication the right to be the first to publish an article; the article would be circulated only in North

America—the United States and Canada. Since the writer was only *licensing* the rights, he retained copyright of the work. After the first appearance, he could resell it elsewhere. In other words, the writer owned what he wrote, renting it out to whomever he wanted.

Back then, many writers made a good living self-syndicating their stories to newspapers across the country. A writer in Chicago, for example, might do a travel piece for the *Chicago Tribune* and, after it was published, resell it to the *Denver Post* or the *Albuquerque Journal.* There were ground rules, of course. For example, you couldn't try to sell that piece to both the *Tribune* and its crosstown rival, the *Chicago Sun-Times.* But if you played within the limits, you could stay quite busy peddling your wares to papers across the country and, if you were adventurous, in other countries as well.

Magazine writers could improve their own bottom line by licensing these so-called "secondary rights." A piece written for a national magazine might be resold—usually slightly rewritten—to a trade journal. An article in a parenting magazine in one region of the country could be resold to another in a different corner of the country. A medical piece published in the United States might find new life in Britain, Canada, or even Japan after being translated. Everyone was a winner. The writer made more money by selling the same piece several times. Publications ran material that was exclusive for their markets. And the public was able to read the work of talented, experienced writers.

Today, of course, things are different. In the age of the Internet and multinational media empires, publications are requesting—*demanding*, actually—much more than FNAR. They want electronic rights. They want syndication rights. They want movie rights. They want to be able to resell and republish your work using any and all technologies—even technologies not yet invented. Here's an example of a particularly grabby, but by no means unique, rights clause from a well-known women's magazine, with the most offending language emphasized:

The author hereby grants [publisher], its licensees and assigns forever, all rights in and to the Material and all rights of copyright therein, including, without limitation, the exclusive right to publish the Material in magazine, newspaper and book form, including the right to publish or authorize the publication of the Material by any and all means, media, devices, processes and technology *now and hereafter known or devised in perpetuity throughout the universe.*

In order to protect their rights and their business, writers today need to challenge such contracts, offer alternative contract language, and explain to publishers why their proposed changes are right and fair. Don't be daunted by the prospect of having to deal with legal language. In the end, it is merely language, and using language is what we writers do. You don't need a law degree to understand, explain, and demand the changes necessary to make even the most unfair contract more writer-friendly. Go through the exercise of reviewing one or two contracts and you'll already know more than 95 percent of the editors out there—and knowledge is power when you're asking for changes. Many editors are taken aback when writers explain how and why a contract is unfair, explaining, "This is what my boss gave me to use." And a surprising number will take a writer's side in asking superior editors or lawyers to make contract changes, once they understand what you're asking for and why.

Only a few clauses cause the majority of the grief for today's writers, including rights, warranties and indemnification, retroactive assignment of rights, and ownership of notes.

Rights

This is perhaps the most important part of a writing contract. The fight for rights often begins with a type of contract called "work made for hire." Here's an example of a typical WMFH clause:

> The Author hereby agrees that the Article is a "work made for hire"
> pursuant to the 1976 Copyright Act, 17 U.S.C., Sec. 101. The
> Corporation is the owner of all rights, title and interest in the
> copyright(s) therein.

Under U.S. copyright law, writing done by newspaper and magazine staffers is typically considered to be WMFH. Staffers are employed by the company and anything they write is owned by the publication—lock, stock, and copyright. In return, staffers get a regular paycheck. They also get a desk and a computer. They may get medical insurance and a retirement plan. In other words, they get much more than a simple check.

What does a freelancer who signs a WMFH contract get? A fee. Nothing more. No desk, no computer, no pension. But the publication nonetheless owns the copyright; by signing the contract, the writer literally transfers ownership of the piece to the publication. An ASJA member who once signed WMFH contracts at a now-defunct consumer magazine hates seeing her articles remain available on Web sites to anyone who pops her name into a search engine. "If I ever have an urge to sign a WMFH agreement," she says, "I just take a look at those articles living on the Web outside my control and earning money for other people. It ruins my day, but strengthens my resolve." Another ASJA member found that a WMFH agreement prohibited her from posting her own article as a writing sample on her personal Web site.

While many contracts boldly declare that they're WMFH, others are sneakier. The rights section may be headed "First Rights." But read further and the contract will list any number of other uses the publication claims for itself. The right to post it on the Web site, the right to put it in a best-of compilation, the right to sell the idea to a Hollywood studio. And what does the writer get? Nothing other than the initial check.

Another danger is the contract that seeks "non-exclusive rights." At first this sounds like a good idea. The writer retains the right to resell the piece, and so does the publisher. If the writer sells it, he keeps the money. If the publisher does, it cashes the check. Everybody's happy, right? Not quite. Writers can't begin to compete with big publishers when it comes to reselling articles. For all intents and purposes, a non-exclusive rights contract can be as restrictive as an all-rights or WMFH agreement.

Dealing with problem contracts requires a certain amount of negotiating skill, but this isn't a chapter about the art of negotiation. For that, try reading the book *Getting to Yes* by Roger Fisher. Still, there are a couple of basic ways to get more rights than initially offered. First, ask for straight first North American Serial Rights. Those are the simplest and fairest terms for all involved. Many publications have more than one version of their contract. The backup, better versions, however, are reserved for writers savvy enough to ask an editor if there's another version in the bottom drawer. The other contract won't necessarily get you First North American Rights, but you'll at least be better off than if you'd said yes to the initial contract without questioning anything. Second, negotiate rights—and separate payments—for each reuse. Most contracts are written by lawyers who are trained to get everything for their clients. But many publications that want reprint rights, syndication rights, and other rights are willing to pay for them.

How much more money should you ask for? As with the main writing fee, you want to get as much as you can. Sometimes writers have little leverage when it comes to rights. Sometimes a publication will not budge on rights but will pay more. For the writer, a heftier paycheck can assuage the sting of a less-than-perfect deal. Just be sure the extra money makes up for what you're giving up in potential future income. For electronic rights, specify a separate fee. Some publications will pay an additional 10 percent or 20 percent for the right to put stories on their Web sites. One ASJA member had a $1,000 contract rewritten so that $900 of the fee was specified for the piece itself and $100 for electronic rights. No, he didn't get any more money, but the contract set a precedent by putting a value on the e-rights. And when a magazine resells a story, many writers feel that a 50/50 split of the gross proceeds—not the net—is fair. After all, the company has made the sale, so it should get a cut. Other writers want full control of their work, especially if they plan to reuse the material, such as in a book. Letting a publisher resell the piece could lessen its future value. Put a contractual time limit on the rights you are granting, after which they revert to you. This is especially important when electronic rights—specifically the right to post something on the Web—can mean a piece stays online forever. Many writers license Web rights for one year, with the right to be renegotiated should both parties desire.

One last thing about rights: *Why* should you fight for them? Signing an all-rights contract immediately kills whatever resale value the article may have. In other words, you won't be able to sell it again, anywhere. Not to a newspaper in another city. Not to a corporate newsletter in another state. Not to a magazine in Bangkok. You might not be able to use it in one of your own books, or even post it on your Web site. But what if you're writing a story you think has no resale value? Ask yourself this: If the piece has no resale value, why does the publisher want those rights? This is a big-picture issue. By agreeing to all-rights contracts, you're setting a precedent. Your story could be turned into a multimillion-dollar movie, and you wouldn't see an additional nickel. Signing an all-rights contract will make it harder for you to retain your rights and get a fair contract in the future, both from that particular publication and from every other employer who hires freelance writers. And you'll be making things harder for every other freelance writer, too. In other words, just because you might not need to aggressively protect your rights today doesn't mean you won't have to protect them down the road.

Warranty and Indemnification Clauses

Whether you're talking about a washing machine or a writing contract, a warranty means the same thing. It's a guarantee. With the washing machine, the guarantee is that the machine will meet a certain level of quality—that it won't break down for at least six months, for example. If it does, the manufacturer promises to repair it free of charge. In a writing contract, the warranty clause can promise a lot of things. Here's a good example of a typical warranty clause from an actual contract:

> I [the writer] warrant that I am the author and sole owner of the rights to the work, that it is original and not in the public domain, that it has never been published, and that it contains nothing unlawful or violative of any person's rights.

Note how the clause starts out innocuously. It asks you to guarantee that you're the person who actually wrote the article you're submitting, that you're not stealing anyone else's words, that you haven't previously published the article somewhere else. Most professional writers should have little objection to making such guarantees. But keep reading and you'll see how the contract also asks you to warrant that the work will not violate any laws or anyone's rights. This one's pretty broad in what it covers. Here's how another contract puts it even more broadly:

> I [the writer] warrant that the article contains nothing defamatory, libelous, or unlawful, and will not violate or infringe any rights of copyright privacy, publicity or any other statutory, common law, or other rights of any party.

That's quite a lot to promise, especially since few writers are experts in copyright, libel, and privacy law. How can you be expected to guarantee that what you write won't violate any laws anywhere in the world? In the age of the Internet, anything you write that's posted online is "published" from Nepal to Naples. What if an article on breast cancer is deemed obscene in Iran? A number of plaintiffs have sued for libel in Britain, where defamation damages are easier to collect, rather than in the United States. Would you be prepared to defend yourself in a British court?

When a contract contains such warranties, you should try to get them struck entirely. If that fails, ask about removing only the really objectionable parts. Ask the editor to strike the promise not to violate any laws that you have no way of knowing exist—and may not exist at the time of the contract. Many editors can see the illogic. Should that fail, try limiting your warranties "to the best of your knowledge." This means literally adding these six magic words to the clause—in the proper spot—as a qualifier. The clause from the first of two on the previous page will read, after making the change, as follows:

> I [the writer] warrant that I am the author and sole owner of the rights to the work, that it is original and not in the public domain, that it has never been published, and that *to the best of my knowledge* it contains nothing unlawful or violative of any person's rights.

Often following close on the heels of the warranty is what's known as the indemnity clause. This clause puts serious financial teeth behind what you've just promised. Here's an example of a typical indemnity clause:

> I [the writer] shall defend and hold [publisher] and its clients harmless from any claims, liabilities or causes of action arising out of, or in connection with, the breach of warranties made hereunder. In the event of litigation, I shall select my own attorney, pay costs, and retain all recoveries.

This means that if someone sues the publisher for something you write, you're basically agreeing to pick up the tab to defend yourself and the publisher. Even if it's a nuisance claim. Even if the publisher doesn't want to fight the lawsuit and simply decides to settle. They settle, you pay. It's hard to overstate this, but in today's litigious society, the bill for the simplest lawsuit can run into the tens of thousands of dollars and, if you're the one paying, result in the loss of your home, your car, your savings. That 600-word, $600 assignment isn't worth it. Your attack plan for dealing with indemnification clauses is similar to that for warranties: When in doubt, strike it out. Should the editor (or, more likely, the publication's lawyer) refuse, there's another simple clause you can add that will effectively limit your obligation to final judgment. That phrase reads: "by judgment sustained." Here's how the clause might look after you get through marking it up:

> I [the writer] shall defend and hold [publisher] and its clients harmless from any claims, liabilities or causes of action arising out of, or in connection with, the breach of warranties made hereunder *by judgment sustained* [emphasis added].

As written, the clause now states that you'll be financially responsible for a settlement only after a lawsuit has gone to court, and only after a final judgment following all possible appeals. What's more, if you've done your homework and effectively neutered the warranty clause, you'll only have to pay if someone successfully sues you.

Retroactive Rights Clause

Some publishers want to stuff you into a time machine. Their contracts today allow them to go back in time and change previous contracts. It's called the retroactive rights clause. Here's an example:

> All rights granted to Publisher herein shall be deemed to be applicable to any and all prior agreements between Author and Publisher to the extent not granted with respect to the works described therein. Author

shall be compensated for such rights in accordance with the provisions of this agreement.

Yes, you've read it correctly. This clause gives the publisher magic "do-over" powers. That's the power to go back and invalidate previous contracts, even those dating back to the days when First North American Rights were the industry standard and the Internet wasn't even a twinkle in Al Gore's eye. The clause says that, in order to get an assignment today, you have to give up the rights to pieces you wrote months, even years ago. No longer can you resell those articles. Instead, you have to turn over the rights to the publisher, which you can be sure will soon have them posted all over the Internet. Back when the short-lived *Rosie* magazine was new, the magazine tried foisting this type of retroactive rights clause on its writers. Writers rebelled, and compared it to a movie producer casting Rosie O'Donnell in a new movie—but only if she surrendered future residuals from *A League of Their Own, Sleepless in Seattle*, and her other previous roles. Thanks to complaints brought by ASJA and others in the writing community, *Rosie* dropped the retroactive rights clause. It's a clause you would do well to fight, too. Signing such a contract not only strips you of your rights today, it strips you of rights you previously owned—and potential income in the future.

Ownership of Notes, Etc.

As a freelance writer, you're an independent businessperson. So why do some publication contracts insist that the publisher owns your notebooks, audiotapes, and other materials you buy to do your research, interviewing, and other reporting? They don't actually want the notebooks themselves, of course. They want the notes inside. Here's how one contract asks for this material nicely:

Pursuant to the Original Agreement, all materials, plans, records and other work product, written, created or developed by the Author in connection with the Work shall be deemed proprietary property of [publisher] and shall at all times belong to [publisher]. Any and all original notes, plans or other materials related to the preparation of the Work currently in the Author's possession shall be delivered to [publisher], no later than ten days after the execution of this Agreement.

If you followed this contract exactly, you'd have to pack up those notes and tapes and send them along to the publisher when you file your story. So what's the big deal? As a writer, you go out and research the story, and then pick and choose from your material what to include in the piece. The final story reflects the reality as you, the writer, see it. Do you really want some editor a thousand miles away scouring your notes to add bits and pieces of information to the article that you've already rejected? Probably not.

Now, this might sound like nothing more than a nasty little turf war. But you're the one who has done the reporting. You know more even than your notes reflect, because you did the interviews, you heard the inflections in your subject's voice, saw the body language that imparts as much information as the words spoken. Yes, you will work with the editor to answer specific questions, to address topics missing from your original piece, and to make whatever other changes are requested. But it's *your* prerogative to decide how to take what's in your notes and put it on the page to satisfy the editor.

Also, you want to keep possession of your notes because you never know when you might need them again. Maybe you'll write another story on the same topic. Perhaps you'll use the notes to write a book. When you see such a clause, try to have it deleted. Use the argument that since you're not an employee of the publication, you own your notes and would rather not surrender them. Indeed, suggest that by surrendering the notes, the Internal Revenue Service could look upon your relationship with the publication as being more like that of an employee than an independent contractor.

Bad contracts are a moving target. Publishers are constantly adding new and not-so-improved clauses. Keep a sharp eye out whenever a contract arrives—even if it's from a publication with which you've enjoyed a long and prosperous relationship. One never knows when a publisher will hire a new, eager-beaver lawyer whose first job will be to review the company's contracts to see whether or not they can be "tweaked."

RICHARD A. MARINI served for two years as chair of ASJA's Contracts Committee. While he continues to freelance for, among others, *American Way* magazine, he is also the health and fitness reporter for the *San Antonio Express-News*. He can be reached at *rmarini@express-news.net*.

22

Creating Brand *You*: Promoting Yourself and Your Work

JENNIFER PIRTLE

Tom Peters, leadership expert and best-selling business book author, insists, "Brand! Brand! Brand! That's the message...."

Such business-speak does not resonate easily among freelance writers. But the notion of "branding," or positioning a business and its services as a unified, cohesive commodity, is a concept that most writers would do well to embrace. You say you'd rather concentrate on the quality of your writing? Though creativity will always be a crucial part of every writer's work, promoting yourself as a reliable, professional brand can make you even more attractive to a client who is in the position to hire you.

So how do you create "brand *you*"? First, write a mission statement. Whether your business revolves around feature writing or furniture restoration, you can't successfully sell your skills to others unless you're crystal-clear about what it is you're offering. To refine your focus, start by taking a self-inventory. Sit down with a pen and paper, commit yourself to some quiet time, and begin brainstorming. Some things to consider: What do you enjoy writing about? Where does your expertise lie? What do you write about now—or what would you like to write about? Aim to summarize your skills in one sentence. Before the release of her fourth book, *You Shouldn't Have: How to Give Gifts They'll Never Forget,* Leah Ingram developed and rehearsed the following tag line: "I'm a gift-giving and wedding expert and have written four books on the subject." Now, as her fifth book is about to be released, she'll use a variation on that theme. "The phrase never fails to inspire a conversation," says Ingram, who has successfully freelanced for over fifteen years. "People always ask, 'How can you write five books on a single topic?' My output shows them that I'm a creative thinker. I like to say I can think outside the foil-wrapped box."

Similarly, fitness instructor and writer Joan Price learned the importance of creating a mission statement after attending a public-relations workshop three years ago. Her team leader asked attendees to introduce themselves in five seconds or less. Though she stumbled then, today she's rarely tongue-tied. "I help people to get lively and make fitness a habit," says Price, reciting the phrase she uses in every face-to-face meeting, posts on her Web site, and even includes in the signature line at the bottom of every e-mail message. "The tag line always brings a smile—and usually the question, 'So, how do you do that?'" says Price. "It's the perfect lead-in for me to talk about myself and my work." Think of your own mission statement as you would a well-cut business suit: If you've invested in one with clean, classic lines, you can adjust its look depending on who you'll be meeting with that day. In the sartorial sense, changing your necktie or adding a colorful scarf or funky piece of jewelry can dramatically change your look; in editorial terms, you can easily craft a new mini-brand targeted to the particular client you're approaching.

I write primarily on health-related topics, but I've also covered everything from floral arranging and packaging design to global positioning software and luxury chocolate shops. If I'm pitching an idea to an editor at a home-and-garden magazine, for example, I'll brand myself to that editor by highlighting the writing I've done for publications that target the décor and do-it-yourself audiences, such as *Martha Stewart Living* or *This Old House*. This focused flexibility gives me the wiggle room to cover topics that might be outside my usual beat, but which I feel particularly passionate about. As Ingram puts it: "You want to present a specialty but you don't want to be pigeonholed, either. Though I write mainly about weddings, I'll often say to editors, 'Wait a minute, I also write about X, Y, and Z.'"

Foster Long-Term Relationships

We should view editors as long-term partners in our business. Though, like many writers, I have a quota of queries I send out each week, much of my work comes as assignments from editors with whom I've built relationships over the years. Often, those associations grew from nothing more than a quick e-mail introduction, in which I laid out the basics: who I am, what I do, and how I'd like to do it for them. In many cases, I've received assignments from top national consumer magazines based on the strength of my "brand name" alone—without offering up a single story idea. Martha Barnette, a former-newspaper-reporter-turned-magazine-writer and author of several books on etymology, including *Dog Days and Dandelions*, rarely queries editors. "I've been really fortunate in that I almost never pitch ideas but editors know that I am good at shaping stories," says Barnette, whose reporting skills and writing style keep her in great demand—she's currently a contributing editor at *Self* and *Allure* and has also written for the *New York Times*, the *Los Angeles Times*, *Glamour*, and other publications. "I got one foot in the door at *Allure*, for example, nearly ten years ago after I met an editor online and developed a relationship with her. Editors don't stay in one place very long, so that relationship led to pieces at *Real Simple* and *Rosie*."

Building relationships can pay off not only in terms of additional paychecks but also in the variety of assignments. One freelancer describes how he'll do an assignment for a magazine or a project for a corporate client, and it goes so well that the boss upstairs says, "Hey, let's use him for something else." Then they start offering the writer new projects, sometimes things he's never done before, simply because they think he can do them. It's a great way to parlay a "brand name" into new areas of business and new markets.

Boost Your Knowledge, Boost Your Brand

Like other successful entrepreneurs, the best freelance writers make a point of keeping current in their respective industries. Joining a trade association is one way to further your expertise and your brand, as Janine Adams discovered when she joined the Association of Pet Dog Trainers two years ago. "Reading their newsletter and participating on their e-mail list has been a great way for me to learn from some of the biggest names in training and given me insight into their business. I'm not a trainer, though I do write about training in my work," says Adams, who has written two books and more than 100 newspaper and magazine articles about pets for publications such as *Family Circle, Good Housekeeping*, and the *St. Louis Post-Dispatch*. "It's definitely helped my specialty by making me more knowledgeable and giving me access to expert sources." Specialty writing organizations, such as the American Medical Writers Association, the Education Writers Association, and the Garden Writers Association of America, are also a way to increase your skills and raise your professional profile. Some, such as the American Society of Journalists and Authors, the Writers Guild of America, the Society of American Travel Writers, and the Outdoor Writers Association of America (OWAA), have stringent entry requirements based on experience and writing samples; others require only a joining fee. Arline Zatz, the author of four guidebooks and numerous newspaper and magazine features about camping, canoeing, kayaking, and other outdoor sports, joined the OWAA several years ago. She has used that membership not only as a rock-solid qualification when approaching public-relations firms, travel bureaus, and book publishers, but also as a networking vehicle. "I recently became interested in fishing, so I contacted another member and received lots of valuable information on the how-to and equipment-related aspects of this sport, such as the best tackle to use to catch bass and how to surf cast."

But don't limit yourself to trade or writing-related organizations. The *Encyclopedia of Associations,* published by Gale Research, is available at most local libraries and contains information on more than 22,000 nonprofit American membership groups aimed at virtually every kind of personal or professional interest. Taking classes, particularly credentialed coursework, is another way to enhance your brand. Freelance writer Nancy Shepherdson pursued certification with the National Genealogical Society in preparation for her book on genealogy for teens. I'm a certified yoga instructor; next is personal trainer certification (with an emphasis on pre- and postnatal exercise) through the American Council of Exercise. Though such courses are time-consuming, they provide a richer knowledge of a specialized subject and an expert credential to offer editors.

Specialized workshops, fellowships, and seminars are also useful.

Health and environment writer Trish Riley was selected to attend a week-long seminar on covering water issues at the Poynter Institute in June 2000. She also attended a weekend-long fellowship in 2001 through the Casey Center for Journalism on Children and Families to study issues surrounding adolescent health. "Both of these seminars featured cutting-edge scientists presenting the latest research and issues—a wonderful means of learning more about the topics I like to write about," says Riley. "And in terms of helping me to define my work, this makes me much more valuable to editors, who think of me when an environmental story comes along, or a health story, or something about how our society affects children."

Building Your Brand Online

The branding benefits of having a Web site are many, but if you're thinking of creating (or updating) one, it's important to consider who will use it—whether the intended audience is an editor, a book agent, or a potential book-buyer. I use my Web site, *www.cityjen.com,* as a virtual "cheat sheet" for editors, public-relations officers, and even expert sources in countries around the world to quickly check my background and get a snapshot of the work I do. One section is geared specifically toward other freelance writers, offering a list of free writing-related resources plus information about my online mentoring program.

"Think about who you want to see it, and construct it with this individual—not your own wishes—in mind," says Marisa d'Vari, who writes about business, marketing, fine cuisine, and luxury-related topics. "Also be clear what your audience *doesn't* care about. This is not the place for pictures of your dog or cat—the key here is professionalism." If you're fairly tech-savvy, it's not crucial to hire someone to create your site, but a good designer can help you focus your ideas and ensure that the site is updated frequently. Above all, information should be clearly delineated, and the site should be easy to navigate. Invite your friends to test the site before you publish it on the Web: Can they move through it quickly and easily without getting lost? Do all the hyperlinks work? If you're using graphics, do they load quickly using a range of connection speeds?

Even if you've already got your own Web presence, don't overlook other online branding opportunities, such as becoming an expert source for *someone else's* site. Sharon Naylor is the author of sixteen wedding books and is the resident wedding expert at NJWedding.com, a position she's held since 2001, when she contacted the site's owner after making a New Year's resolution to pursue more local media. "In return for the roughly thirty minutes a week I spend answering the visitors' questions through e-mail, he gave me a full biography, write-ups about each of my books, announcements about my upcoming books, listings in the site's online wedding store (with purchasing links to Amazon.com), a link to my own Web site, plus a special feature page with the most-frequently-asked questions and my responses," she says. "Better yet, he includes me in all of his public-relations mailings, which has resulted in coverage in all the big New Jersey newspapers as well as in the *New York Times*. It's a great setup and has done wonders for my visibility in the tri-state area."

Participating in Web-based forums and e-mail discussion groups is another great way to round out your knowledge and to increase awareness of your work, says Connie Benesch. When she was working on a book about sugar, she joined two e-mail discussion groups—one about sugar addiction and another about hypoglycemia. "People are often writing e-mails seeking advice, information, support, and encouragement, and in many instances, I can offer that. Doing so boosts my visibility and helps establish me as an expert," she says. "For example, this week, I shared a list of some fifty-plus names for sugar so people can know what sweets to avoid. All week, people have been writing to thank me, and the founder of the list even posted it in a prominent place on her Web site—with a byline about me and my work."

Build a Better Business Card

Though Web, fax, and e-mail are invaluable in today's business world, there are times when you'll want to meet potential and existing clients face-to-face. In these instances (or when you're sending something, such as clips, by snail mail) having a professional business card is crucial. Your cards should include your name and contact information, including Web site and e-mail address; whether you choose to include a title (freelance journalist, writer, author) is up to you. Cards need not be fancy and shouldn't be gimmicky—avoid including artwork of pens, pencils, or typewriters, all of which scream "amateur" to editors. And although words are our business, don't ignore the look and feel of your business cards and other collateral pieces, such as stationery and envelopes. "Design is a crucial element of presenting a professional face. Make sure you get everything designed in one shot—including your cards, stationery, mailing labels, and anything else that might brand you," says Chris Sandlund, a business and technology writer who formerly worked as an editor at several prominent magazines. "When I was an editor, I hired one individual because his clips were killer and his stationery was so professional. I think that good design is a sign of your professionalism to editors. To this day, I continue to refer overflow work to this writer—and have never had a client regret working with him."

With today's desktop publishing programs you can make these things yourself, but a graphic designer has a specific skill set, an expertise, that you may not. (After all, as writers, we'd never assume that a graphic designer could write a great article.) Think of the cash outlay for design and printing—which can range from a few hundred dollars for a stack of business cards to $2,000 or more for a total package (depending on the items you choose and the complexity of their design)—as an investment in your brand. It's also a tax-deductible business expense.

Sing Your Praises—And Get Others to Do So, Too

If you're profiled or have a story published, don't be shy about telling others. Sometimes simply getting the word out about your own good news can result in more work. I've sent recently published articles to editors I've been wooing for months but haven't yet connected with on an assignment—and included a lighthearted, handwritten note saying "Here's what I've done for your competitor—when are *we* going to work together?" That friendly little nudge proved, on several occasions, an easy way to cement the deal. One well-known freelancer capitalizes on the occasional profiles of her that appear in publications by and for other writers. She sends e-mails about such articles to her editors, accompanied by a note thanking them for all the great assignments they've given her over the years. She typically receives not only nice notes in return, but usually a small raft of new assignments. Testimonials from people you've worked with are also useful. I make a point of asking my former students what they thought of our time together. I post a selection of those comments (with the authors' permission) on my Web site and direct potential new students to that area.

Deborah Knuckey, a newspaper and magazine writer and the author of two books on personal finance, uses a similar tactic when she approaches new clients. "I use two written testimonials that I have embedded into a simplified writing resume when I am approaching a new publication, particularly one where the clips I have are not as directly relevant as I would like." Not only can testimonials make a good impression with a *new* client, studies have shown that simply asking a former client to write one can make *that* person more committed to you, too.

Get Out of the Office

Though most writing by freelancers gets done alone in a room, smart writers make a point of getting out of their offices to meet editors, attend workshops, network with their peers, or speak at conferences. "I've just offered myself as a panelist at South by Southwest in Austin, Texas, probably the nation's biggest music-industry conference," says Daylle Deanna Schwartz, who has authored several music-industry books, including *The Real Deal: How to Get Signed to a Record Label* and *Start & Run Your Own Record Label.* "The visibility helps establish me as an expert, and also gives me an inside track to interview or pick the brains of other industry pros who are speaking." Such events can be a way to recharge your enthusiasm for your work, and can result in book sales or lay the groundwork for future business.

For the past several years, writer Andrea Warren has been transitioning from magazine writer and corporate seminar presenter to children's author. Her nonfiction histories about children set in extraordinary times include the acclaimed *Orphan Train Rider: One Boy's True Story* and *Surviving Hitler: A Boy in the Nazi Death Camps.* She's learned to think creatively to supplement low publishing advances and "slow, but steady" royalty checks by positioning herself as a speaker with something to say. Two of her recent speaking engagements took place at a library less than an hour away from her home in Kansas. "At one, the library was jammed with everyone from elementary-school students to senior citizens. My talk was followed by a 'pie supper,' with some of the best homemade pie I've ever eaten. I was paid three hundred and fifty dollars plus mileage for my forty-five-minute presentation, followed by a book signing at which I cleared two hundred and fifty dollars in book sales. Last Friday I gave a two-hour teacher in-service program for an area high school. Social studies and English teachers were there and received 'credit.' I talked about my research, offered ideas on how to bring nonfiction into the classroom, and shared information about my books. There's a strong likelihood that some of the teachers will incorporate my books into their classes, which means additional sales and wider exposure for my work."

Some writers find ways to brand themselves, tap their creativity, and have some fun at the same time. Peter LaFrance, a New York writer and author who covers the beer, wine, and spirits businesses, hosts an annual prix fixe "beer dinner" at a local restaurant. Chefs get a chance to show off their skills, and their food is paired with house or special beers. LaFrance gets to hold court—and sell his books. "I charge a fixed fee and the restaurant must purchase enough books so that each guest gets a personally inscribed copy. If the event is based outside the New York area, the restaurant must provide transportation and one night's lodging. Each dinner grosses between seven hundred and one thousand dollars, gets books in readers' hands, builds contacts and my reputation as a moneymaker for the house, and creates menus that form the base for more books and articles."

JENNIFER PIRTLE has written hundreds of articles on health, fitness, nutrition, and other topics for international publications, including *Health, Self, Shape, Fitness, Elle, Martha Stewart Living, Martha Stewart Weddings, Ladies' Home Journal*, and *Cosmopolitan*. She is also a former senior features editor for *Family Circle*. She teaches writing courses and runs an online mentoring program for freelance writers. For more about her, visit *www.cityjen.com*.

23

Writers and the Law

SALLIE RANDOLPH AND TIMOTHY PERRIN

For a freelance writer, the world is full of legal pitfalls—and we're not even talking about the quagmire we call contract law. (See Chapter 21 on contracts.) Issues include your rights as a writer, the rights of your subjects to privacy and to their reputations, taxation and how to organize your business, and, of course, copyright. In this chapter, we provide an introduction to some of these issues—highlights only, not legal advice. The details of the law vary from country to country, state to state, and even city to city; this chapter merely raises red flags that say, "Here's something you should discuss with a lawyer."

Freedom of the Press—Your Rights as a Writer

One of the marks of a democratic society is a free press. The roots of America's free press are found in the First Amendment of the U.S. Constitution. Freedom of the press is really a right of the public, not just the writer. Federal law provides no special journalistic privilege, though some states have statutes, often called shield laws, that offer writers some protection. But in states without shield laws, journalists have no special status. As a result, be careful about promising sources that you will not reveal their names. You may not be able to keep those promises. Also be careful about promising that a source can review or veto a story before publication. Besides hurting your credibility, failing to follow through could put you in breach of contract. And be careful about a promise to interview someone "off the record." Many courts will enforce this promise, and give it different interpretations. Moreover, failing to keep it kills your credibility. Many experienced journalists *never* go off the record.

If you engage in investigative reporting, sooner or later you're going to tick someone off. In extreme cases, you'll be served with a subpoena or find yourself on the wrong end of a lawsuit. Because of this not-uncommon scenario, good journalistic practice and legal prudence require that you:

TAPE CONVERSATIONS. Laws about the taping of interviews vary among jurisdictions. In New York, for example, it is legal to tape a conversation as long as one of the parties is aware of the taping. In other states, however, taping is illegal unless both parties consent. Check on the law where you live and work. When in doubt, inform your interview subjects that you are taping and obtain their consent.

KEEP NOTES AND TAPES. Always hang on to your notes and tapes of all conversations. Keep copies of all documents. Ten years is a good rule of thumb.

CORROBORATE. In *All the President's Men,* Carl Bernstein and Bob Woodward would not go with anything they were told by Deep Throat without corroboration from another source. Make that your practice as well.

OFFER AN OPPORTUNITY FOR REPLY. Offer the subject(s) of your investigation an opportunity to state their side of things, preferably in the same story as your initial findings. They can refuse—"No comment"—or not, as they wish. But make sure they get the opportunity.

REVIEW DOCUMENTS CAREFULLY. Are you sure you understand the documents you are reviewing? Do you need expert help? A forensic accountant? A doctor or dentist? Don't assume that you understand everything you read.

DON'T SACRIFICE TRUTH FOR DRAMA. We all want those highly dramatic stories, but sometimes it's just not there. If a court gets wind that you've played fast and loose with the truth in order to heighten the drama of your story, you're toast.

BE CAREFUL WITH CONFIDENTIAL INFORMATION. Just because you get something from a whistle-blower doesn't mean you can use it, no matter how newsworthy it is. A document that appears to be reliable might in fact be a fake. Or stolen. And even a legitimate document might be legally protected or privileged, such as the product of a lawyer-client or doctor-patient relationship. Citing such privileged information in a story could make you liable to civil or criminal charges.

AVOID THE SPY TRAP. The work done by journalists and spies is sometimes similar. Both learn things that others don't necessarily want us to know. In some countries, journalists walk a fine line; reporters being charged with espionage is not uncommon.

Defamation—A Writer's Risk

Defamation takes two forms: libel (written) and slander (spoken). A statement is defamatory if it adversely affects the reputation of the person in question in the estimation of ordinary persons; deters ordinary people from associating or dealing with that person; or injures the person in his/her occupation, grade, office, or financial credit. Defamation affects the entire chain of publication: author, editor, publisher, distributor, vendor, even a radio announcer. As with most things legal, the law of defamation varies from jurisdiction to jurisdiction. That means that it is different in Massachusetts than it is next door in New York. Between countries, the differences are even greater.

In trying to decide whether a particular statement you are about to make might be defamatory, first look at the plain meaning of the words. Second, is the innuendo defamatory? Third, given the overall context of the story, is it defamatory? Defamation must be specific. Does your statement refer to the plaintiff? You need not refer to the plaintiff by name to defame her; even referring to her indirectly might be construed as defamation. Even fiction may be defamatory if readers can figure out on whom your character is based. You cannot defame a group, however—only individuals. Defamation must be published, either in writing or speech. Saying something defamatory is not actionable unless it is heard by someone else. Publication may be accidental—such as being recorded without the speaker's knowledge—and repeating a defamatory statement is, in many countries, just as actionable as making the original statement.

If you are accused of libel, talk to a lawyer about your possible defenses. First, if what you said is true, you're in the clear, although you should be careful about what constitutes truth. There are also several legal justifications for defamation, such as consent by the subject to publication of the statement and waiving of the privilege. Certain statements are protected by law. For example, judges and members of Congress or the state legislature are all protected for what they say in the course of litigation (in the case of judges) and debate (in the case of legislators). However, a statement made on the floor of Congress could be the source of a lawsuit if repeated outside the Capitol building. Some statements are protected by the qualified privilege of fair comment—as in the case of a public issue. You may also have a qualified privilege if your reporting is "fair and accurate"; it is substantially correct; and it is on an important matter of public interest. In the United States, a defamatory statement made about a public figure must also have been made maliciously; the law assumes that public figures have chosen to be in the public eye and so are not entitled to the same level of protection as private citizens.

If you defame someone, there are some ways you can make it better—and potentially avoid a large damage award. First, apologize and retract the statement. Doing so *before* you are sued carries more weight than afterward. As long as the apology is "full and fair," you might be able to avoid an award of general damages. If you're clearly in the wrong, the publication that printed the defamation or the broadcaster that aired it will probably offer to settle the case.

Privacy and Publicity

You may have a First Amendment right to write truthfully about people, but individuals also have a right to privacy. You should be careful not to reveal private facts about people, such as medical information, in your reporting. The right to privacy is strongest in a person's own home and more limited in public places, but you should be careful about revealing any highly personal details without permission. Of course, the right to privacy varies from one jurisdiction to another. Individuals also have something called a *right of publicity,* which, again, varies between jurisdictions. This is the right not to have your name or image used for commercial purposes without your consent—prohibiting using a person in an advertisement, product endorsement, or on commercial goods. It's important to note, however, that editorial use of a person's name or image does not violate her right to publicity. Editorial use is not commercial use, even if a writer or publication earns money in the process.

Business and General Law

Freelance writers are business professionals who need to comply with various laws governing businesses. The question of incorporating may be explored with a capable business attorney, although that generally does not allow a writer to shield herself from responsibility for such individual acts as libel or copyright infringement. Incorporating can also have negative tax impacts. Writers must comply with relevant tax laws by honestly reporting all income and deducting only allowable expenses. Every freelancer should make a thorough study of tax requirements and, whenever there is doubt, consult a reliable tax professional. (See Chapter 24 on taxes.) All people, including writers, should have a will and do some estate planning. Writers with a significant literary opus should consider appointing a literary executor to manage it.

Copyright—Who Owns the Words?

Probably the most significant area of law affecting writers is copyright. Copyright is the exclusive right of the copyright holder to reproduce a work—in our case, a piece of writing—in any form. As the creator of a work, you own the copyright in your writing from the moment it is first fixed in a "tangible medium of expression." Other than creating your work and fixing it in a tangible medium of expression—by writing it down or printing it out, for example—you don't have to do anything special to obtain your copyright. It is yours automatically and its protection lasts for your lifetime plus seventy years. It is not necessary to "take out" a copyright or to register it. However, for U.S. writers, registration with the U.S. Copyright Office at the Library of Congress is necessary to enforce some of your rights under the U.S. Copyright Act. (More on registering copyrights in a moment.)

In order to be subject to copyright, a work must be original—that is, it must be the author's work. It must be the product of an independent creative effort, not just a mechanical or automatic arrangement. Further, it must somehow be fixed in a tangible format. If you tell someone an idea—even an entire story—there is no copyright protection. Copyright only springs into being when a work is set down in some way that fixes it permanently, such as a printout.

There are three exceptions to the rule that copyright vests in the author from the moment of fixation. First, if you are an employee and you create the work in the course of your employment, your employer owns it. Second, if you sign an agreement with a publisher of articles (or other specific categories enumerated under the law) that refers to your work as a "work made for hire" or "work for hire," then it is as if you were an employee for the purposes of the creation of that work, and the "employer" owns the work outright. Third, if you do a job for the federal government, the work will usually be in the public domain. This last is not true for state and local governments, however.

Your copyright is more than just the right to make copies. It includes the right to resell your work, to translate your work into another language, to perform your work in public, to convert it to another medium (for example, to convert a novel to a film), and the right to prepare a derivative work. In Canada, Britain, and virtually everywhere else except the United States, you also have "moral rights," which include the right to have your name associated with the work (or not, as you wish) and the right not to have your work changed in such a way as to reflect poorly on your reputation.

The publisher of a collective work such as a periodical, encyclopedia, or anthology also has a special "collective copyright" in the entire work as a unit. This arises because of the originality, skill, judgment, and labor the publisher applies to create the collective work. The publisher's collective copyright is separate from your underlying copyright in an article published in that collective work. A federal court has held that the publisher's registration of the copyright in the collective work *does not* suffice to register the copyrights in the underlying articles, photos, and other elements that make it up—like your article. That's one reason ASJA urges you to register your published articles regularly.

Copyright is not an absolute right. Rather, it is society's way of recognizing the value that creative people contribute to the world and giving them a period of exclusivity in which to exploit that value. There are a variety of exceptions to that exclusive right. The most important of these is "fair use." The U.S. Copyright Act says "the fair use of a copyrighted work ... for purposes such as criticism, comment, news reporting, teaching [including multiple copies for classroom use], scholarship, or research, is not an infringement of copyright." The statute says there are four factors that must be evaluated in determining whether a particular use of a work is a "fair use." These are the purpose and character of the use, the nature of the copyrighted work, the amount and substantiality of the portion used in relation to the copyrighted work as a whole, and the effect of the use upon the potential market for or value of the copyrighted work.

Fair use is not an exception to the copyright; it is a defense to a charge of copyright infringement. Fair use is subtle and complex because its meaning must be determined by context. In fact, one federal court justice called it "so flexible as virtually to defy definition." To make things more complicated, courts have not hesitated to expand or restrict the scope of fair-use protection to serve the "interests of justice." Is all this complexity really necessary? The answer is yes. The fair-use doctrine is a judicial and legislative attempt to balance the interests of copyright holders, society at large, and individual information users. Fair use cannot do that if it is overly simplistic.

Copyright exists automatically as soon as you create a work that meets all the requirements necessary for copyright. Do you need to register your copyright? Yes and no. First, registering a copyright creates a presumption of ownership. Second, in the United States, if a work is registered with the copyright office within three months of publication, a copyright holder can elect to receive statutory damages (instead of having to prove actual damages), attorneys' fees, and court costs. And you *must* register your copyright prior to bringing an action for copyright infringement.

Registering each work individually can be expensive; it costs $30 for each registration. However, if once every three months you collect everything you have published in that period and register it in a group (use Form GR as an addendum to form TX) you will end up paying only $120 each year. You can use Form GR to group-register all of your published works in a calendar year, but you need the quarterly registration to make sure each qualifies for statutory damages and attorney fees. There are detailed directions on the ASJA Web site (*www.asja.org*) for how to do this, and the Copyright Office also has forms, information, and instructions on its Web site (*www.loc.gov/copyright*).

If copyright is the exclusive right to reproduce the work, then copyright infringement is reproducing a copyrighted work without permission. There is strict liability for copyright infringement, which means that everyone who had anything to do with the infringement is potentially liable, even if the infringement seems innocent. Infringement occurs whenever anyone violates any of the exclusive rights under copyright law. However, you cannot infringe on someone's idea. There is no copyright in an idea, only in a tangible expression of an idea. If there is no copyright, there can be no infringement.

If your copyright is infringed, you have several available remedies, ranging from an injunction (a court order to stop the infringement) to damages (legalese for money). Actual damages are based on how much you lost because of the infringement. As you can imagine, calculating and proving actual damages is difficult, and the actual damages are often much less than the cost of bringing an infringement lawsuit. Statutory damages are damages set by the Copyright Act. You don't have to prove that you actually lost any money to be awarded statutory damages. In the United States, however, you must have registered your copyright within ninety days of publication or before the infringement begins in order to qualify for statutory damages (or for court costs). Statutory damages range from $750 to $30,000 per infringement and can go up to $150,000 if the infringement is found to be willful. This is why the quarterly registration of your published articles can pay off big-time in the event that your copyright is infringed.

There is another remedy available to copyright owners under the recently enacted Digital Millennium Copyright Act (DMCA). It's called "Notice and Takedown." The DMCA was enacted in part to facilitate access to the Internet by giving Internet access providers a safe harbor from charges of infringement for the infringing acts of their subscribers. Providers are shielded from infringement charges if they file with the Copyright Office of the Library of Congress the name and contact information of an individual to be notified in the event of infringement, and if they promptly take down any infringing material upon receiving good-faith notice of the infringement by the copyright owner. So if you have been infringed on the Internet but you don't want the expense and hassle of filing a lawsuit, you can get the infringing matter taken down by sending written notice to the ISP. Invoking the notice and takedown provisions of the DMCA does not in any way compromise your right to sue the primary infringer.

Professional Guidance

This quick tour of the legal terrain might have answered some questions for you, but freelancers often face complicated legal dilemmas. When you have a legal question, you might be able to find the answer by consulting a book, visiting a reliable Web site, or checking with other writers and writers' organizations. The Authors Guild offers its members a free contract review service and will have legal interns answer some member questions. ASJA does not have staff attorneys, but its Contracts Committee and Legal Resources Committee can provide invaluable information. If the question is about something important to you and you still have doubts, you should consult an attorney. You definitely need an attorney if you are threatened with a lawsuit or are planning to sign a complex book-publishing contract. You probably need an attorney to draft or review a collaboration agreement for you. You probably don't need an attorney to answer basic questions about copyright and other freelance issues or to assist in negotiating a magazine contract.

How do you find an attorney? One thing you *don't* want to do is to ask your local real estate attorney. You need someone experienced with publishing law—the more experienced the better. The best source of information about such attorneys is word of mouth, so start by asking other writers and writers' organizations. You may have read an article or book by a publishing attorney or found an attorney's Web site. Your agent may know someone suitable. Make a list and then contact two or three prospects. Tell each one a little about your problem and ask if they handle such matters. Ask about fees and how they are determined. Ask if they give a discount to members of any writers' organizations to which you belong. Make your choice based on their experience, areas of practice, fees, and your own comfort level. Don't be timid and don't hesitate to negotiate.

NOTE: *The information in this chapter is provided for information purposes only and is not intended as legal advice, which can only be provided by an attorney.*

SALLIE RANDOLPH is a recovering freelance writer who is now an attorney in Buffalo, New York, with a practice representing authors. Her Web site is *www.authorlaw.com.* Her latest book is *Author Law: A Desktop Guide to Writers' Rights and Responsibilities* (Capital Books).

TIMOTHY PERRIN is a writer and recovering lawyer in Westbank, British Columbia. After close to thirty years in the business, hundreds of articles, and five books, he's decided that, on the whole, he'd rather be sailing. His Web site is *www. timothyperrin.com.*

24

Taxes and Deductions

JULIAN BLOCK

All writers—and many would-be writers—don't do anything without wondering, "Can I write this off?" Well, the answer is almost always a resounding maybe. Freelance writers have way too many tax questions to answer in a single chapter, but I'm going to cover some of the questions that fellow writers most often ask me—along with some tips that the most tax-savvy writers have been using for years.

In essence, any expenditures required to do your business can be deducted: travel, lodging, meals, research, publications, phone, stationery, equipment, and so on. Many writers who work at home choose to take the home-office deduction, but this is so complicated—often with ramifications when you sell your house—that it's best to seek advice from a tax professional about your specific situation. Similarly, some freelancers deduct all or part of their family vacation costs if they sell stories about family vacations, but this is another area that can be fraught with intricate problems and usually deserves the attention of a professional. All these deductions assume, of course, that your freelance writing constitutes a business intended to make "profits." Long-standing rules disallow deductions for losses incurred in pursuing "hobbies." Because of that distinction, the feds program their computers to bounce returns that show full-time salaries and other sources of income offset by losses from sideline undertakings that turn out to be hobbies—writing, photography, and painting, to cite just some of the activities that are likely to draw the attention of the tax collectors. How do IRS examiners determine whether your intention is to turn a business profit from, say, your writing—or just to have fun? They get their cues from Internal Revenue Code Section 183, which provides guidelines on how to distinguish between a hobby and a business. To take advantage of Section 183, you have to establish a profit motive.

To cut down on disputes, the law presumes that you are engaging in a business rather than a hobby—with the IRS as a partner who is entitled to a portion of your profits—as long as you have a net profit in any three out of the last five consecutive years. *Net profit* is IRS-speak for an excess of receipts over expenses. So you usually don't have to worry if you have at least three profitable years during the last four. Satisfy that stipulation and you are entitled to fully deduct your expenses this year, even if this is a loss year. Even if you have red ink in more than two out of five years, you still can establish that you conduct a "for-profit" business, provided you pass an IRS "facts and circumstances" test. This test looks at a number of factors, including the way you conduct your writing activities; whether you rely on expert advice or you know what you're doing on your own; how much time and effort you expend on your writing career; your success in other business endeavors; your history of income or losses from writing, and the amount of profits you make; and elements of personal pleasure or recreation.

One note before we delve into a few specifics: To back up your deductions in the event of an audit, save all your records. This includes receipts for purchases and pay stubs, of course, but also such records as queries to publishers and programs from writers' conferences. Note, too, that employment full-time in some other field does not automatically disqualify you as a professional writer. You can earn a paycheck somewhere else and still have a legitimate freelance-writing business.

Depreciation Deductions

Freelance writers and other self-employeds who are tax-savvy know that they have two choices on how to write off their outlays for purchases of equipment and other kinds of personal property: the "standard route" with depreciation, or the lesser-known "expensing" alternative. But because of their mistaken belief that there is only one way to deduct equipment purchases, countless freelancers pay way more in taxes each year than is legally required. When tax time rolls around, they go the "standard route" that allows them to recover their expenditures through depreciation deductions over varying periods. The general rules for depreciation specify periods that range from as low as three years to as high as thirty-nine years, with the majority closer to three than to thirty-nine.

Freelancers get to depreciate most of their equipment over five years (computers, copiers, and the like) or seven years (furniture and fax machines, for example). That usually translates into a cap on the first-year deduction of only 20 percent for five-year property and about 14 percent for seven-year property.

Many freelancers overlook the other choice: Internal Revenue Code Section 179 authorizes an important exception to the general rules for depreciation. This exception bestows an option on businesses, whether full- or part-time, that qualify as "small businesses" (typically, freelance writers do). Qualifying outfits can dispense with depreciation and elect "expensing," if that is more advantageous. This tactic entitles them to write off the *entire* cost in the first year the equipment is "placed in service" (IRS lingo for made ready and available for a specific use, whether or not it's actually used), rather than the year it's purchased or paid for. First-year expensing is subject to several limitations. However, in my experience, few freelance writers are going to spend sufficiently to run afoul of the limitations. The key stipulation sets a dollar cap on the deduction. Under the rules that apply as this book goes to press, the ceiling is $25,000 per year.

Here's a caution: The amount you expense cannot exceed the taxable income from your business. Put another way, the first-year deduction cannot create a loss. But for purposes of this limit, *taxable income* has its own special meaning. Because, among other things, wages and salaries can be included, and because couples filing joint returns are allowed to use their combined income, this requirement can even be met by a start-up operation that shows little or no profit the first year.

And here's a tip: Write-offs for equipment purchases enable self-employeds to save more than just income taxes. They also reduce self-employment taxes on net (receipts minus expenses) earnings, as calculated on Schedule SE (Self-Employment Tax) of Form 1040. For more information, take a look at IRS Publication 946, *How to Depreciate Property*. Publication 910, *Guide to Free Tax Services,* lists all the IRS booklets. Get free copies of the booklets by calling (800) TAX–FORM (they'll be mailed to you); or call (703) 368–9694 for an automated fax service; or download copies from the IRS Web site (*www.irs.gov*). For more on IRS publications, see the discussion under "Free Help for Writers from the IRS" later in this chapter.

Freelance Health Insurance Deductions

For full-time freelance writers, health insurance and medical bills can be a huge concern. Unfortunately, while these outlays may loom large in your eyes, they may not measure up to a large deduction in the view of the IRS: As you laboriously list your itemized expenses on Schedule A of Form 1040, you'll find that the only expenditures deemed allowable are those exceeding 7.5 percent of your AGI, short for adjusted gross income, the figure on the last line of page 1 of the 1040 form. However, freelancers, consultants, and other self-employeds do get some relief. They can take a complete deduction, without regard to that 7.5-percent threshold, for medical insurance premiums for themselves and their spouses and dependents.

Profit from Paying Your Kids

Putting your children on your writing business' payroll is a perfectly legal way to keep income in the family, but shift some out of your higher bracket and into their lower bracket. The business gets to deduct the wages, which are taxed to the child *at his or her own rate*. The child can offset some or perhaps all of the income with a standard deduction, the no-questions-asked amount authorized for a person who does not itemize. In case you're worried about paperwork, the Internal Revenue Code authorizes an exemption from Social Security and Medicare taxes for wages you pay to your under-age-eighteen sons or daughters, provided you do business as a sole proprietorship or husband-wife partnership. Another break for child employees is that they can put part of their wages into a Roth IRA, where contributions can grow without being taxed.

IRS auditors are understandably suspicious of deductions for wages paid to your own children. For the write-offs to survive scrutiny, you must be able to establish that the children *actually* render services. Expect the feds to throw out a deduction for hiring, say, a six-year-old to make photocopies; someone that age likely lacks the skills or discipline for office work. Another hurdle is the "reasonableness" requirement. Wages paid to children cannot be more than the going rate for unrelated employees who perform comparable tasks. Treat your children the same as any other employee and keep the usual records showing amounts paid and hours worked.

Q&A on Common Tax Issues

Here is some expert advice on common tax problems. If you need additional information or guidance in specific areas, you should contact the Internal Revenue Service or consult your personal tax advisor.

QUESTION: A magazine agreed to pay me $1,500 for first rights for an article, plus reimbursement of expenses. I delivered the article, along with my bill for the fee as well as travel, telephone, and research expenses totaling $500. But I received nothing because the magazine went bankrupt. In the expenses part of Schedule C, the second entry is a line reading "Bad debts from sales or services." Is that where I list my bad-debt deduction for the unpaid $1,500?

ANSWER: No. Unfortunately, despite that line, you cannot take any deduction for the $1,500. The snag: You are what is known as a "cash-basis taxpayer." That is the IRS designation of individuals (including most of us) who do not have to report payments for articles, books, and other income items until the year that they actually receive them and do not get to deduct their expenses until the year that they pay them. Since you did not previously count the $1,500 as reportable income, you are not allowed to deduct an equivalent amount.

QUESTION: I am an architect and moonlight as a freelance writer. I went to a get-together with some of my fellow writers. There was no speaker; it was more of a social event. While I see it as network-ing with my professional colleagues, and most of the talk was about work-related issues, writing is only a part-time activity for me. Can I take a business-expense deduction for the cost of getting there? How about my cash contribution to the refreshments for the group?

ANSWER: It is immaterial that you are a part-time freelancer. Your writing endeavors do not have to be full-time for this kind of event to qualify. You are entitled to claim the entire cost of round-trip travel between your home and the party's site. As for noshing outlays, they fall into the category of meals and entertainment, and are subject to a cap. They are only 50-percent deductible.

QUESTION: I write for several magazines. One magazine's 1099 form reports not only the fees they paid me during the year in ques-tion, but also includes sums that compensated me for out-of-pocket expenses. Of course, this doesn't correspond to my records; I don't count those payouts as expenses, since I know that I'm going to get them back—and I don't count expense checks as income, either; it's just a wash. Suppose I receive a 1099 form that shows $2,587.53, which actually includes a $2,500 payment for an article and $87.53 worth of reimbursement for telephone calls. It doesn't make sense that I'd have to include the latter amount in totaling my income for line 1 of Schedule C, since it wasn't income.

ANSWER: Contrary to what many writers (and other self-employed people) mistakenly believe, it's not "just a wash." This is much like payments from agents; you should make sure your return reflects the consistency that will keep the IRS computers in a calm, unagitated state. You should include in your line-1 total the full amount shown by the magazine, $2,587.53. Then include the $87.53, though reimbursed, with your other deductible expenses, since you should not be paying taxes on it. That way, you avoid an overstatement of net profit and overpayment of self-employment taxes, as well as federal, state, and city income taxes.

QUESTION: My income soared because of an unusually large book advance. What is the form I use to take advantage of income averaging?

ANSWER: You have to calculate your taxes the same as anyone else. Averaging ceased to be available after 1986.

QUESTION: I came in from Chicago to New York City to attend a writers' conference. I'm pretty sure that I'm entitled to claim some deductions, but what sorts of expenses can I deduct, and can I deduct them totally?

ANSWER: You get to deduct 100 percent of what you spent for the attendance fee, tapes of sessions, books on writing, and the like, plus travel between your home and New York, and expenditures for hotels. There's a limitation, though, for meals not covered by the attendance fee, including both what you ate en route and food consumed while you were in New York: Deduct only 50 percent of those expenditures.

QUESTION: I will be paid for a talk that I will give at a writers' conference. Is a charitable-contribution deduction available to a speaker who declines an honorarium and asks that the money be donated to a charity he or she picks?

ANSWER: Yes. But the speaker still has to declare the honorarium as income.

QUESTION: I receive books to review, and then donate them to a charity. Can I deduct the value of the books?

ANSWER: The IRS says that a writer who donates unsolicited property that is received "for free," such as books received from a publisher for review, must declare the value of the books as income if he or she donates them to charity.

QUESTION: A university asked to reprint one of my magazine articles in its alumni publication. I gave permission without asking for any payment. Can I take a charitable contribution deduction equal to the fee I would have asked of a commercial publisher? Do I need a letter from the school?

ANSWER: Sorry, a letter won't help. You are not allowed any deduction.

QUESTION: I have written several bestselling books on World War II. I plan to donate papers, including original manuscripts and historic correspondence with famous persons, to a university. Should I consult a tax expert on how to calculate the value of my charitable contribution?

ANSWER: Don't bother. The measure of your allowable deduction is your cost for the property. Because your cost basis for the property is zero, you can claim no deduction.

QUESTION: Can I deduct money spent for magazines purchased at a newsstand for pre-query research? These are not magazines I'm now writing for but magazines I hope to write for. And if I can, where on Form 1040 do I list those deductions?

ANSWER: The law allows you to deduct business-related publications, and these magazines are in that category. Like your other writing expenses, you claim them on Schedule C.

Free Help for Writers from the IRS

Most successful freelance writers find it worthwhile to get professional advice, particularly if they can find a tax preparer who specializes in freelance writers and artists and other self-employed craftspeople and artisans. Meantime, however, the IRS also provides a broad variety of free services for freelance writers. For openers, there is the agency's annual bestseller, *Your Federal Income Tax* (Publication 17), a guide that covers the basics of Form 1040 and various accompanying schedules and forms.

An absolute must for writers is *Tax Guide for Small Business* (Publication 334). It spells out the reporting requirements for writers and other self-employeds who operate their businesses as sole proprietorships and have to file Schedule C (Profit or Loss from Business) and Schedule SE (Self-Employment Tax) with their 1040 forms.

Not sure which publications or forms you need? Get Publication 910, *Guide to Free Tax Services*. It summarizes what the publications cover, identifies the many IRS materials and services available to you, and explains how, when, and where to get them. They are obtainable by phone, fax machine, or on the Internet. The easiest way is to dial a toll-free number, (800) TAX–FORM (829–3676), or access the IRS Web site at *www.irs.gov*. For person-to-person advice, dial (800) 829–1040.

ASJA member JULIAN BLOCK is a writer specializing in taxes and an attorney in Larchmont, New York. His book, *Tax Tips for Freelance Writers*, is self-published. He can be contacted at *julianblock@yahoo.com*.

25

Forays into Fiction

KATHRYN LANCE

> *It is my belief that if we truly honor the story in us*
> *by being ruthless yet tender in its telling,*
> *we have reached into other hearts as well.*

—Charlene Baumbich, ASJA member, journalist, and novelist

Your nonfiction career is humming along. You have a couple of books under your belt, the article credits are piling up, you have "writer" listed on your business card, and yet...something seems to be missing. Whatever happened to your dreams of becoming the next Tom Wolfe or James Michener? If any of this sounds familiar, you may want to rekindle your love affair with writing by turning (or returning) to fiction. Although the money is usually not wonderful compared to articles and nonfiction books, the satisfaction in writing fiction can be greater. Successful nonfiction writers who write fiction often speak of a deep feeling of gratification and other sometimes surprising emotional rewards.

Bruce Most, a financial writer who also publishes mysteries, says that what he loves most about writing fiction is "the ecstasy of discovery—of a plot, of a character, a situation, a section of dialogue, a setting. It's exhilarating in a way I've never found with nonfiction." Laura Tiebert, a freelancer who writes mostly about travel and lifestyle, agrees: "For me, fiction is much more challenging than nonfiction, and much more personal. Putting a piece of yourself out there is incredibly exhilarating and terrifying. I am never more in the zone than when I write fiction. At the same time, it's so hard to get myself to sit down and write, especially when nonfiction is paying the bills."

In my own case, I can say without exaggeration that I have found writing novels to be the single most satisfying activity I have pursued in my entire writing life. Of the fifty-some books I have written, approximately half are novels for young adults and adults. Although the effort involved in writing these books is very similar to the work that goes into my nonfiction books, I look forward to working on them in a way I seldom do with nonfiction. I love being in a world of my own making, among characters created from my imagination who become every bit as real to me as those in my actual life. And I love being able to use the skills I have honed as a longtime nonfiction writer to create scenes that evoke emotion in me as I am writing them, and in readers afterward.

How Nonfiction Prepares You for Fiction

How, you may be wondering, do you begin to write fiction? The answer, according to most writers, is you just do it. Laura Tiebert admits that she was nervous about her first venture into fiction. "About six years ago I took two fiction-writing classes and was awful," she says. "In fact, one of my teachers said, 'You must be a nonfiction writer.' I then took a class in nonfiction narrative and started realizing how many techniques transferred between nonfiction and fiction."

Most writers find that the basics are the same. For fiction as well as nonfiction you need to use all the tools of the trade, including setting a scene, creating characters, inserting background information, and shaping a story. In recent years, the lines between fiction and nonfiction have become blurred. You may think that you don't know how to write dialogue, but you've probably been doing it all along as you've shaped and polished quotes and anecdotes. The only difference is that in fiction, instead of using real conversations, you shape those that you have heard in your head.

Mary Higgins Clark, longtime ASJA member and bestselling author of dozens of thrillers, expresses it this way: "The bottom line is one simple thing: No matter what you write, you've got to tell a story." Clark emphasizes that fiction is stronger when a nonfiction discipline is brought to it. For example, though you might think of research as primarily a nonfiction tool, it is every bit as important in lending verisimilitude to your stories and novels. "You can write a much better story if you're a good researcher," Clark says. "Having a detailed knowledge of what you're writing about—whether for a factual piece or a novel—brings authority to the writing." In researching her thrillers, Clark studies the techniques and procedures in various Manhattan police precincts. "I know exactly how they would handle stolen property in a given precinct," she says. "You don't make those things up. Even though this [fictional] case didn't happen, it could have happened that way."

Many less-thorough researchers encounter reader ridicule when they write about, say, guns, without understanding how many bullets a particular pistol will hold, or not researching the effects of a certain caliber of bullet on a body. Bruce Most points out that "one of the tricks in learning to write nonfiction is how to sift through mounds of research and include only the best, most germane twenty percent in the article or whatever you're writing." The same thing is true, he asserts, for novels. "I research pretty heavily," Most explains. "The trick is not to throw in everything you find, but only those details that make the fiction come alive. Unfortunately, it's not uncommon to come across fiction that reads more like instructive magazine articles than fiction."

On the other hand, as a nonfiction writer you've probably had the experience of learning much, much more than you can ever put into any given article or book. Fiction projects—especially novels—give you a chance to recycle or use for the first time all those cool things you've learned that never quite fit into a nonfiction story or book. Charlene Baumbich has written about a wide variety of subjects during her career as a reporter and freelance journalist. Her series of novels give her a perfect outlet for recycling some of these subjects. "As a reporter, I'd written about senior citizens' softball," she says. "Got a senior softball league in my books. I'd written about demolition derby. Got a demo-derby in one of the books. Relationships have always been a specialty for my nonfiction writing, and that certainly came in handy as I developed characters and how they related to one another in the novels."

In my own fiction writing, which is mostly science fiction, solid research is crucial. For example, the plot of my first adult novel, *Pandora's Genes,* involves a recombinant-DNA disaster that spawns a deadly hereditary disease with the potential to wipe out the human race. I completely invented this illness, but only after steeping myself in genetic studies to make sure it was plausible. A few months after the book came out, a population-geneticist friend told me that I had inadvertently recreated the genetics for an existing, rare—but real—hereditary disease among fruit flies. My scenario never actually happened, but it could have—and maybe still could.

How Fiction Hones Writing Skills

Not only can fiction writing make use of the tools you have learned while writing nonfiction, you will find that fiction in turn sharpens your nonfiction skills as you learn to do things in a slightly different way. According to Maxine Rock, a journalist with eight nonfiction books to her credit, writing fiction can reinvigorate a nonfiction-writing career. Rock, who began writing fiction after twenty-five years of strictly nonfiction, explains that fiction can allow you to relax and spread your wings in a way that's not possible with tightly written journalism pieces. "Writing as a journalist has honed my skills in reporting swiftly," Rock explains, "but it has also driven out some of the more fanciful aspects of my writing, which I would like to summon back for fiction." She adds: "One of the things that hooked me was the freedom to control people and situations. To have the story come out as I want it, not as it has to, as when you write nonfiction. It's a pleasure to nudge facts a little, as if to thumb my nose at how precise I must be in nonfiction. What a relief!"

Janine Latus, a freelancer who writes about personal finance and parenting for national publications, agrees. "Fiction gives me much more opportunity to play with words," she says. "I don't have to be crisp as in a service piece. I can wander through a scene and describe whatever I think will bring it into focus for the reader. In fiction, I am not writing for an editor, I am writing for my readers. And sometimes, not even for them. Sometimes I am writing only for myself, just to flex my imagination."

Another carryover between the two sorts of writing is that nonfiction often provides ideas for fiction. One of the most famous examples is that of *Pale Fire,* the brilliant novel in the form of a poem and notes written by Vladimir Nabokov in 1962. Several critics have pointed out that Nabokov conceived and wrote the book—perhaps as a fictional parody—while embroiled in the nonfictional task of translating and annotating *Eugene Onegin,* the epic poem by the great Russian writer Alexander Pushkin, into English.

For many writers, the connection of ideas is more direct. Bruce Most is working on a new mystery that revolves around modern-day cattle ranching. The idea, he says, grew out of two magazine articles on cattle rustling that he wrote fifteen years ago. Likewise, Laura Tiebert reports that her latest novel-in-progress grew out of an article on travel in the Middle East: "It's such a mysterious, intriguing area of the world that my imagination just ran away with me."

Controlling Your Own Universe

In a fictional world of your own making, you control what happens (at least until your characters become so real that they begin to dictate what will happen next). If you write science fiction, for example, you literally can create societies, planets, or even universes. You can use fiction to visit places you would never go in real life, or to have adventures that are beyond your physical or emotional powers. The late Isaac Asimov—author of innumerable books of fiction and nonfiction, including the epic Foundation series, a science fiction saga about the rise and fall of a galactic civilization—was well known for his reluctance to travel more than a few blocks from his midtown Manhattan apartment. Nevada Barr, author of the bestselling mysteries featuring Anna Pigeon, a National Parks ranger, got the idea for her first mystery while on a lonely patrol in the wilderness of Guadalupe Mountains National Park in Texas, where she herself was a law-enforcement ranger. "There were two bad guys I knew about who I thought should be dead," she told an interviewer. "I wandered around [the back country] thinking of how to kill them and get away with it." These murderous meanderings came together in a plot that led to *Track of the Cat,* Barr's first Anna Pigeon mystery.

"[Fiction] gives me a chance to bring my imaginary friends to life, to create and control whole worlds," says Janine Latus. "It walks me into a world where I set the rules. I can pick up a character and set her down in suburbia and see how she behaves, and then pluck her out of her own backyard and set her in the city to see what happens. . . . It's a way for me to take the road not taken." The truth is that no matter what we write, we all write from our own experience, however disguised or even unconscious. Fiction offers an opportunity not only to orchestrate fate, but to create characters out of the real-life people you've known. Charlene Baumbich, who has written six nonfiction books, recently had her first fiction, the two-book "Dearest Dorothy" package, published by Guideposts Books. "My eighty-seven-year-old heroine is based upon the energies of a real-life 'character' I know," she says. "Several other of my fictional town's residents have character traits not unlike older folks I've known, including family members and many people I've interviewed throughout the years."

When I was a teenager, I spent my study hours writing endless stories (as well as bad poems) featuring thinly disguised versions of my friends and family. In retrospect, I see that these early fictional forays were a way to help myself deal with and make sense of such adolescent traumas as boyfriend woes and power struggles with my parents. Charlene Baumbich speaks of using her current fiction writing as an outlet for grief. Her multiple-book project began shortly after the deaths of her father, her godmother, and a mentor. "It's amazing how working on fiction became a wonderful grief outlet," she says, "even though what I was writing was humor. It was a quirky way to continue to live in the company of those whom I loved so dearly and who had modeled such vibrancy in their lives." Fiction can be used even more directly to bring the dead back to life: In the early 1990s I published a young adult novel, *Going to See Grassy Ella,* in which the protagonist was based on my sister, who had died at the age of thirteen in the early sixties. Writing *Grassy Ella* was a way for me both to honor my sister's memory and imagine what her life might have been like had she not died so young.

Why a Writing Group Helps

No matter how many nonfiction books and articles you have published, you will encounter some new approaches or techniques when you first turn your hand to fiction. I strongly recommend joining a writers' group, if you can find a good one, or enrolling in a continuing education course in fiction writing. Being part of a fiction group has at least two advantages. First, it will provide motivation to write, something very difficult for someone whose writing has been mostly on assignment and for pay. And you will undoubtedly receive much useful feedback, if you are willing to listen. I have always used a writing group for feedback on my fiction, and though I don't always agree with the group's judgments, I wouldn't consider turning in a novel without soliciting the group's opinions. I recall laboring over one long story that just wasn't working, until someone in the group suggested changing the narrative voice from third person to first. I tried it and was amazed at how much better the piece read—and how much easier it was to write the rest of it. Laura Tiebert reports that she often uses writers' groups or classes. "They help keep me motivated and force me to produce. In the classes, I am always amazed at how many talented writers exist, and sad at how few of us actually publish novels."

Getting into Print

How few of us actually publish is the unspoken reality that may keep many nonfiction writers from giving fiction a try. Unfortunately, with fiction, you may not sell your work at all, and even if you do, you probably won't see much money for your effort. In other words, don't give up your day job. For many of us, writing nonfiction is an enjoyable way of putting bread on the table, while writing fiction is a way to feed the soul. Maxine Rock laments that while she has won some short-story contests, she has yet to sell her first novel. "The most frustrating thing about fiction," she says, "is that you generally have to do the full manuscript before sale, whereas with nonfiction, a query letter [or book proposal] is the selling point." ASJA member and literary agent Elizabeth Pomada stresses that all writers—fiction and nonfiction—need agents, but that fiction is not for every writer. "Nonfiction writers should know that the audience does not carry over. You can be famous in nonfiction, but that won't help sell the novel."

Even if you do sell your novel, you may not be thrilled with the bottom line. Unless publishers perceive your book to truly have mass-market appeal, expect a very small advance (perhaps $5,000 or less) for your first novel and little more or even less for the second, unless the first manages to quickly find an audience. My first novel, *Pandora's Genes,* was turned down by twelve publishers before finding acceptance at Questar. One of my recent YA novels, handled by the same agent, was turned down by virtually every young-adult publisher in the known universe. As for locating an agent, it is generally harder to get one for fiction than for nonfiction; if you already have an agent who handles both types of writing, you are ahead of the game.

Because of the somewhat gloomy odds against publication, I have learned to accept that my fiction writing is primarily for *me*, rather than a means of earning a living. When a novel is accepted and published, it is icing on the cake of a satisfying freelance career. We write fiction because we love to write fiction. All the warnings in the world will not deter someone who has to scratch a fiction itch. Charlene Baumbich sums up the way most fiction writers feel about their craft in describing the experience of finishing her first novel: "When the fiction project was complete, it was as though I had to grieve all over again, as though I'd said goodbye twice, to those whom I knew in real life and those who appeared from the cosmos. There are five more books I'd like to write in this series, so perhaps one day soon we can all play together again. But in the meantime, I continue to pay close attention to life, interviews, and all stories, for they are the nonfiction fodder that just keeps on feeding me and the fictional stories."

KATHRYN LANCE, a member of ASJA since 1979, is the author of more than fifty books of nonfiction and fiction. She can be reached through her Web site at *www.klance.com*.

26

Moving to
Full-Time Freelancing:
It's Not a Leap

ROBERT BITTNER

I dreamed of full-time freelancing for most of my working life, including fifteen years as a full-time textbook editor and part-time freelance writer. Looking back on those part-time freelance years, I now realize two important things. First, the wait was worth it. Second, I could probably have cut those fifteen years to seven—or less—had I devoted more planning to my writing career.

The first step, of course, is making the decision to actively work to move from full-time employment to successful full-time freelancing. When people talk about going from part-time to full-time freelancing, they often talk about "the leap." As in, "I'm hoping to make the leap in about six months" or, "I'd love to freelance full-time, but I'm afraid to take that leap"—as if freelancing full-time were like running off a cliff in the dark. The implication is that we're leaving behind the stability and certainty of our day jobs for the risk of surviving by our own wits. Well, anyone who has set foot in an office cubicle in the last decade should be painfully aware of the uncertainty and instability of the modern workplace. There are no guarantees that the job you love will exist tomorrow. Or that your decades-old company will last out the year. Or that you'll get the raise you need and deserve. For some of us, it seems riskier to trust the future to the whims of an employer than to take charge of our own careers.

So if the image of taking a dangerous leap has been standing between your day job and your dreams, erase that screen. Picture instead a career path with multiple branches. You're not stepping off into an abyss; you're looking down the road and saying, "I think I'd like to head in *that* direction now." Sure, the path might get rocky, might twist and turn. But if you plan ahead, have a good map of the terrain, consult a guide occasionally, and take it one step—one day—at a time, you have a great chance of successfully reaching your goals.

The Power of Planning

When it comes to planning for full-time freelancing, just about every other book on writing offers guidance that is undeniably sensible. Most recommend that you don't even think about leaving the security of full-time employment unless:

* You have at least six months' salary in the bank.
* You are earning at least half of what you need to live on as a part-time writer.

* You have at least one regular market or client that you can count on for assignments.

This is terrific advice. I don't know anyone who has followed it to the letter. The reason is that everyone's situation is different. Some very successful freelancers are afraid that a lot of money in the bank might be the kiss of death for their careers; if they have the security of a financial cushion, they won't work as hard. To thrive, they need to know that something real is at stake. They need pressure. For others, the threat of Debtors' Prison is too much pressure. If their minds are going to be free enough to find and do creative work, they need to know that their financial responsibilities are covered, that they can handle the unexpected car repair or get the dryer fixed. Only you can say just how much longer you can maintain the balance between full-time employment and part-time writing. When I left my day job, it was because I had the chance to try something I'd wanted to do for years, not because I hated the work I was doing. Not everyone is so lucky. Only you can decide when or whether leaving truly is better than staying.

Tania Casselle left her job as a fashion-industry magazine editor when she realized there was nowhere to go in the corporate hierarchy. "Although I was promised all kinds of future promotions," she says, "I couldn't see what that would be, or that I wouldn't be gray before they came about. I also wanted more choice and autonomy in my life. I'd done the nine-to-five—or more likely the nine-to-nine—for long enough and wanted more time for my personal life and to pursue creative and spiritual interests."

Writer Wendy Lyons definitely has the desire to freelance full-time, but she's not ready to make the switch, for practical reasons. "To date, I've sold two nonfiction magazine articles and quite a few humorous/advertorial pieces for a major online-dating Web site. I'm at over four thousand five hundred dollars' worth of income from these efforts so far, which sounds like good part-time money right out of the chute, but it's hardly enough to merit a career change." Before she can make the move, Lyons says she needs "more substantial clips, more clients, and more money in the bank. I also could use more experience with journalistic research."

Christine Woodside tried full-time freelancing twice before she was able to make the move successfully. She admits she just wasn't thinking about freelancing as a real business. "I was too much of a dreamer and not realistic about how hard it was," she says. "I didn't work at it enough and I didn't know anything about how much money to seek in a job. I believed when I was twenty-two—and again when I was twenty-five—that if I spent all day writing one thing on speculation for *Bird Watcher's Digest* or sent one letter to the *Wall Street Journal*, I was doing enough. I was wrong to believe that all it took was being smart and having a few good ideas. It required four times as much work as I was putting into it. I let myself get discouraged quickly—and, because I didn't have enough contacts in the journalism world at that time, I slipped too fast into looking for other paying work, which further distracted me from freelance writing."

Keeping Your Day Job Without Losing Your Mind

My former boss should be enshrined in the Freelancing Hall of Fame. He encouraged my freelancing (and continues to encourage other staff members who freelance), never failing to mention it whenever he took visitors on a company tour and happened to stop by my office. If you meet even one boss like this in your entire career, consider yourself blessed. Freelancing makes most employers nervous. They think it means you aren't devoting yourself 100 percent to the company, that you might publish something that will make them look bad, that you're on your way out the door. Sometimes, they'll be right.

The office situation can get especially tense—for both you and your employer—when your day job also involves writing or editing. Your bosses will wonder whose work you're really doing at your desk. And you might wonder how much longer you'll have to keep slogging away on other people's stuff. Sharon Edry began freelancing when she was a full-time magazine editor for magazines such as *Child, Family PC*, and *National Jeweler*. "It got to the point where I was not a very good employee," she admits. "I was doing a lot of freelancing on the job. I was actually having to turn down assignments because I couldn't make the calls at work. I was just longing to give full-time freelancing a go." Another freelancer, Janine Adams, avoided some of that tension by exchanging her full-time public-relations job at a botanical garden for part-time work. "I took a part-time job in a big hospital, doing whatever my boss needed me to do. I worked two days a week in the hospital and worked three days a week sending out query letters." She gradually built up her freelance business until she was ready to pursue it full-time.

Handling the Transition

Quitting your job—or not looking for another job—is the easy part of the transition from part-time to full-time. (For most of us, crafting a great resignation memo should be a snap.) The challenging part will be learning how to manage your newfound freedom effectively and profitably. I'm not talking about establishing a retirement account, planning for taxes and insurance and Social Security payments, or beefing up your office machinery and supplies. While those are all important concerns, I'm talking about learning to manage the sudden flood of possibilities you'll face as a full-time freelancer.

Within days of quitting my job, I was floundering. I had left at a point when I was financially prepared, but I wasn't yet carrying a full-timer's work load. As a result, one week into my glorious freedom, I had zero assignments. Worse, I had zero ideas about how I should be spending my time. *Do I work on developing and sending out a couple of queries a day?* That sounded good. *Maybe I should spend this slow time polishing a book proposal I'd really like to write.* That sounded good, too. *Maybe I should dig into* Writer's Market *and the* Writer's Handbook *and turn up some great, undiscovered markets. Maybe I need to spend more time going through my local paper looking for story leads. Maybe I should clean out my files and look for stories that I could sell as reprints. Maybe I should attend an upcoming writing conference.* Good, good, good, and good.

Since I was suddenly free to spend my days any way I pleased—and had no way of knowing which actions would yield the best return—I was overwhelmed. To get some breathing room, I spent the next few days cleaning up my office and really thinking about which things I wanted to accomplish and how I might best accomplish them. It took me about six months to settle into the new rhythm and responsibilities of my workdays. Perhaps the following four tips will help shave a couple of those months off when it's your turn.

1. FOCUS ON YOUR CURRENT ASSIGNMENTS AND YOUR EXISTING RELATIONSHIPS. Your first priority, obviously, should be to meet your current deadlines. Yes, you might want to spread your wings and fly in a hundred different directions at once. But full-time freelancing is precarious enough without unnecessarily annoying an editor who, not unreasonably, expects you to keep your feet on the ground and turn in your work on time. Honor those commitments. But don't forget that those good working relationships can last far beyond your current assignment. Review your last dozen or so assignments. Have you continued to send those editors your ideas? If not, now is the time to start. These editors have purchased your work before and know you can deliver. In other words, they're your existing customers. And it's a lot easier to sell to your existing customers than it is to snag new ones.

2. IN THE BEGINNING, FOCUS ON DOING WHAT YOU CAN DO. Yes, you suddenly have the freedom to explore all those in-

depth, meaty stories you never had time for before. But don't let freedom blur your focus. You may have the time to spend a year shadowing a police detective and writing a dramatic tale of life on the streets—but do you have other responsibilities that make such projects impractical, if not impossible? Do you have the financial wherewithal to attend distant conferences in your special-interest areas on your own dime—or should you instead plan to attend only those meetings held within driving distance? Once we take a realistic look at our own personal situation—whether that means family responsibilities or financial constraints or something else altogether—we can begin to winnow down the seemingly infinite number of choices available to us. For example, when I started freelancing full-time I had the opportunity to co-author the autobiography of a woman who had lived through the Holocaust as a child. Our initial conversations went well, and I started to put together a book proposal. However, as I began to scratch the surface of the literature on the Holocaust, and as I thought about the research challenges (the woman had kept no diary, had no surviving family members, and had only a child's recollection of people and places, including many places that had changed names several times since then), I realized that the project was beyond me. Instead of getting back to her with a book proposal, I thanked her for her time and wished her the best in finding the *right* co-author.

3. GAIN FOCUS THROUGH SPECIALIZATION. Whether you've specialized from the start or you're just beginning to develop some primary subjects you'd like to concentrate on, specialization can help eliminate a lot of the guesswork—and "second-guessing-work"—that can be so daunting in the early days of full-time freelancing. If you've written about wine and food in the past, focus your energies on building on that specialty. If

you've followed construction trends, British music, microchip innovation, or dog breeding, use that specialized knowledge as your key for opening new markets. Brainstorm ways you can take specialized research that you did for a trade magazine, say, and transform it for a consumer magazine. Or if you've only pitched to newsstand publications in the past, pick up the phone and call some trade magazine editors. If you haven't yet developed any specialties, ask yourself what three or four areas you'd most enjoy focusing on. Start there when it comes to brainstorming new article ideas, developing queries, and approaching markets. (See also Chapter 13 on specializing.)

4. FINE-TUNE YOUR MARKETING. First, limit your markets. That may sound counterproductive. After all, more markets equal more assignments and more income, right? Not necessarily. The markets you pitch to should be helping you reach the next level in your career—whether through bigger paychecks, longer assignments, or clips from higher-profile publications. If the markets you're querying aren't helping you work your way up the writing ladder in some way, they may actually be costing you career growth. Try to weed out markets that aren't doing you any good. If you've been sending a market a query every month for a year without success, ask yourself whether your efforts might be better directed elsewhere. Of course, there's nothing wrong with continually working to break into tough markets. But eliminate marginal markets and invest your time and energy in the publications that reflect your current interests and goals.

Next, consider taking a multitiered approach to marketing. List six magazines you'd really love to sell to, magazines that would be at the absolute top of your list in terms of pay, prestige, whatever. Consider these your "top-tier" markets. Next, seek out at least two second-tier magazines for every top-tier title on your list. Second-tier magazines are a notch or two below your ultimate goal, but they should still be good-paying, quality markets. Let's say you'd like to write longish investigative stories related to health/medicine. And let's say that *Atlantic Monthly* is one of your top-tier magazines in that category. Look at all the other magazines out there that might also be interested in investigative stories related to health/medicine. Maybe they publish shorter stories, maybe they don't pay as well—but they'll be publications that are easier to break into and that can provide the clips that will help you open doors at your ultimate-goal publications. Keep a steady stream of queries going to your second-tier markets while continuing to knock on the door at the top-tier magazines.

Living the Full-Time Freelance Life

Living the full-time freelance life does come with a price. Instead of having one boss, you may end up with a different boss for almost every magazine article and book you write—with all the baggage that implies. If you're used to sending out one query a week, you may be shocked at the amount of personal marketing required to generate the work needed to pay your bills. You may also be shocked at the number of rejections you receive. You'll face frequent requests to revise something you thought was perfect when you submitted it. You'll have deadlines that must be met, no matter what—which sometimes means sixteen-hour workdays, including weekends. Not to mention unreturned phone calls, unfair contracts, days when you just don't feel like writing, paychecks that should have arrived four weeks ago, and queries that go unanswered. They're all part of the wonderful freelance-writing life, and you need to brace yourself for them.

But they are just *part* of the freelance life. There are also incredible benefits to being a full-time freelance writer—benefits that, for many of us, far outweigh the frustrations. "The luxury of working from home is something I never take for granted," says Tania Casselle, adding that other benefits include "the ability to dictate my own hours, not to have to wear suits and make office chat when I'm not in the mood. If I want to work till late at night sometimes and take a day off at other times just because the weather is good, I can do that. I've continued to travel and explore my personal interests in a way that would be impossible in an office job. I have the choice to work for three months—very, very hard, around-the-clock—and then take a few months off."

For former newspaper journalist Alison Wellner, the benefits are more craft-related: "I think I'm a better writer and reporter as a free-lancer than I was as a full-time staffer. In part, it's because I dig deeper, on the prowl for info that I can use to blow my clients away and for the tip to the next story that I'm going to pitch to a new editor. I'm also harder-working as a freelancer, because that work accrues directly to my bottom line. On staff, more work simply equals more work, and it's sometimes difficult to go through an additional round of tough editing simply for professional glory.

"Finally," she says, "there is simply no way to beat the freedom of being self-employed. You are the master of your own destiny."

ROBERT BITTNER is a full-time freelancer based in Charlotte, Michigan. His fourth book, *Your Perfect Job: A Guide to Discovering Your Gifts, Following Your Passions, and Loving Your Work for the Rest of Your Life* (Shaw Books), was released in March 2003. Visit him online at *www.robertbittner.com*.

Sondra Forsyth

Always finish a story two days before your deadline. Print it out, let it cool, then read it with a red or blue pencil in hand. You'll find typos, repeated words, awkward transitions, and other egregious errors you couldn't have seen when the piece was freshly written.

Greg Daugherty

Some writers may do their best work in offices that are piled floor to ceiling with clutter, but I've learned the hard way that I'm not one of them. So I set aside some time at the end of each week to throw out old drafts, clippings, notes, magazines, and anything else I no longer need. Every little scrap I can get rid of is a victory. I also find the hum of the paper shredder to be very therapeutic.

Cathy Dold

Always ask for more money. It works sometimes.

Eleanor Foa Dienstag

I use DOME Simplified Weekly Bookkeeping Record (about $12) to record all my cash expenditures (like cabs to airports, etc.), my income, and my reimbursed expenses, so that I can reimburse my business.

Irene Levine

I always send an e-mail invoice, along with a note saying, "Hard copy to follow in snail mail." This gives editors two opportunities to remember or forget to pay.

Erik Sherman

Be wary of those who tell you that it's impossible to make a living as a writer. They are almost always inexperienced or unsuccessful, or both.

Kathryn Lance

The Outline feature of Microsoft Word, found in the View menu, allows you to outline a story, article, or book with consistent headings, down to as many levels as you like. You can easily add, delete, or move any of the heads and subheads, along with their contents, simply by clicking and dragging. Even better, you can easily toggle between Outline View and regular view, so the outline doesn't get in the way while you are writing. You can begin a project using Outline View, or easily convert an existing document. I discovered Outline View when I was given a month to write an "instant" book. There was no time to organize the book in the usual way, but with Outline I was able to simply dump information in the proper categories whenever I came across it, to be worked on later. As the big picture of the book changed, I easily changed the outline to match it.

Bernie Asbell

Think of the advance as all the money you will make on a book. Don't count on further royalties. If the advance isn't satisfactory, don't do the book.

Ann Monroe

Use Infoselect, a free-form database that lets you file, cross-file, and find anything instantly. I couldn't live without it.

Tim Harper

Check with your tax advisor to make sure you don't overlook potential deductions or business expenses. For example, you might be able to write off all or part of your family vacation expenses, even if you don't sell a story.

Florence Isaacs

Always keep a glass of water handy when doing radio interviews by phone. Then you'll never have to worry about getting a catch in your throat or going on a coughing jag.

Katy Koontz

Keep a Progress Report database that lists each assignment with the name of the magazine, the deadline, if it's been handed in, if it's been accepted, the fee, the expenses and when they were invoiced, the issue it is scheduled for, and any follow-up. Use a macro command to sort out instantly who has articles they haven't accepted yet, who has accepted articles that haven't been paid for yet, who owes you expenses, and who owes you issues. Do that at the end of every month, and put expenses in the spreadsheet, too.

Greg Daugherty

When you have to cut big chunks out of an article or a book manuscript to get it down to an assigned word count, don't simply delete them. Instead, copy and paste whatever is left over into another computer file. You may be able to recycle some of that material later on, especially if you write about the topic often.

Barbara DeMarco-Barrett

Keep at least one idea file going, and spin through it every so often. In your idea file include those slips of paper you wrote a title on, or an article you clipped that inspired you and you planned to draw from for a story with your own slant.

Florence Isaacs

Two books on creativity, both by Julia Cameron, have changed my life and helped me make leaps in my career. The first is *The Artist's Way.* The second is *Walking in This World,* which is excellent if you read *The Artist's Way* a long time ago, but now need another kick in the pants.

Linda Wasmer Andrews

Set diversification goals. Many writers establish goals to break into certain markets or make a particular amount of money each year. I do, too—but I also set goals geared toward keeping my business diversified. First, I identify three market sectors for my work. In my case, these are magazines and other periodicals, Web sites and other electronic media, and books and reference works. For another writer, they might be three specialty areas. Then, I set comparable sales or publishing goals for each. This approach has kept my income steadily rising through publishing's recent ups and downs.

Paulette Cooper

When leaving a telephone message for an editor, in addition to my phone number I leave my e-mail address. I'm more likely to get a response that way since many editors prefer to work by e-mail.

Maxine Rock

I have fact sheets for people seeking my services as collaborator, co-writer, or editor. There's a different sheet for each. The sheets list essentials, such as my fee, deadlines, agent, method of operation, and other basic details, so I don't have to go through it all, each time, for every different person who queries. If they agree on the basics, we can discuss the individual project. At least they know the ground rules and there's no confusion later, because they have it all in writing.

Susanne M. Alexander

Use an electronic calendar like Outlook that allows you to set an electronic reminder that an interview is coming up. This way, if you are deep in the middle of writing, you won't forget to either call the person or leave for the appointment. Setting a timer when you are cooking or doing laundry helps you not forget what else is going on in your life.

Jan Jasper

I use software to keep track of people, appointments, reminders, and all manner of miscellaneous information. I've been using Goldmine for years—though if you're just starting out, Act is easier to learn, and Outlook is in some ways superior. One of the many nice things is that you can link every draft of an article, query letter, etc., to an editor's or agent's "record" in your database, so you don't have to scramble to find things while you're on the phone. You just open the record of the editor or agent you're talking to and immediately you see a list of computer files of everything you sent her and when you sent it. One of the biggest benefits, though, is that you never need to clean up your zillion notes and reminders. You edit them on the computer, and you can also cut and paste from other applications. You can do a search, in a second, to find what you would have spent hours looking for in a pile of paper notebooks. I can't overstress how much time you can save. For more, check my Web site, *www.janjasper.com/articles_keeping_track html#article.*

Bernie Asbell

If you can manage it, have two separate desks. On one, do your bill-paying, bill-sending, and other maintenance work. Keep the other for your writing.

Bonnie Remsburg

When stuck, or troubled, clean up your office. Neatening files, getting rid of obsolete papers, etc., has a wonderfully restorative effect on the creative mind.

Greg Daugherty

If you have a book out, do a Web search periodically to see if it's been reviewed anywhere that you've missed. If it has (and the review is a good one), send a copy to your publisher. That may help keep your book in print or bolster your case when you suggest updating it. And if the review says something particularly glowing about you, consider using that in your biographical materials.

Paulette Cooper

I try to obtain easy-to-remember Web pages. For example, for my pet books, *277 Secrets Your Dog Wants You to Know,* and *277 Secrets Your Cat Wants You to Know,* I have the Web page *www.277secrets.com,* and for my destination wedding book I have *www.destinationweddingbook.com.* That way, I can give out the address on the air when I'm on the radio, and people are likely to remember them easily.

Susan K. Perry

For book promotions, set up talks at writers' organizations about your book, even if it has nothing in particular to do with writing. It gets your name listed in the newspaper and in the group's newsletter, and you might sell some books. All beginners want to know more about the process of getting published. Type up a sheet titled "Why This Book Is Different," with a bulleted list and in a large font. Cover it in plastic and have it on display whenever you talk about your book. I use this same material on my Web site to help differentiate my books from their competitors.

Sherry Suib Cohen

When interviewing people, be clear. Make certain that your subject understands the exact nature of the story you are working on. When you are asking questions, always keep your readership in mind. Make sure that any jargon that your expert uses (particularly if he/she is a scientist or a doctor) is put into reader-friendly terms so that any layman can understand it. Never be shy about asking for further explanation if something the expert has said is unclear to you.

Barbara DeMarco-Barrett

Purge! Go through your file cabinet every couple of months and see what's there, throw stuff out, and be inspired by ideas in your idea file. Clearing clutter encourages clearer thinking.

Susanne M. Alexander

If you do many telephone interviews, buying a good-quality headset is a must to save strain on your neck and back while you write or type your notes as you listen. Radio Shack can also set you up with options to allow you to record your interviews in case you need to listen to a quote again later.

Janine Latus

Never keep more then a half-pint of Ben & Jerry's in the house at any one time.

Andrea Warren

I have had two canceled book projects. In both instances, more protection in the contracts could have avoided considerable trouble. Here's how my new contract reads: *"Acceptance or rejection by the Publisher will be given in writing within 45 days of receipt of the final manuscript. Should the Publisher find the manuscript unacceptable, before termination of this agreement the Publisher shall submit to the author in writing its editorial comments and suggestions for revision of the manuscript, and the Publisher shall give the Author an additional period of time, to be determined in the Publisher's sole discretion, in which to deliver a revised manuscript to the Publisher."*

Claire Tristram

Write your best all the time, no matter how small the publication or how little you are getting paid in the beginning. Over and over again in the course of my career I've had editors working at magazines I'd never dream to query call me up and ask me to write something for them; they saw a story of mine in some no-name magazine and liked it. Also, be nice to editors at these little-known magazines. More often than not they are going to advance their careers, and advance you right along with them when they do. Over and over again I've garnered great assignments, from new and better-paying markets, when editors who liked working with me moved up.

Paulette Cooper

I make up colorful or cute business cards for each of my available books. When possible, the picture matches the subject of the book, such as a travel scene for a travel book. The cards include the book's title, author, ISBN number (important!), and price. People are more likely to keep these than to remember a title. Also, I sometimes autograph the cards when handing them out.

Sondra Forsyth

Consider setting the alarm so that you can rise before the sun in order to clock some productive early-morning hours. At 4:00 A.M., the kids and spouse are not yet awake, the phone isn't ringing, and the paper hasn't been delivered. You can crank out a lot of pages while the world still sleeps. Then you can sneak in a snooze during your toddler's naptime or when your schoolkids still aren't home. Or you can simply go to bed early. This plan has worked for me for years.

Kathy Koontz

Keep a record of queries in a database, and list in each entry where you want to send the query next if it is turned down. That way, if you do get a "Sorry, but no" letter, you already know where it's going next. If you have several ideas for one magazine and don't want to send them all in one query, keep a list in the same way for what idea to send in next after a rejection.

Erik Sherman

Create a set of folders for stories you are currently researching. As related e-mails arrive, put them in those folders. That way, you have all sorts of documentation that will come in handy.

Paulette Cooper

When I get a request to go on a radio show, I agree only if I can get an airdate at least two weeks away. Then, I check *www.switchboard.com* and find the Barnes & Noble and Borders bookstores in that city. I call each major store, get the names and faxes of the "community relations" people, fax them that I'll be on a certain show at a certain time, tell them that I'll be plugging their stores, and ask them to order my book. Or if they already have the book in stock, I'll ask them to put it in an accessible spot and/or face out. When I write up the intro that I want the program to read when they introduce me, I say that my books are available at those particular stores.

Mary Mihaly

As you work, you always should be able to see a symbol of your desires, dreams, goals. What are you working for? If it's to provide well for your kids, you should be able to see pictures of them as you work, to remind you of the good reasons why you labor. I want to be able to afford travel more, especially to exotic places, so I have a map of the world above my desk with big red pins showing every city where I've slept.

Greg Daugherty

New magazines—or old magazines with new editors—are almost always open to new writers. So prowl the newsstand and read the business pages for announcements of magazine launches and personnel changes. Also see if you can get your hands on trade publications such as *Advertising Age*.

Paulette Cooper

When people tell me they're going to look for my book in a bookstore, I tell them that if they can't find it, they should order three copies, not one. When the books come in, the buyer takes just one. Then the store puts the other two books out on the floor.

Tim Harper

Here are some useful sites: for anything related to the government, *www.govspot.com*; for links to a wide range of news organizations, sources of information, search engines, or all of the above, *http://reporter.umd.edu/*, *http://209.8.151.142/vlj.html*, *www.headlinespot.com*, *www.assignmenteditor.com*, *http://looksmart.com*, *www.ceoexpress.com*, *www.nytimes.com/library/tech/reference/cynavi.html*.

Sondra Forsyth

If you will be doing an interview in person for a "real people" piece, do a pre-interview on the phone with the person in order to get the essence of the story before you are on-site.

Donna G. Albrecht

Bribery sometimes works. When my kids were young, I'd offer to take them somewhere they wanted to go, like the local pet store, if they would first give me the uninterrupted time I needed to write or concentrate, usually an hour or so. I could often get a lot of work done in an hour. The only down side was that I had to take care of the goldfish they talked me into buying.

Jennifer Pirtle

I write off the entire business phone line (as well as my high-speed DSL line) as a tax-deductible business expense. Much quicker and less fiddly than having to invoice individual publications for phone calls.

Anita Bartholomew

For in-person interviews, I videotape rather than simply audiotape. When I go back to my office to write, I have people's expressions, mannerisms, the interaction between subjects, etc. I can write, "Simonson scratched compulsively as he reminisced about the twelve-foot flea."

Greg Daugherty

Editors love writers who always meet or beat their deadlines; they are quick to dump writers who consistently miss them. However, it rarely pays to beat your deadlines by more than a couple of days. For one thing, the editor will probably be too busy working on other things to focus on your manuscript. For another, getting a piece in too early may make it seem like the assignment was too easy or that you didn't put enough effort into it. Writers, like trapeze artists, should always make what they do look a little harder than it actually is.

Cathy Dold

Get Quicken. I use it to track all the financial aspects of freelancing, and I couldn't live without it. At a moment's notice I can tell exactly who owes me money, how much money I've made so far, and lots more.

Erik Sherman

For invoicing, I use an accounting program that will create a PDF invoice that I can e-mail. That invoice gets attached to the same e-mail carrying the article. So, if the editor has the copy, I know the invoice has also arrived.

Ann Monroe

I use a combination of long-distance companies' accounting codes and Pocket Quicken on my Palm to automate the expense-invoicing process. I can do quarterly invoices for five to six clients, with phone calls, faxes, and more itemized, in about fifteen minutes.

Susan K. Perry

Don't let fear bog you down. There is *no* risk in writing. While there may be certain risks in publishing particular kinds of material, a writer mustn't censor herself for fear of unknown "dangers." Just write down what you're feeling an urge to write, even if it's personal, controversial, or feels daring in some way, and worry about whether to edit it out later. Some of the best and most original writing gets done that way.

Irene Levine

More often than I would like, I accidentally press SEND and an e-mail message flies away before I have time to review it or make corrections. To guard against my fast-flying fingers, I am trying to discipline myself to always fill in the SEND TO field last.

Sondra Forsyth

Organize your clips in hanging files with labels such as "Sex/Relationships," "Child Care," "Psych/Self-Help," "Real People." I've been in the business for thirty-some years, and I still get asked to submit clips when editors play musical chairs.

Erik Sherman

Follow up on all queries. Don't buy this "If we don't get back to you, we aren't interested" attitude. Many magazine use slush piles upon which your query can languish—unless you ask about it.

Ann Monroe

Use baskets instead of file folders; it's easier to get stuff in and out.

Linda Wasmer Andrews

Become the expert. After twenty years of writing about health and mental health, I finally decided to go back to school to get an advanced degree in health psychology. This way, I'll always have an expert source on call—me. More importantly, I'll be able to market myself as the expert consultant/lead author and the professional writer/co-author rolled into one.

Tim Harper

If you've got a topic or specialty that you've turned into an entertaining and informative talk, search the Web for resorts, spas, or cruises that offer free vacations to people who speak or lead workshops for guests.

Florence Isaacs

The best advice I ever got was, "Never write Chapter One of a book first." It will bog you down because you don't really know what to include in that chapter until you're well into the book.

Greg Daugherty

After you've been writing for the same publication for a year or so, it never hurts to ask for a raise. You may not get it, but very few editors will be offended that you tried.

Susanne M. Alexander

Keep a six- to twelve-month view calendar with holidays marked on it immediately next to your computer so you can easily type the date in your notes when you are doing phone interviews, plan how long an assignment might take, and use it as a reference during goal setting.

Tim Harper

Anyone who does Web research should check out tips from Columbia University journalism Prof. Sreenath Sreenivasan at *www.sreetips.com*, which is loaded with shortcuts for finding good information faster. For example, Sree suggests *www.statistics.com* and *www.robertniles.com/data/* as good starting places for anyone looking for statistics.

Erik Sherman

Yes, you like the editor you deal with. But negotiate contracts as though this person will be replaced at any moment by Simon Legree. Your written word binds you not to an individual, but to a company.

Cathy Dold

Learn to budget your money. When you freelance, money arrives in chunks. No one pays you a salary. And just because you got a big check, that doesn't mean you can go on vacation. Figure out how to pay yourself a salary every month.

Florence Isaacs

Work on two (or even three) chapters at a time, rather than waiting for one to be completely finished before starting on the next. Psychologically, you'll feel as if you're moving right along and making progress. In addition, you may discover an insight in Chapter 4 that sheds light on a quandary in Chapter 2.

Linda Wasmer Andrews

Move around every hour. Although I often work long days, I try to never spend more than forty-five to fifty minutes straight sitting at the keyboard. Instead, I pop up frequently to water the flowers or fold the laundry or walk on my treadmill. This simple strategy helps keep up my energy level up and keep down my problems with a stiff neck, sore eyes, and lack of motivation.

Erik Sherman

Learn to like sales. You want to do a lot of it, and you want to be good at it.

Susanne M. Alexander

Keep your current project folders in a rack on your desk—one color for journalism stories and a different color for any other kind of writing project. When a project is submitted to a client or editor, put it in alphabetical order in a separate section of a file drawer for pending files. Once you have received the final copy of the story or the client has signed off on the project, then project files go to their permanent location and journalism files go to theirs. This way, you won't lose track of obtaining the final published clips and payment for your work.

Greg Daugherty

Terrific as the Internet is, don't forget your local library and all the free resources it offers. A good reference librarian can often direct you to sources you wouldn't have found on your own or that simply aren't available online.

Paulette Cooper

Whenever I have to give out free copies of one of my books I point out to recipients that I buy them at half price (many people seem to think that authors are given a million free copies), and that it'd be a nice thank-you gesture for them to leave a review of the book at Amazon.com or BarnesandNoble.com.

Susan K. Perry

The best investment I ever made was a several-hundred-dollar transcription machine. After too many years of taping my phone interviews with one of those cheapie stick-on devices, my transcription machine allows me to be plugged in all the time. Just press a button and I'm recording any phone call. When I'm ready to transcribe, I can slow down or speed up the playback while using the foot-pedal to stop and start. It's been a foolproof way to turn one of freelancing's most tedious chores into a slightly less tedious and faster task.

Sherry Suib Cohen

One of the first things I always do in an interview is to thank the expert for taking the time to speak to me. Then I ask how he/she wants to be credited. I make sure to also get an e-mail address, phone number, and mailing address so I or the editor can forward a copy of the article. It's also crucial to make sure subjects spell out their first and last names so that no mistake is made. I also ask them if I can contact them via phone or e-mail with follow-up questions; they always say yes.

Cathy Dold

Get a dog to keep your feet warm and keep you company in the office.

Florence Isaacs

Try to use provocative titles for article queries, such as "Killer Foods" for a piece on food poisoning, or even "Fat Kids" for an article on overweight children. Although the titles may not actually be used as cover lines, they do grab an editor's attention and can help get your proposal to the top of the pile.

Erik Sherman

There are great deals on long-distance calling—some as low as five cents a minute. Review your current phone plan. You might be paying hundreds of dollars a year more than you need. Also check with your local phone company to see if there are ways of saving money for the services you currently use.

Tim Harper

If there's a book or big article you want to do but you can't sell it in advance, look around for government or private grants and fellowships, especially if the topic has something to do with social, economic, political, and cultural changes.

Susanne M. Alexander

Use your scanner for making single copies of documents; it's much less time-consuming than running to the library or copy center.

Erik Sherman

Get a raise. Or give yourself a raise. One of the easiest ways to make more money is to raise your rates. To do that, first ask your current clients about increasing the pay. If you've been writing for a publication for some period, it's probably time to see about increasing the word rate.

Sherry Suib Cohen

If you belong to any journalism group, such as ASJA, the members are a rich source of information and resources. Often they are the experts, and if they are not, they know who is and how to find them. Many other writers will hand you the expert's e-mail address or phone number, no questions asked. ASJA and other groups offer a range of electronic forums and bulletin boards where you can post questions to members.

Erik Sherman

Always, always, always be polite to the accounts payable people (the bookkeepers who pay your invoices). If payment is late, they can tell you if it's being held up, or if the editor hasn't bothered to forward the invoice.

Tim Harper

Check with a financial advisor about business insurance. And plan for retirement even if you don't intend to ever quit writing. Set up a pension through an IRA, SEP, Keogh, solo 401(k), or some other plan. The solo 401(k), launched in 2002, looks particularly appealing for successful freelance writers.

Sondra Forsyth

Before you tape an interview, record the following: "This is an interview by Jane Doe with John Smith for Something Magazine, conducted on (date) at (time)." Also, write the information on the stick-on labels for both the cassette tape and its case before you begin. For your own reference, and especially if the magazine wants the tape or there turns out to be a legal issue, this system lets you find what you need.

Florence Isaacs

Don't let fears that your idea will be stolen stop you from seeking feedback from colleagues and/or a writing group. In my experience, it never happens—and in any case, you have to take risks once in a while to get moving. Nothing will get you unstuck faster than fresh insights from someone else.

Greg Daugherty

Jot a note on your calendar for when you expect to receive article payments, book royalties, and so forth. That will alert you to gently remind your editor when your money is late. It will also make it less likely that you'll completely forget about a payment you're owed.

Susan K. Perry

For book contracts, once you've negotiated the advance as high as possible, focus on the smaller stuff (or ask your agent to). It adds up. For instance, I've never agreed to provide or pay for an index. I also ask for and get many more author copies than are initially offered. Once when a contract said I had to provide twenty large photos of myself for publicity, I got them to agree to accept a single electronic photo.

Paulette Cooper

Let editors know a manuscript is coming. If you're sending a submission to a newspaper or magazine and you don't know the editors, and you're not sending it at their request, call them first. Leave a brief message that the manuscript is coming: Give the title, a one-line description, and your name. The advance notice may make it more likely that they'll pay attention to it.

Tim Harper

You can access the Ten Key Negotiating Points in an Author-Publisher Agreement at *http://www.ivanhoffman.com/points.html*.

Erik Sherman

Be careful about how you save money. An expenditure such as broadband Internet connectivity, which might cost $50 a month, could free up enough waiting time to fit in work worth $300 or $400.

Florence Isaacs

DiscountMagazines.com, at *www.discountmagazines.com*, offers great bargains on subscriptions. You have to order five subscriptions the first time you buy from them, but after that there's no minimum. The ordering interface is done well and you can easily buy gift subscriptions.

Sondra Forsyth

If you routinely type your notes during an interview, prepare a Word document ahead of time with the subject, date, and contact information.

Susanne M. Alexander

Buy a used Dictaphone machine for listening to or transcribing parts of tapes from interviews. It automatically backspaces a few words and you can slow the tape down—helpful features not on tape recorders.

Tim Harper

There is a wealth of writers' resources on ASJA member Bella Stander's Web site at *www.bookpromotion101.com*.

Barbara DeMarco-Barrett

Look around you for other items in your home that can help you organize. I needed a filing cabinet. I thought about putting it where the old unused dishwasher sat. Voilà! I unplugged the electricity, turned off the water, and put my files in the old dishwasher. The racks are perfect for folders. Make organizing fun and you'll want to do it more.

Mary Mihaly

Your chair should be strong and have a full back (not a huge space between shoulder and rump) so you'll "feel supported" at work.

Sherry Suib Cohen

As an interview is winding up, I always ask the expert one crucial question: Is there anything else I should know about you or this topic? That's where I sometimes hit the mother lode. "Yes, there is a new invention you should know about that comes to mind," or "I have a new book I'm working on," or, "That reminds me of a subject we haven't mentioned yet." That tiny little question usually provides me with a fantastic quote or some additional insight that makes the story shine.

Kathy Koontz

Tax time is easier if you keep track of expenses each month instead of waiting until a whole year has passed. I made a spreadsheet that lists all the categories of expenses on Schedule C that apply to my business down one side, with a column for each month and then a total for the year across the top. Each time I have an expense, I write the category and amount spent in red ink in my desk calendar on the day I paid for it. (I keep track of mileage the same way, too.) I also include an office-in-the-home section and record the expenses that belong on that form, as well. At the end of each month, I add up the amounts I spent for each category and record the total for the month on the spreadsheet. That way, my expenses never get away from me, and I never have to add more than a manageable amount of numbers at one time. I use a second spreadsheet for income, with the source down the side and the months across the top, with a total. That way, when I get each 1099, I can easily see if it is correct—as well as see what companies have yet to send me 1099s.

Sherry Suib Cohen

To prepare for interviews, read up on the subject and the person you will be interviewing. Make sure to get the book, press kit, or bio on the person or author before the interview so you have time to digest the information. Check that your tape recorder has batteries, you have other pens in case one runs out of ink, and prepare your major questions ahead of time for easy reference throughout the interview. I usually type them on a piece of paper with lots of space in between questions.

Susan K. Perry

Find a way to make your most pedestrian assignments fun. I've found renewed interest in my writing by injecting amusing anecdotes about my friends, illuminating insights from my kids, or long-hidden bits of my own past into my work. Sometimes these anecdotes get cut (by a more restrained me or by a conservative editor), but they've served their purpose by keeping me emotionally engaged in the work.

Greg Daugherty

Tempting as it may be, try not to juggle too many writing projects at the same time. For me the limit is four or five. I find it's almost always more efficient to finish something and get it into the mail (or e-mail) before taking on anything else.

Sondra Forsyth

I have a Hewlett-Packard OfficeJet all-in-one printer/fax/scanner/copier for which I paid a mere $300 and change. I copy my own clips as needed, fax them when asked, scan pix for my Web site, print color letterheads and business cards, and much more.

Tim Harper

When you receive an e-mail warning about a computer virus, check it out to see if it's a hoax before doing anything to your own files or passing along the warning to others. Here are some sites to check: *http://hoaxbusters.ciac.org, http://urbanlegends.about.com, www.snopes.com, http://vmyths.com, http://securityresponse.symantec.com, www.antivirus.com.*

Greg Daugherty

Aim high. Try the best-paying, most prestigious markets first. You may find, as I have, that you're rejected less often and simply treated better there.

Linda Wasmer Andrews

Read for fun. Most writers undoubtedly start out as avid readers, but, somewhere along the way, they often lose the joy under the mounds of books, magazines, press releases, studies, and manuscripts they have to read for their jobs. Don't forget to indulge your love of poetry, adventure novels, or fashion magazines. This pleasure doesn't even have to be a guilty one. You're actually working, since you're rejuvenating your love of the language.

branding, 231–41, 233–34
  mission statement as part of, 232
  role of trade associations in, 234–35
  testimonials as part of, 239
  Web sites as part of, 236–37
Brenoff, Ann, 186
Bunin, Brad, 129
Bush, George W., 101
business cards, 238
business plans, 9–17
  accounting procedures as part of, 15
  definition of goals within, 10–11
  financial needs as part of, 12
  invoicing as part of, 16
  marketing goals as part of, 16
  revenue calculations as part of, 13–14
  sales planning within, 15

California's Writer's Club, 157
Casselle, Tania, 277, 284
Celestine Prophecy, The (Redfield), 143
Chicago Tribune, 181
Christian Science Monitor, 185
Christmas Box, The (Evans, Richard Paul), 143
Clark, Mary Higgins, 267
Clausen, Connie, 66
Cleveland Plain Dealer, 183
Cohen, Sherry Suib, 86, 291, 300–301, 304–5
collaboration, 121–33
  agents and, 128–29
  book proposals and, 131
  experts and, 122, 132–33
  legal contracts for, 128–31
Colorado Author's League, 157
Complete Guide to Self-Publishing, The, 148
computers, 24–30
  bookkeeping software for, 30
  printing software for, 30
  word processing software for, 28–29
"concept," 66–67
  role in book proposal, 66–67
Connecticut Press Club, 157
"content" writing, 73–78
  employment opportunities for, 74–76
  online journalism and, 73–78
  payment for, 76–77

reprints as part of, 77
specialization in, 78–79
Cool, Lisa Collier, 62
Cooper, Paulette, 288, 290, 292–94, 299, 302
Copernic browser program, 29
Copyright Act, 252
copyright infringement, 251–52
  legal actions against, 252
copyrights, 222–23, 248–52
  author's rights under, 222, 251–52
  "collective," 250
  exceptions to ownership, 249
  "fair use" clause, 250–51
  "moral rights" in addition to, 249–50
  registering for, 249, 251
corporate writing, 166, 169–73
  assignment length for, 170
  conflicts of interest in, 172–73
  deadlines, 170–71
  diversification and, 166
  rate-setting, 169–71
Cosmopolitan, 50
Country Journal, 40
Crane, Elizabeth, 75
Crawford, Tad, 129
Crowe, Cameron, ix

Dallas Morning News, 183–84
Daugherty, Greg, 285, 287, 290, 294–95, 297, 299, 305–6
Decorating for Comfort (Cohen/Seidman), 64
Decorating Rich (Cohen/Seidman), 64
defamation, 226, 246–47
  legal justifications for, 247
  libel as part of, 246–47
  retractions and, 247
  slander as part of, 246
  warranty clauses and, 226
DeMarco-Barrett, Barbara, 287, 291, 304
Dienstag, Eleanor Foa, 285
Digital Millennium Copyright Act (DMCA), 252
Dishner, Jackie, 118
diversification, 166–76
  corporate writing as part of, 166
  educational opportunities as part of, 173

ABOUT THE EDITOR

T<small>IMOTHY</small> H<small>ARPER</small> is an ASJA member and former Associated Press national writer who became a full-time freelance writer in 1984. His stories have appeared in many major U.S. newspapers and dozens of magazines, including *Atlantic Monthly, Reader's Digest*, and *Sky*. His eleven books include *License to Steal* (HarperCollins), about stockbrokers; *Moscow Madness* (McGraw-Hill), about Americans doing business in Russia; and *Doing Good* (ASJA Press), a collection of his inspirational magazine stories. He is a member of the adjunct faculty at the Columbia University Graduate School of Journalism, serves as a writing coach for corporations, and acts as a publishing and editorial consultant for companies and individuals who want to write and publish books. He lives with his family in Ridgewood, New Jersey. For more on him and his work, or to get in touch with him, go to *www.timharper.com*.

✓ 808.02 ASJ

The ASJA guide to
freelance writing
$ 15.95
2003-9125

FINKELSTEIN
MEMORIAL LIBRARY
SPRING VALLEY, N.Y.
Phone: 845-352-5700
http://www.finkelsteinlibrary.org

NOV 13 2003